Financialization and the Economy

There can be no doubt that the influence of the financial sphere has intensified rapidly in recent years, but there is much debate about the effect of that influence. The aftermath of the Financial Crisis has led to numerous discussions of the phenomenon of so-called financialization: the increasing impact of financial institutions on the activity of all business entities; emerging threats related with dynamically developing financial markets and the growing importance of financial themes. In light of these issues, which appear in all economies and touch all entities and every area of economic activity, there is a need for a summary and evaluation of the role of financialization in the world today.

This monograph presents the role of financialization in the modern world. It shows positive as well as negative effects of financialization on the stability of the whole economy, the functioning of different types of markets, activity of enterprises, state institutions and behaviours of households. Written by expert contributors, this book plays an important role in the debate concerning future directions of development of the financial sector and financial markets.

Financialization and the Economy is of great importance to those who study political economy, macroeconomics and banking.

Agata Gemzik-Salwach is the Deputy Dean of the Faculty of Administration and Social Sciences at the University of Information Technology and Management (UITM), for Economics, Finance and Accounting, Management Courses, Poland.

Krzysztof Opolski is Professor of Economics and Head of the Department of Banking, Finance and Accountancy at the University of Warsaw, Poland.

Routledge Critical Studies in Finance and Stability
Edited by Jan Toporowski, School of Oriental and African Studies, University of London, UK

The 2007–8 Banking Crash has induced a major and wide-ranging discussion on the subject of financial (in)stability and a need to revaluate theory and policy. The response of policy-makers to the crisis has been to refocus fiscal and monetary policy on financial stabilization and reconstruction. However, this has been done with only vague ideas of bank recapitalization and 'Keynesian' reflation aroused by the exigencies of the crisis, rather than the application of any systematic theory or theories of financial instability.

Routledge Critical Studies in Finance and Stability covers a range of issues in the area of finance including instability, systemic failure, financial macroeconomics in the vein of Hyman P. Minsky, Ben Bernanke and Mark Gertler, central bank operations, financial regulation, developing countries and financial crises, new portfolio theory and New International Monetary and Financial Architecture.

For a full list of titles in this series, please visit www.routledge.com/series/RCSFS

6. **Civil Society and the Reform of Finance**
   Taming capital, reclaiming virtue
   Charles McDaniel, Jr.

7. **Financial Regulation in the European Union**
   Edited by Jan Kregel, Mario Tonveronachi and Rainer Kattel

8. **Achieving Financial Stability and Growth in Africa**
   Edited by Stephany Griffith-Jones and Ricardo Gottschalk

9. **Financial Development, Economic Crises and Emerging Market Economies**
   Edited by Faruk Ülgen

10. **Financialization and the Economy**
    Edited by Agata Gemzik-Salwach and Krzysztof Opolski

Financialization and the Economy

Edited by Agata Gemzik-Salwach
and Krzysztof Opolski

Routledge
Taylor & Francis Group
LONDON AND NEW YORK

First published 2017
by Routledge
2 Park Square, Milton Park, Abingdon, Oxon, OX14 4RN

and by Routledge
711 Third Avenue, New York, NY 10017

Routledge is an imprint of the Taylor & Francis Group, an informa business

British Library Cataloguing-in-Publication Data
A catalogue record for this book is available from the British Library

Library of Congress Cataloguing-in-Publication Data
Names: Gemzik-Salwach, Agata, editor. | Opolski, Krzysztof, editor.
Title: Financialization and the economy / edited by
Agata Gemzik-Salwach and Krzysztof Opolski.
Description: Abingdon, Oxon ; New York, NY : Routledge, 2017. |
Includes index. Identifiers: LCCN 2017001657 |
ISBN 9781138241039 (hardback) | ISBN 9781315281537 (ebook)
Subjects: LCSH: Finance. | Financial institutions. | Economic development.
Classification: LCC HG173.F51949 2017 | DDC 332–dc23
LC record available at https://lccn.loc.gov/2017001657

ISBN: 978-1-138-24103-9 (hbk)
ISBN: 978-1-315-28153-7 (ebk)

Typeset in Times New Roman
by Out of House Publishing

Contents

Figures

Tables

Contributors

Editors

Agata Gemzik-Salwach, University of Information Technology and Management in Rzeszów, Poland
Krzysztof Opolski, University of Warsaw, Poland

Authors

Anna Białek-Jaworska, University of Warsaw, Poland
Bruno Bonizzi, SOAS University of London, United Kingdom
Gary A. Dymski, University of Leeds, United Kingdom
Anna Iwańczuk-Kaliska, Poznań University of Economics, Poland
Christina Laskaridis, SOAS University of London, United Kingdom
Marta Maciejasz-Świątkiewicz, Opole University, Poland
Oksana Martanus, Lomonosov Moscow State University, Russia
Elena Merekina, Lomonosov Moscow State University, Russia
Tomasz Potocki, University of Rzeszów, Poland
Malcolm Sawyer, University of Leeds, United Kingdom
Andrzej Szopa, Cracow University of Economics, Poland
Hanna K. Szymborska, University of Leeds, United Kingdom
Jan Toporowski, SOAS University of London, United Kingdom

Introduction

Agata Gemzik-Salwach and Krzysztof Opolski

In the discussion on the role of the financial sector in the economy, it can be observed that different views collide. On the one hand, there are arguments in favour of the status quo, those that present financialization as a driving force of the economy. It is believed that a properly functioning financial system contributes to economic growth, and financial institutions as banks and insurance companies support the processes of development and efficiency of other sectors. On the other hand, there are plenty of very critical remarks about the negative impact of the financial sphere on all elements of economic and social life. Financialization is blamed for a whole range of undesirable effects, such as economic collapse, excessive consumption and debt, the crisis of moral values, stratification of income, the rebellion of the masses, political revolutions, etc. The extremity of both of these assessments invites us to take a closer look at the subject.

This monograph comprehensively presents the role of financialization in the modern world. It shows the positive and negative effects of financialization on the stability of the whole of the economy, the functioning of different kinds of markets, enterprises, state institutions and behaviours of households. It is a kind of an account of profits and losses that are associated with this process. The aim of the book is to synthetically show the effects of financialization relating to state institutions, companies and households in terms of international, regional and local levels. The book is intended to show which of the phenomena caused by financialization can be selected and accepted, and which areas need to be improved and regulated. This monograph can play an important role in the debate on the future direction of the development of the financial sector and financial markets.

There already are available publications on the market explaining the essence of financialization and showing the growth of its importance. This monograph goes a step further; it sums up what is known about this phenomenon so far, but above all, assesses and gives guidance as to the way ahead. The book gives an original outlook on the actions taken to protect citizens from the effects of financialization. Previous actions undertaken after the economic crises caused by financialization, were oriented to quickly alleviate the current situation, but according to the authors of this book, they lacked a bit of long-term perspective. Through showing the different faces of financialization, the monograph forces us to take a closer look at its effects in the long term and formulates goals and recommendations for institutions responsible for monetary and fiscal policy. Also new is the view of many phenomena from the perspective of countries in Central and Eastern Europe, that is, the countries catching up in current economic backwardness, where little about financialization is said or written.

The FESSUD project (Financialization, Economy, Society and Sustainable Development) became the inspiration for the book, where the editors had the opportunity to observe its development and effects. Cooperation with the following professors played a huge role: Gary Dymski, Trevor Evans, Malcolm Sawyer, Jan Toporowski and Alessandro Vercelli, thanks to whom our attention has turned to the topic of financialization and its significance. We are grateful to professors Gary Dymski, Malcolm Sawyer and Jan Toporowski for having agreed to prepare chapters of this book, and especially would like to thank Jan Toporowski for his valuable tips, still in the planning stages of this monograph. Following the observations of the FESSUD project participants' work, science representatives from countries in Central and Eastern Europe make an attempt to analyse the status and the course of the financialization phenomenon in their countries, where the process of financialization due to varied economic, social, historical and political conditions often runs in different ways. As a result, the book created by an international composition of authors, can initiate discussions between representatives of different countries. The subject of financialization is relatively well known in Western Europe, while relatively little recognized in the countries of Central and Eastern Europe. Thanks to the experience and knowledge of authors from more developed countries, and understanding of the markets, reality and conditions for the operation of authors from Central and Eastern Europe, a network of mutual cooperation is formed and a base to promote achievements of Western Europe to other countries is created.

The book consists of three parts, each of which shows the impact of financialization on a different area of economic life. The first part is devoted to issues of the impact of financialization on the economy and occurring mechanisms. The second part shows the way financialization shapes the new financial markets and processes in financial institutions, and the third part shows the influence of financialization on individual entities: businesses and households as well as society. In each chapter the authors try to answer the posed questions relating to the impact of financialization on various areas of economic life.

The first part is devoted to the economy as a whole, and it is opened with Chapter 1 written by Malcolm Sawyer, who with a broad literature review of research conducted so far shows in a synthetic way the impact of growth of the financial sector on changes in real economy. What is the impact of rapid growth in the financial sphere on real economy? Are these relationships constant over time, or rather, on the contrary – changing with the rise in processes of financialization? What significance for real economy are such manifestations of financialization as: the development of new instruments, securitization, growth in trade of derivatives and changes in the ways of business management? All these phenomena, according to the author of the chapter, are not without relevance to real economy.

Chapter 2, by Jan Toporowski and Bruno Bonizzi, presents the developing and emerging countries as finance providers: foreign exchange reserves and direct investment to the European Union. Will the financial flows that exist between countries support economic development and financial stability of the European Union member countries? Or is the nature of flows such that it can hardly be expected that they will contribute to financial stability? Jan Toporowski and Bruno Bonizzi carry out a thorough analysis of the phenomena occurring in this area.

In Chapter 3, Gary A. Dymski poses the question of the need for global financial management dictated by the need to ensure economies' sustainable development and global prosperity. Are the necessary global investments, like those associated with the need to protect the environment, resulting from the ongoing climate changes, possible without international financial support? Is the current method of financial management able to provide funding for such global investments? Chapter 3 is an important voice in the discussion about these issues.

In Chapter 4 Tomasz Potocki and Krzysztof Opolski discuss macroeconomic factors determining the level of financial expertise in the societies of the European Union on the example of numeracy. Why can even the well-educated and wealthy people not make the right financial decisions? Could these skills be determined by more than those factors, e.g. a group of determinants that describe the level of financial development of a country? The authors attempt to answer this question through analysing relationships that take place in all European countries between the financial know-how and macroeconomic variables, state of countries' financial development data and the level of development with the quality of the education system.

The second part of the book deals with the impact of financialization on financial institutions and financial markets. In Chapter 5 Anna Iwańczuk-Kaliska asks about the consequences for payment intermediation that result from the bankruptcy of banks in conditions of financialization. What are the consequences for the contractors of banks and intermediaries on the national and international level? What is the threat of systemic risk that arises from bank failures? The research in this chapter focuses on the consequences arising especially from banks' roles as payment services providers and settlement agents. The conclusions of these considerations can play a big role in the debate on the future direction of development and regulations for financial institutions and markets.

Chapter 6, by Christina Laskaridis, examines the process of financialization in low income countries in the context of the new EU relationship to developing countries. The author turns her attention to the Franc Zone.

What are the key historical factors that have shaped the development of the financial sector in the Franc Zone? Can the Operations Account mechanism, designed to sustain convertibility through overall trade balances, be effective with a build-up of cross-border debt in the private or public sectors of member countries? The discussions on the Franc Zone appearing in the literature are supplemented in this chapter by elements associated with debt in the public and private sectors.

In Chapter 7 Oksana Martanus and Elena Merekina describe the phenomenon of growth of alternative investment funds, which, according to the authors, is a consequence of the process of financialization. How to assess the attractivity of alternative investment funds? What factors must be taken into account in the assessment of such funds? Can the methods used in this field in the European market be also used in Russia? All the issues presented by the authors are presented from the viewpoint of two markets: the European and Russian.

Andrzej Szopa in Chapter 8 continues the theme of the impact of financialization on financial instruments, focusing on the problem of increasing financial risk. How to measure financial risk for the instruments available on the market? Are the hitherto used risk measurement methods effective, or should we strive to develop new proposals in the face of financialization? The chapter provides an overview of the methods used so far and proposals for a new solution.

The third part of the book, that shows the impact of financialization on society, households and enterprises is begun by Chapter 9 by Hanna K. Szymborska. This chapter revisits the existing theoretical approaches to analysing inequality in order to answer the following questions. Are current theories capable of reproducing the trends in inequality experienced in the twenty-first century? Do their predictions survive the transformation of economic relations in the light of deregulation and financial innovation? Is economics in need of a new theory of inequality?

Agata Gemzik-Salwach in Chapter 10 presents the relationships between the phenomenon of financialization and the level and structure of indebtedness of households in Poland. What changes have taken place in the structure and level of household debt in recent years? What impact on these factors did the new supervisory regulations introduced after the crisis have? Can the structure of household debt in Poland be considered beneficial? Financialization, which results in an increase of the number of financial institutions offering loans and growth of strength of financial motives that drive households, has an impact on the status and type of household debt.

The topic of financial exclusion, which is raised in Chapter 10, is continued and developed by Marta Maciejasz-Świątkiewicz in Chapter 11. Should the phenomenon of financial exclusion always be perceived in a negative light? How to treat the phenomenon of self-exclusion, understood as voluntary resignation from using financial products and services? The author's aim is to answer the question in which situations could financial exclusion be the result of rational behaviour of an individual.

In Chapter 12, Anna Białek-Jaworska explains the source of the savings in business in the era of financialization. Is the increase in companies' savings resulting from a faulty measurement used in the National Accounts or from changes in the way businesses operate? How much of an impact does the valuation at fair value – which by virtue of the Accounting Act concerns financial investment and investment property, and due to International Financial Reporting Standards additionally concerns fixed assets and intangible assets – have on companies' behaviour? The carried out statistical analysis, as well as panel and logit analyses of determinants of savings of companies listed on the Warsaw Stock Exchange, including operating risk, aim to answer these questions.

This book, due to an international composition of authors and a wide range of problems, may be of interest to a broad environment of scientists, and not only those who represent economics and finance, but also for social scientists, sociological and political, as well as for entrepreneurs who can identify prospects and barriers to economic development in the context of the opportunities and constraints posed by financialization.

Part I

Financialization: impact on the structure of economy and economic mechanisms

1 Financialization and economic and social performance

Malcolm Sawyer[1]

Introduction

The growth and evolution of the nature of financial systems over the past few decades have a multitude of effects for good or ill on the real economy. In this chapter the focus is on the effects which financialization in the present era has had on the performance of the real economy. Financialization has involved the growth of the financial system in its economic scale, its growing political and social importance, the development of new financial instruments, securitization and derivative trading. Financialization has changed the relationships between the financial sector and the real sector, and as ownership of corporations passes into the hands of the financial sector there is increasing the emphasis on the 'pursuit of shareholder value'.

The growth of the (formal) financial sectors has often been viewed as involving positive effects on economic growth – through stimulating savings opportunities, allocating and monitoring the use of funds, and thereby promoting more investment in terms of quality and quantity and contributing to faster growth. However, the ways in which the financial sector has grown in the past decades has shifted their activities (in relative terms) away from the savings–investment linkages and towards creating, managing of and trading in financial assets. The question arises whether those changes have undermined the financial development–economic growth linkage. There are other ways through which financialization (particularly in the guise of ownership by the financial sector of the corporate sector and the pursuit of shareholder value) sets the framework for a wide range of decisions taken by corporations including investment and employment.

The processes of financialization are intimately wrapped up with the operations of capitalist economies, and the recent decades of financialization have been accompanied by globalization and neo-liberalism. Disentangling the effects of financialization on the economy from the broader operations of capitalism is particularly difficult, if not impossible. However, we attempt to provide some partial answers to the question of the effects of financialization on economic performance. In this regard, economic performance is broadly interpreted, and it is specific aspects of financialization such as the growth of the financial sector and the rise of the pursuit of shareholder value which can be examined.

Financial deepening and economic growth[2]

There has been a large literature extending back many decades on the relationship between finance and economic growth, notably using measures such as bank deposits to GDP, stock market value to GDP as measures of financial deepening. This literature has used the terminology of financial development and deepening but can be viewed as one significant component of financialization. Financial deepening focuses on the growth of the formal financial sectors and does not reflect the role of informal financial sectors and 'curb markets'. In a similar vein, economic growth (and development) often relates to the formal sector and (implicitly) industrialization. This literature has generally found a positive relationship between financial deepening and economic growth, though the causal relationships involved are matters of debate. A more recent literature has tended to find weaker relationships than hitherto and now is often finding negative relationships at high levels of financial deepening. There is a sense in which the financial sector has become too large which is also considered, and particularly in terms of the scale of financial asset transactions (relative to the levels of savings and investment).

Levine (2005) in his extensive review of the empirical literature concluded that

> a growing body of empirical analyses, including firm-level studies, industry-level studies, individual country-studies, time-series studies, panel-investigations, and broad cross-country comparisons, demonstrate a strong positive link between the functioning of the financial system and long-run economic growth. … Furthermore, microeconomic-based evidence is consistent with the view that better developed financial systems ease external financing constraints facing firms, which illuminates one mechanism through which financial development influences economic growth. Theory and empirical evidence make it difficult to conclude that the financial system merely – and automatically – responds to economic activity, or that financial development is an inconsequential addendum to the process of economic growth.
>
> (p. 921)

Arestis *et al.* (2015) conclude from their meta-analysis of the empirical evidence on the effects of financial development on growth that 'the results suggest the existence of a statistically significant and economically meaningful positive genuine effect from financial development to economic growth' (p. 559). However, there is considerable heterogeneity in the results, and that

> the usage of market-based proxies of financial development seems to result in lower correlations than the usage of either liquid liabilities or market-based variables. [However], the estimated coefficients of bank-based measures and complex indices are found statistically insignificant in all specifications. ... Additionally, panel data, which are frequently used from the late 1990s onwards, produce smaller correlations.
>
> (p. 558)

The relationship between financial development and economic growth during the era of financialization (from circa 1980) is of particular interest.[3] Casual observation may suggest that the general growth of the financial sector and the enhanced size of that sector have not obviously been associated with any faster economic growth. Further, the literature on financialization has indeed suggested a variety of ways in which the processes of financialization may have diminished investment, as further discussed below.

Authors have reported on at least some weakening of the links between financial deepening and economic growth. Rousseau and Wachtel (2011, p. 276) argue that 'we show that it [the finance-growth link] is not as strong in more recent data as it was in the original studies with data for the period from 1960 to 1989'. Another study finds 'that in the long run financial intermediation increases growth and reduces growth volatility. Both effects have, however, become weaker over time' (Beck *et al.*, 2014, p. 62). A study of

> the complex real effects of financial development ... come[s] to two important conclusions. First, financial sector size has an inverted U-shaped effect on productivity growth. That is, there comes a point where further enlargement of the financial system can reduce real growth. Second, financial sector growth is found to be a drag on productivity growth. Our interpretation is that because the financial sector competes with the rest of the economy for scarce resources, financial booms are not, in general, growth enhancing. ... More finance is definitely not always better.
>
> (Cecchetti and Kharroubi, 2012, p. 14)[4]

Sahay *et al.* (2015, p. 5) use a broad measure of financial development and find that

> the effect of financial development on growth is bell-shaped; it weakens at higher levels of financial development. This weakening effect stems from financial deepening, rather than from greater accessor higher efficiency. The empirical evidence also suggests that this weakening effect reflects primarily the impact of financial deepening on total factor productivity growth, rather than on capital accumulation. [Further] the pace of financial development matters. When it proceeds too fast, deepening financial institutions can lead to economic and financial instability.

Cournède *et al.* (2015, p. 6) based on 50 years of data for OECD countries conclude that 'in most OECD countries, further expansion [of the financial sector] is likely to slow rather than boost growth'.

Overall, it could be concluded that a positive relationship between the financial sector and economic growth has generally been found though issues of causation have not been resolved. The positive relationship has weakened and indeed may have been reversed in recent years, noting that the econometric studies generally use data spanning the past few decades. The empirical work has focused on measures of the financial sector such as bank deposits, size of the stock market, and has not in general reflected the expansion of the financial sector in recent decades in terms of derivatives, securitization and volume of trade in assets and liabilities.

Financial liberalization and growth

Financialization has been closely associated with financial liberalization and de-regulation with financial interests pushing for de-regulation and financial liberalization aiding the growth of finance. McKinnon (1973) and Shaw (1973) propounded the 'financial liberalization' thesis arguing that government restrictions on the banking system restrain the quantity and quality of investment. Financial liberalization was to remove 'financial repression' which referred to a high degree of regulation of the banking and financial system in many countries, and specifically control by Central Bank and government of the level of interest rates and the allocation of credit.

Bumann *et al.* (2012) note that

> whereas some have claimed that liberalisation of financial markets contributes to the efficiency with which these markets can transform saving into investment, which ultimately fosters economic growth, others have pointed out that these liberalisations have contributed to various financial and economic crises in the past. … The evidence that emerges from these studies [of the relationship] remains inconclusive.
>
> (p. 41)

They undertake a meta-analysis based on 60 empirical studies. From their meta-regression analysis they

> conclude that although our results indicate that, on average, there is a positive effect of financial liberalisation on growth, the significance of this effect is only weak. [Further], for most of the variables that may help explaining the heterogeneity of results about the relationship between financial liberalisation and economic growth we do not find any significant results. There are two exceptions. Our analysis suggests that data from the 1970s generate more negative financial liberalisation coefficients which suggests that financial liberalisation policies carried out during the 1970s seem to have a stronger negative relationship with growth.

> Moreover, our results show that studies that take into account a measure of the level of development of the financial system report lower t-statistics for the relationship between liberalisation and growth.
>
> (pp. 43–45)

Demirgüç-Kunt and Detragiache (1998) remark that the 'frequency of systemic banking problems has increased markedly [in the past 30 years, i.e. 1970s through 1990s] all over the world, raising the issue of whether greater fragility may be a consequence of liberalization' (p. 4). After controlling for factors such as bad macroeconomic policies and adverse macroeconomic developments, 'financial liberalization exerts an independent negative effect on the stability of the banking sector, and the magnitude of the effect is not trivial' (p. 33). They find (p. 6) that banking crises are more likely to occur where there is a liberalized financial sector even when other factors such as the real rate of interest are taken into account. Further, banking sector fragility tends to occur a few years after the start of financial liberalization, rather than as an immediate effect. Over the period 1980–1995 in the sample of 53 countries, '78 per cent of banking crises occurred in periods of financial liberalization' (p. 13).

Arestis (2016, p. 3) points to two striking findings from the experiences of financial liberalisation in developing and developed countries over the past four decades. First, in that period, banking crises have been frequent and severe. Second, 'there have been exacerbated downturns in economic activity, which have imposed substantial real economic costs for the local economies involved' citing, inter alia, Arestis and Sawyer (2005).

Financial crises

Although the history of capitalist economies is littered with financial crises, the era of financialization since circa 1980 has witnessed a much greater volume and intensity of financial crisis than hitherto (with the 2007–2009 financial crises being the most recent intensive crisis). As indicated in the previous section, financial crisis is often related with financial liberalization, itself a key element of financialization. Laeven and Valencia (2013) identify 147 banking crises, of which 13 were borderline events, over the period 1970–2011, and a further 211 currency crises and 66 sovereign crises. In the recent financial crisis period from 2007, the authors identify 13 systemic banking crises and 8 borderline cases in the period 2007–2011. They report that 'advanced and emerging economies tend to experience larger output losses than developing countries … to some extent driven by deeper banking systems that makes a banking crisis more disruptive' (p. 226).

The IMF (2009, p. 122) summarized its findings on the effects of financial crisis on output, growth and employment as follows:

> The path of output tends to be depressed substantially and persistently following banking crises, with no rebound on average to the precrisis

> trend over the medium term. Growth does, however, eventually return to its precrisis rate for most economies. ... The depressed output path tends to result from long-lasting reductions of roughly equal proportion in the employment rate, the capital-to-labour ratio, and total factor productivity.

Laeven and Valencia (2012) provide estimates for banking crises. From their Table 4, overall output loss is reported as a median of 23.2 per cent of GDP across all countries, with 32.4 per cent in advanced economies, 33.6 per cent in emerging economies with 0.7 per cent in developing countries. Fiscal costs average 6.8 per cent of GDP though in this case heavier for developing countries at 10 per cent and advanced at 4.2 per cent.

Overall costs of the financial sector

Epstein and Montecino (2016) examine the costs of the financial sector to American households in terms of three components: (1) rents, or excess profits; (2) misallocation costs, or the price of diverting resources away from non-financial activities; and (3) the costs of the 2008 financial crisis.

The rents obtained by the financial sector come 'through a variety of mechanisms including anticompetitive practices, the marketing of excessively complex and risky products, government subsidies such as financial bailouts, and even fraudulent activities, bankers receive excess pay and profits for the services'. Epstein and Montecino (2016) estimate the total cost of financial rents as in the range of $3.6–$4.2 trillion between 1990 and 2005. Mis-selling, anti-competitive and fraudulent activities in the financial sector impose their costs. Dzimwasha (2015) indicates that the 20 largest global banks paid $235 billion in fines for a range of mis-selling in the seven years following the 2008 financial crisis. Zingales (2015) reports that fines paid by financial institutions to US regulatory agencies amounted to $138.59 billion over period 2010–2014. Fines imposed in the UK by the Financial Services Authority and its successor the Financial Conduct Authority amounted to just under £3.5 billion during the years 2009–2015.[5] Robert Jenkins provides a listing of the 'misdeeds' of banks. He gives over 50 proven cases and 25 currently under investigation. These range from mis-selling (e.g. of payment protection insurance, interest rate swaps), manipulation of markets (e.g. precious metals markets, US Treasury Market auction/client sales, energy markets), aiding and abetting tax evasion and money laundering for violent drug cartels, collusion with Greek authorities to mislead EU policy makers on meeting Euro criteria, etc. (Jenkins, 2016).

Misallocation costs come from speculative finance which

> harms the economy on a daily basis ... by growing too large, utilizing too many skilled and productive workers, imposing short-term orientations

> on businesses, and starving some businesses and households of needed credit. We estimate that the cost of misallocating human and financial resources amounted to \$2.6 trillion–\$3.9 trillion between 1990 and 2005.
> (Epstein and Montecino, 2016)

Malkiel (2013, p. 97) argues that neither the argument that the increase in fees reflected increasing returns for investors from active management nor if it was necessary to improve the efficiency of the market for investors who availed themselves of low-cost passive (index) funds is supported by the data. 'Thus, the increase in fees is likely to represent a deadweight loss for investors. Indeed, perhaps the greatest inefficiency in the stock market is in "the market" for investment advice.'

For the costs of the financial crisis, Epstein and Montecino (2016) use the estimates from the Dallas Federal Reserve (Atkinson *et al.*, 2013). They report the cost of the crisis ranges from 40 per cent to 90 per cent of 2007 output over the period 2008–2023 during which output is forecast to remain below long-term trend as a consequence of the financial crisis. These estimates relate to the US and the recent financial crisis: in the section above costs of other financial crises have been indicated.

Epstein and Montecino (2016) overall place the total costs imposed on society by the financial sector as between \$12.9 trillion and \$22.7 trillion in the period 1990–2023, which represents between 66 per cent and 133 per cent of one year's US GDP. These results have to be read in conjunction with the discussion above on the relationship between the size of the financial sector and economic growth.

Shareholder value, investment and industrial restructuring

Financialization has been associated with the rise of the push for the maximization of shareholder value. Van der Zwan (2014) views the pursuit of shareholder value as one of the three key characteristics of financialization, and Minsky's notion of money manager capitalism places an emphasis of financial institutions as shareholders. Financialization often involves the growth of the financial sector's ownership and dealings in equity, and the growth of financial markets. There has been the speed-up in the trading of equity (as with other financial assets), and emphasis on short-term share-price performance rather than on longer-term growth prospects. The particular significance of these developments here comes from the impact on decisions on investment, employment, output, etc., as made by corporations. Do these developments foster more or less investment, more or less research and innovation? – questions often summarized under issues of short-termism. Further, do these developments favour some sectors over others? What would the impact be on the quality and quantity of jobs?

Financial institutions, notably in the form of pension funds, insurance companies, investment banks, whether trading on their own account or on behalf of others become owners of equity and have interests in the price of equity. The financial institutions and their managers have material interests in the corporate performance, at least as reflected in the equity price. At the same time, and in some ways paradoxically, the frequency of trading has speeded up and hence the average length of time for which an equity is held is reduced. The exercise of ownership interest in the performance of a corporation can be enhanced with the growth of financial institutions in so far as a large number of small individual shareholders are replaced by a small number of financial institutions with a sizeable interest. The higher frequency trading though means that a financial institution's portfolio is continuously changing, and there is reliance on price changes (rather than interest) for profits.

The advocacy of the pursuit of shareholder value is a route through which shareholder interests are imposed on managerial interests. It also acts in the interests of the financial sector which gains from increasing stock market valuations. It is interesting to note that the 'managerial theories' of the firm would 'predict' that growth would be slower under 'shareholder value' maximization than previously. The re-alignment of management interests with shareholder value was advocated through the use of share options, profit-related bonuses, etc. The growth of inequality resulting from the high pay of 'top' managers is one result of that attempted re-alignment.

Lazonick and O'Sullivan (2000, p. 13)

> provide an historical analysis of the rise of shareholder value as a principle of corporate governance in the United States, tracing the transformation of US corporate strategy from an orientation towards retention of corporate earnings and reinvestment in corporate growth through the 1970s to one of downsizing of corporate labour forces and distribution of corporate earnings to shareholders over the past two decades. We then consider the recent performance of the US economy, and raise questions about the relation between the maximization of shareholder value and the sustainability of economic prosperity.

They argue that although during the 1990s stock prices were bid up as funds flowed in the stock market, 'the stock-market boom has not made capital available to industry … [with] net corporate equity issues … negative over the course of the 1990s because of corporate stock repurchases' (p. 32). Overall, they conclude that 'the experience of the United States suggests that the pursuit of shareholder value may be an appropriate strategy for running down a company – and an economy' (p. 33).

Hein summarizes a range of arguments on the generally adverse effects of the pursuit of shareholder value' under financialization on investment:

1. Shareholders impose higher distribution of profits on firms, i.e. a higher dividend pay-out ratio and hence a lower retention ratio and/or a lower

contribution of new equity issues to the financing of investment, or even share buybacks. Therefore, internal means of finance for real investment are reduced, and the ability to invest hence suffers ('internal means of finance channel').

2. Managers' (firms') preference for growth is weakened as a result of remuneration schemes based on short-term profitability and financial market results. The preference for growth, and hence the willingness to invest in capital stock, therefore suffers, too ('preference channel').

(Hein, 2012, p. 39)

Financialization is viewed in terms of increasing shareholder power relative to management and workers, and also a higher rate of return to rentiers on holdings of bonds and equity, and depressed 'animal spirits' of management, all of which have a negative impact on firms' real investment.

A rather similar view comes from Dallery (2009):

> Whether a firm's orientation is decided by managers under shareholders' pressure or by shareholders themselves, financialisation effectively leads to a decreasing tendency to accumulate. … On the one hand, managers do not blindly pursue growth, and they also care about target utilization rates and the indebtedness threshold. On the other hand, shareholders are not only motivated by profit rate; they are also concerned with debt-leverage and growth. … What I have shown is that financialisation taken as a constraint for managers entails a relatively small drop in accumulation, and it could even lead to a constant accumulation through increased pressure on workers and/or increased real fragility. Considering the opposite case where shareholders preside over firms' fates, I find that the decrease in accumulation is far greater, but the scale of this reduction is dependent on what is assumed to be shareholders' objectives and time horizons (the longer it is, the more need for growth). The way financialisation has been presented here offers a theoretical representation of the historical change in corporate governance, 'from an orientation towards retention of corporate earnings and reinvestment in corporate growth through the 1970s to one of downsizing of corporate labour forces and distribution of corporate earnings to shareholders over the past two decades' (Lazonick and O'Sullivan, 2000).
>
> (Dallery, 2009, p. 513)

Inequality and poverty

The relationships between financialization on the one hand and inequality and poverty on the other are not straightforward. Since financial development and growth can take many forms and work through a variety of institutional arrangements the relationships of financial development and inequality and poverty will vary over time and space. It is easy to point to features of the financial system and institutions which are intended to aid the poor – micro-finance institutions, credit unions being notable examples. At the other end of the spectrum private equity companies operate to make high returns for the already rich.

It is possible that there is some form of Kuznet's curve type relationship[6] involved – initially financial development favours the wealthy but as banking spreads to the less well-off it can favour the less wealthy. It can be remarked that over the past three to four decades the growth of the financial sector and rising inequality have gone together.

> The majority of theoretical studies on the relationship between income inequality and financial development argue that financial deepening might be a feasible instrument for improving income distribution. This paper finds that the prediction crucially depends on the stages of financial development that the country is undergoing. The benefits of financial depth only occur if the country has reached a threshold level of financial development. Below this critical value, financial development counteracts income inequality. Our policy implication is that a minimum level of financial development is a necessary precondition for achieving reduction in income inequality through financial development.
>
> (Kim and Lin, 2011, p. 310)

Beck *et al.* (2007) find that financial development helps the poor.

> Greater financial development induces the incomes of the poor to grow faster than average per capita GDP growth, which lowers income inequality. ... Although the results show that financial development is particularly beneficial to the poor, this research is silent on how to foster poverty-reducing financial development.
>
> (p. 46)

Some argue that 'theory provides sound reasons for believing that the poor disproportionately benefit from financial development'. In effect financial development reduces financial exclusion, and more are able to borrow from the financial sector. However, financial development may take the form of improving financial services for the rich. Demirgüç-Kunt and Levine (2009) suggest that empirical evidence in general supports the view that

> there is a strong beneficial effect of financial development on the poor and that poor households and smaller firms benefit more from this development compared with rich individuals and larger firms. Empirical research suggests that an improvement in financial development expands economic opportunities, particularly for those whose opportunities had previously been tightly curtailed.
>
> (p. 47)

However, Jauch and Watzka (2011, p. 27) observe in the last five decades two phenomena can be observed: 'increasing financial development and increasing gross income inequality in many countries, especially in the developed world'. They reach conclusions running counter to those indicated in the previous paragraph.

> Using a broader data set and time-invariant country specifics in our panel estimation, we … reject these earlier theories and previous empirical research. Integrating time-invariant country characteristics, we find a positive relationship between financial development and income inequality within countries. Better-developed financial markets lead to higher gross income inequality. … We do not exclude the possibility that all income groups within a country benefit from more financial development, but we do find that those who are already better off benefit more because income inequality is increasing.
>
> (p. 27)

They argue for the importance of targeting financial development towards the poorest, which suggests policy interventions rather than market forces.

Onaran *et al.* (2011) find that the redistribution of income in favour of rentier income and of profits at the expense of wages, which has gone alongside financialization suppresses consumption; however, the secondary redistribution of profits in favour of rentier income has a positive effect on consumption. Their results suggest that the changes in functional income distribution and wealth effects in the era of financialization have had an overall neutral effect on aggregate demand.

A more direct linkage with financialization comes from the observation

> increasing dependence on financial income, in the long run, is associated with reducing labor's share of income, increasing top executives' share of compensation, and increasing earnings dispersion among workers. Net of conventional explanations such as deunionization, globalization, technological change, and capital investment, the effects of financialisation on all three dimensions of income inequality are substantial. Our counterfactual analysis suggests that financialisation could account for more than half of the decline in labor's share of income, 9.6% of the growth in officers' share of compensation, and 10.2% of the growth in earnings dispersion between 1970 and 2008.
>
> (Lin and Tomaskovic-Devey, 2013, p. 1284)

Das and Mohapatra (2003), present

> evidence of a strong statistical association between the event of liberalization and income shares. The data strongly support a positive coefficient between liberalization and the highest income quintile's share of mean

> income, and a negative coefficient between liberalization and the middle class income share .... We find no evidence of any statistical association between liberalization and the lowest income quintile. ... However, it is important to note that there are mechanisms which should relate capital market liberalizations to income shares under a wide variety of hypotheses that are true in emerging markets (e.g., differential access to credit markets, limited stock market participation, and the tight links between upper quintiles and policy makers).
>
> (p. 245)

Employment and work

The discussion above does not speak directly of the effects of financialization and financial development on the quantity and quality of employment. Financialization has been accompanied by increased incidence of financial crisis, and crises, particularly banking crises, have a devastating effect on output and on employment. The longer-term effects of financialization on employment are not at all clear-cut. In so far as financial development fosters growth and higher output, then it could be thought favourable for employment. But the causal links between financial development and economic growth are not well-established, and higher output does not necessarily translate into higher employment depending on productivity trends and capital formation. Some other trends, which may be associated with financialization, which have been discussed in the preceding section, would operate to constrain employment.

Slater and Spencer (2014) have highlighted four routes through which the processes of financialization have consequences for work and work relations. The first is that

> financialisation has impacted directly on the employment relationship. Specifically, it has enabled employers to increase their power over workers. As workers have accumulated financial assets and taken on greater amounts of debt, they have become less able and willing to push for higher wages and better working conditions. To the contrary, their weakened economic position has made them more vulnerable to real wage cuts, longer work hours and more precarious forms of employment.

The second echoes the shareholder value route with

> the interests of shareholders have been elevated above those of other stakeholders, including workers. Pressurized by financial markets to maximize short-term profits and to raise dividends for shareholders, managers have looked to reduce wages, lay off workers, and downsize production (Lazonick and O'Sullivan, 2000; Froud, *et al.*, 2006; Thompson, 2011). ... The simultaneous growth of private equity investors that have bought

> and sold productive assets, in addition, has resulted in poorer employment outcomes for workers (Clark, 2009).

The third issue which is discussed is the impact of the financial crisis of 2007–2009 which 'has its origins in the financialization process and among its outcomes has been a decline in employment, job security, wages and working conditions', to which could be added that financial crises have become more frequent under financialization.

The fourth impacts on the organization of work, where it is argued that

> financialisation impedes the adoption and sustainability of forms of participatory work practices that rely on the elicitation of commitment, and flexibility from workers. Despite their perceived economic benefits … these practices have not been adopted to any great extent, in part because they represent too high a cost for firms, but also because they pose a challenge to employers' 'right to manage' …. Managers demand commitment and flexibility from workers but their drive to maximize shareholder value means that they cannot maintain the conditions required to secure the continued cooperation of workers.
>
> (Slater and Spencer, 2014, pp. 142–143)

Cushen (2013) speaks of 'startling trends concerning employment outcomes under financialization which indicate the hegemonic force of financialized interests within organizations' (pp. 317–318). Lazonik (2014) speaks of an organizational failure in which 'U.S. business corporations have failed to use their substantial profits to invest in new rounds of innovation that can create new high value-added jobs to replace those that have been lost' to the financialization of the US corporation. US corporations are pursuing 'employment strategies purely for financial gain' which includes manufacturing plant closure, off-shoring production to low wage areas. But 'business corporations failed to invest in new, higher value-added job creation on a sufficient scale to provide a foundation for equitable and stable growth in the U.S. economy' (p. 859).

On the contrary, with superior corporate performance defined as meeting Wall Street's expectations for quarterly earnings per share, companies turned to massive stock repurchases to 'manage' their own corporations' stock prices. Trillions of dollars that could have been spent on innovation and job creation in the US economy over the past three decades have instead been used to buy back stock for the purpose of manipulating the company's stock price. This financialized mode of corporate resource allocation has been legitimized by the ideology, itself a product of the 1980s and 1990s, that a business corporation should be run to 'maximise shareholder value'. Through their stock-based compensation, corporate executives who make these decisions are themselves prime beneficiaries of this focus on rising stock prices as the measure of corporate performance.

Assa (2012) argues that the

> strengthening of finance vis-à-vis the rest of the economy did not come without a price. The empirical evidence clearly confirms the relationships discussed in the literature on financialisation, and in particular its negative effects on equality, growth and employment. Each percentage increase in financialisation is associated with between 0.49% and 0.81% more inequality (depending on which indicator of financialisation is used). A similar increase in financialisation is related to a 0.2% slower growth of GDP, and between 0.12% and 0.74% higher unemployment.
>
> (p. 39)[7]

Conclusion

The impacts of financialization on the performance of the real economy are clearly far from agreed upon. However, we would hazard the following remarks. The financial sector has grown rapidly in the past three decades, and it can be doubted that this has aided growth. In earlier periods a positive relationship between financial deepening and economic growth was generally accepted, even if the direction of causation remained disputed. The relationship has become much weaker, and the larger scale of the financial sector has been associated with somewhat slower growth in industrialized countries. Financialization has been associated with a greater frequency of financial crises, which are often associated with substantial unemployment and loss of output. Inequality has in general risen (at least as far as industrialized countries are concerned) in recent decades. Some authors have viewed the growth of the financial sector as tending to reduce inequality, while others have seen financialization as encouraging inequality. Financialization has been associated with the pursuit of 'shareholder value', and many authors have postulated to negative effects on corporate performance coming from that pursuit in the form of discouragement of long-term investment and innovation, and the impact on employment conditions.

Notes

1 Acknowledgements: This chapter draws on the results of research undertaken within the project Financialization, Economy, Society and Sustainable Development (FESSUD), which received funding from the European Union Seventh Framework Programme (FP7/2007–2013) under grant agreement n° 266800, and for which I am the principal investigator. The views expressed in this chapter are mine, and do not reflect the views of the partners within the FESSUD project nor of the European Commission. For Information on FESSUD and for the working papers arising from the project, consult fessud.eu.
2 This section draws heavily on Sawyer (2013) for which see for further references.
3 See, for example, Sawyer (2014, 2016); Vercelli (2014).
4 For other studies see, for example, Aghion *et al.* (2005); Rioja and Valev (2004, 2005); Barajas *et al.* (2012, 2013); Dabla-Norris and Srivisal (2013).

5 Calculated from www.fsa.gov.uk/about/press/facts/fines and www.fca.org.uk/firms/being-regulated/enforcement/fines/2015-fines.
6 Kuznet's curve expressed the idea that economic development and industrialization would at first be associated with rising inequality, and then with falling inequality generating (over time) an inverted U-shaped relationship between level of GDP per capita (or similar) and inequality. The evidence of the past 30 years with rising inequality and higher levels of GDP per capita has severely undermined the Kuznet's curve.
7 His measures of financialization are: Value added in finance as a percentage of total value added and Employment in finance as a percentage of total employment, where finance sector is the broadly defined FIRE. The estimation is panel for OECD countries, and for the years 1970–to 2008 for growth and unemployment, and six period observations for inequality (Gini coefficient).

References

Aghion, P., Howitt, P. and Mayer-Foulkes, D., 2005. The Effect of Financial Development on Convergence: Theory and Evidence. *Quarterly Journal of Economics*, 120, pp. 173–222.

Arestis, P., 2016. Financial Liberalisation, the Finance–Growth Nexus, Financial Crises and Policy Implications. In: P. Arestis and M. Sawyer, eds. *Financial Liberalisation: Past, Present and Future*. Annual Edition of International Papers in Political Economy. Houndmills, Basingstoke: Palgrave Macmillan, pp. 1–42.

Arestis, P. and Sawyer, M., 2005. Financial Liberalisation and the Finance–Growth Nexus: What Have We Learned? In: P. Arestis and M. Sawyer, eds. *Financial Liberalization: Beyond Orthodox Concerns*. Houndmills, Basingstoke: Palgrave Macmillan, pp. 1–42.

Arestis, P., Chortareas, G. and Magkonis, G., 2015. The Financial Development and Growth Nexus: A Meta-Analysis. *Journal of Economic Surveys*, 29(3), pp. 549–565.

Assa, J., 2012. Financialisation and its Consequences: The OECD Experience. *Finance Research*, 1(1).

Atkinson, T., Luttrell, D. and Rosenblum, H., 2013. How Bad is it? The Costs and Consequences of the 2007–09 Financial Crisis. *Staff Papers, The Federal Reserve Bank of Dallas*.

Barajas, A., Chami, R. and Reza Yousefi, S., 2012. *The Finance and Growth Nexus Re-examined: Do All Countries Benefit Equally*. Washington: unpublished IMF Working Papers.

Barajas, A., Beck, T., Dabla-Norris, E. and Reza Yousefi, S., 2013. *Too Cold, Too Hot, or Just Right? Assessing Financial Sector Development Across the Globe*. Washington: IMF Working Papers WP/13/81.

Beck, T., Levine, R. and Demirugüç-Kunt, A., 2007. Finance, Inequality and the Poor. *Journal of Economic Growth*, 12(1), pp. 27–49.

Beck, T., Degryse, H. and Kneer, C., 2014. Is More Finance Better? Disentangling Intermediation and Size Effects of Financial Systems. *Journal of Financial Stability*, 10, pp. 50–64.

Bumann, S., Hermes, N. and Lensink, R., 2012. *Financial Liberalisation and Economic Growth: A Meta-Analysis. Technical Report*. London: EPPI-Centre Social.

Cecchetti, S. G. and Kharroubi, E., 2012. *Reassessing the Impact of Finance on Growth*. BIS Working Papers No. 381, The Bank for International Settlements.

Clark, I., 2009. Owners and Managers: Disconnecting Managerial Capitalism? Understanding the Private-Equity Business Model. *Work, Employment and Society*, 23(4), pp. 775–786.

Cournède, B., Denk, O. and Hoeller, P., 2015. Finance and Inclusive Growth. *OECD Economic Policy Paper*, Issue 14.

Cushen, J., 2013. Financialisation in the Workplace: Hegemonic Narratives, Performative Interventions and the Angry Knowledge Worker. *Accounting, Organisations and Society*, Issue 38, pp. 314–331.

Dabla-Norris, E. and Srivisal, N., 2013. *Revisiting the Link Between Finance and Macroeconomic Volatility*. Washington: IMF Working Papers WP/13/29.

Dallery, T., 2009. Post-Keynesian Theories of the Firm under Financialisation. *Review of Radical Political Economics*, 41(4), pp. 492–515.

Das, M. and Mohapatra, S., 2003. Income Inequality: The Aftermath of Stock Market Liberalisation in Emerging Markets. *Journal of Empirical Finance*, 10(1), pp. 217–248.

Demirgüç-Kunt, A. and Detragiache, E., 1998. *Financial Liberalisation and Financial Fragility*. Washington: IMF Working Papers WP/98/83.

Demirgüç-Kunt, A. and Levine, R., 2009. *Finance and Inequality: Theory and Evidence*. Cambridge, MA: NBER Working Paper 15275.

Dziwasha, T., 2015. *20 Global Banks Have Paid $235bn in Fines Since the 2008 Financial Crisis.* [Online] Available at: www.ibtimes.co.uk/20-global-banks-have-paid-235bn-fines-since-2008-financial-crisis-1502794 [Accessed 21 November 2016].

Epstein, G. and Montecino, J. A., 2016. *Overcharged: The High Cost of High Finance.* [Online] Available at: www.peri.umass.edu/236/hash/fd100f263f6805db4562d-7816b225e5f/publication/711/ [Accessed 11 October 2016].

Froud, J., Leaver, A., Johal, S. and Williams, K., 2006. *Financialisation and Strategy: Narrative and Numbers*. London: Routledge.

Hein, E., 2012. *The Macroeconomics of Finance-dominated Capitalism – and its Crisis*. Cheltenham: Edward Elgar Publishing.

IMF, 2009. *World Economic Outlook 2009*. Washington: IMF.

Jauch, S. and Watzka, S., 2011. *Financial Development and Income Inequality*. Munich: CESifo Working Paper No. 3687.

Jenkins, R., 2016. *Robert Jenkins' Partial List of Bank Misdeeds.* [Online] Available at: www.finance-watch.org/hot-topics/blog/1186-jenkins-bank-misdeeds [Accessed 17 October 2016].

Kim, D. H. and Lin, S. C., 2011. Nonlineary in the Financial Development–Income Inequality Nexus. *Journal of Comparative Economics*, 39(3), pp. 310–325.

Laeven, L. and Valencia, F., 2012. *Systemic Banking Crises Database: An Update*. Washington: IMF Working Papers WP/12/163.

Laeven, L. and Valencia, F., 2013. Systemic Banking Crises Database. *IMF Economic Review*, 61, pp. 225–270.

Lazonick, W., 2014. The Financialization of the U.S. Corporation: What Has Been Lost, and How it Can Be Regained. *Seattle University Law Review*, Issue 36, pp. 857–909.

Lazonick, W. and O'Sullivan, M., 2000. Maximising Shareholder Value: A New Ideology for Corporate Governance. *Economy and Society*, 29(1), pp. 13–35.

Levine, R., 2005. Finance and Growth: Theory and Evidence. In: A. Philippe and N. Steven, eds. *Handbook of Economic Growth*. Cambridge, MA: Elsevier.

Lin, K. H. and Tomaskovic-Devey, D., 2013. Financialisation and U.S. Income Inequality, 1970–2008. *American Journal of Sociology*, 118(5), pp. 1248–1329.

McKinnon, R. I., 1973. *Money and Capital in Economic Development*. Washington: Brookings Institution.

Malkiel, B., 2013. Asset Management Fees and Growth of Finance. *Journal of Economic Perspectives*, 27(2), pp. 97–108.

Onaran, O., Stockhammer, E. and Grafl, L., 2011. Financialisation, Income Distribution and Aggregate Demand in the USA. *Cambridge Journal of Economics*, Issue 35, pp. 637–661.

Rioja, F. and Valev, N., 2004. Finance and the Sources of Growth at Various Stages of Economic Development. *Economic Inquiry Journal*, 42, pp. 127–140.

Rioja, F. and Valev, N., 2005. Does One Size Fit All? A Reexamination of the Finance and Growth Relationship. *Journal of Development Economics*, 74, pp. 429–447.

Rousseau, P. L. and Wachtel, P., 2011. What is Happening to the Impact of Financial Deepening on Economic Growth? *Economic Inquiry*, 49(1), pp. 276–288.

Sahay, R., Čihák, M., N'Diaye, P. *et al.*, 2015. Rethinking Financial Deepening: Stability and Growth in Emerging Markets. *IMF Staff Discussion Note 1508*.

Sawyer, M., 2013. *Financial Development, Financialisation and Economic Growth*. Leeds: FESSUD Working Paper Series No. 21.

Sawyer, M., 2014. What is Financialization? *International Journal of Political Economy*, 42(4), pp. 5–18.

Sawyer, M., 2016. Confronting Financialisation. In: P. Arestis and M. Sawyer, eds. *Financial Liberalisation: Past, Present and Future*. Annual Edition of International Papers in Political Economy. Houndmills, Basingstoke: Palgrave Macmillan.

Shaw, E., 1973. *Financial Deepening in Economic Development*. New York: Oxford University Press.

Slater, G. and Spencer, D., 2014. Workplace Relations, Unemployment and Finance-dominated Capitalism. *Review of Keynesian Economics*, 2(2), pp. 134–146.

Thompson, P., 2011. The Trouble with HRM. *Human Resource Management Journal*, 21(4), pp. 355–367.

Van der Zwan, N., 2014. State of the Art: Making Sense of Financialisation. *Socio-Economic Review*, 2014(12), pp. 99–129.

Vercelli, A., 2014. Financialisation in a Long-run Perspective: An Evolutionary Approach. *International Journal of Political Economy*, 42(2).

Zingales, L., 2015. *Does Finance Benefit Society?, Prepared for the 2015 AFA Presidential Address.* [Online] Available at: http://papers.ssrn.com/sol3/papers.cfm?abstract_id=2585194 [Accessed 11 October 2016].

2 Developing and emerging countries as finance providers

Foreign exchange reserves and direct investment to the European Union

Jan Toporowski and Bruno Bonizzi

Introduction

At the global level, financialization represents an extraordinary increase in cross-border financial transactions and claims. Such flows and claims have also increasingly involved the developing world. It is a well-known fact that, over the past decade these countries as a whole recorded high private capital inflows and trade surpluses. The mirror image of this phenomenon was the accumulation of foreign exchange reserves. This highlights the subordinate role that these countries play in the global financial system: they are mostly recipients of foreign direct and portfolio investments, and accumulate reserves to prevent and contain the volatility that these investments might induce. Nevertheless, flows from the developing world to advanced economies have increased, representing thus another subject of analysis for a proper understanding of financialization at the international level.

In order to understand capital inflows from the developing countries into the European Union (EU) it is necessary to understand the debt structures that link the developing countries with the EU. These debt structures are not only the debt obligations, denominated in Euros, or to EU official, multilateral or private sector creditors of governments and the private sector in developing countries. They are also assets and companies in the EU owned by residents of the developing countries, emerging markets and off-shore financial centres frequently located in less developed countries. For convenience therefore, capital inflows into the EU may be classified as holdings of European currency reserves by governments of developing countries and emerging markets; portfolio investment in EU capital markets, including holdings of European assets by Sovereign Wealth Funds in developing countries and emerging markets; and foreign direct investment (FDI) in the EU from developing and emerging markets.

Figure 2.1 represents a snapshot of emerging and developing countries' external assets. Clearly, reserves remain a crucial component, constituting about half of total external assets. The chart does on the other hand show in more recent years that other components have seen an expansion. Emerging

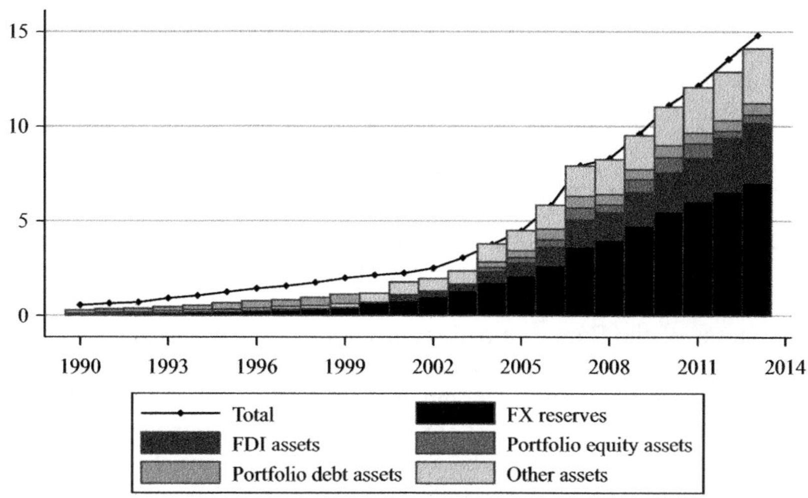

Figure 2.1 Total external assets of emerging economies, 1990–2014, in trillions of USD
Source: Authors' calculation based on Lane and Milesi-Ferretti (2007) and IMF balance of payment statistics

and developing countries have started to invest abroad, and diversify part of their reserves into a more mixed composition of currencies. Moreover, as the chart shows, outward direct investments have substantially increased since 2004.

This chapter focuses on two channels through which emerging and developing countries may provide finance to Europe: foreign exchange reserves and foreign direct investments.

The importance of the Euro as a component of foreign exchange reserves has been an intensely studied subject. Before 2008, the importance of the Euro was rising, and a consensus emerged arguing that the Euro could eventually challenge the supremacy of the US dollar as a global reserve currency (Chinn and Frankel, 2005; Papaioannou and Portes, 2008). The continuous depreciation of the US dollar and the expansion of the Eurozone and the EU as a financially and economically stable institution, in a context of increasing trade and financial integration, were considered to be drivers of an increase in the usage of the Euro as a reserve currency.

Foreign direct investment (FDI) to Europe by emerging and developing countries on the other hand has not attracted the same level of attention. Several studies focus on the increasing outward orientation of BRIC – Brazil, Russia, India and China – countries, and study the determinant of their investments (Sauvant, 2005; Gammeltoft, 2008; Holtbrügge and Kreppel, 2012). However, few focus specifically on the analysis of the FDI from these countries to the EU. Clegg and Voss (2012) is an exception, but focuses exclusively on China.

This chapter contributes to the existing literature in two ways. First, it reassesses the role of foreign exchange reserves accumulation as supply of finance to the European financial markets. Second, it presents an overview and analysis of FDI from emerging and developing countries and their potential contribution to economic development of Europe.

The Euro within foreign exchange reserves

The Euro has been, since its birth, the second most important currency after the US dollar. A quarter of global debt securities for example are denominated in Euro (ECB, 2014).

The status of the Euro as a major currency is also suggested by its inclusion in the portfolio of Central Banks' foreign exchange reserves. Despite the relatively small size of Euro-denominated trade invoicing (ECB, 2014), the Euro has been the second biggest component of global currency reserves as shown in Figure 2.2: since 2002, between 20 and 22 per cent of reserves[1] have been held in Euro-denominated assets, while US dollar-denominated reserves decreased from 72 per cent to 62 per cent.

The presence of official investors provides European debt markets with a wider investor base, which could contribute to lower bond yields. Indeed having lower yields on foreign liabilities and high returns on its assets is what

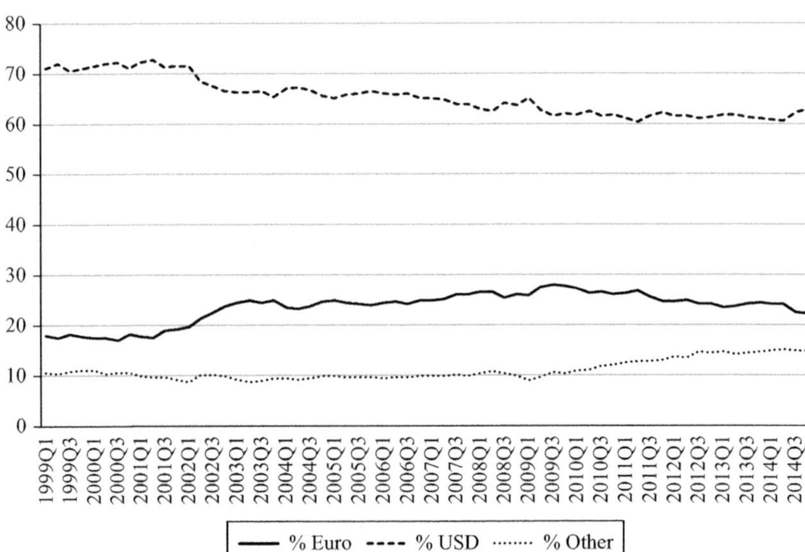

Figure 2.2 Share of world foreign exchange reserves, 1999–2014

Source: Authors' calculation based on IMF Composition of Foreign Exchange Reserves (COFER)

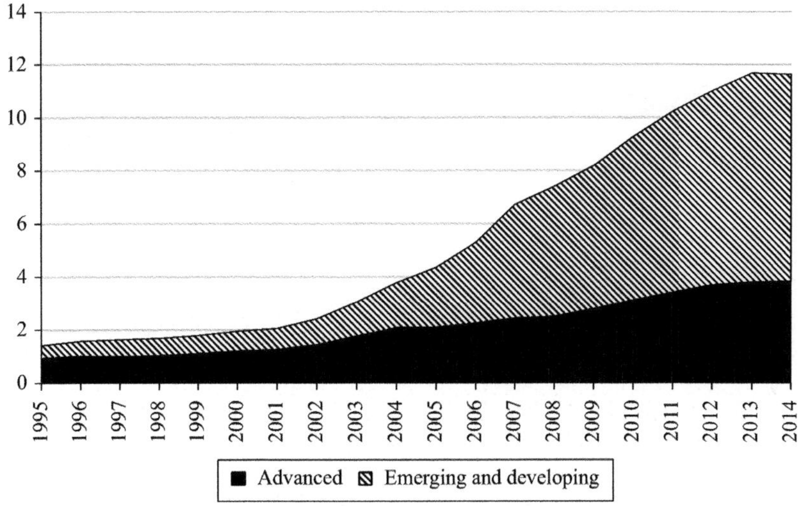

Figure 2.3 Total reserves, 1995–2014, in trillions of USD
Source: Authors' calculation based on IMF COFER

constitutes the 'exorbitant privilege' of the US (Gournichas and Rey, 2005). While the Euro does not seem to have enjoyed the same excess return on its foreign assets (Habib, 2010), its creation has made the costs of borrowing for many governments much lower, effectively equalizing their interest rates (Economist, 2011). This may be partly due to the Euro status as a reserve currency.

Developing and emerging countries could have a major role in this process. As shown in Figure 2.3, foreign exchange reserves accumulation has proceeded at a very fast pace since 2000, and this has been mostly driven by emerging and developing countries. As of 2014, they hold about two-thirds of total – allocated and unallocated – currency reserves. Emerging and developing countries, therefore, may contribute substantially, if indirectly, to provide stable financing conditions that favour economic development in Europe.

This process however seems to be heavily dependent on the financial stability outlook of Europe. The percentage of reserves held by emerging and developing countries in Euro-denominated assets has noticeably dropped since the first quarter of 2009, from over 29 per cent to about 21 per cent as shown in Figure 2.4. This seems to be the result of two patterns. First, it follows the increasing diversification of reserves, as testified by the increasing share of 'other' currencies in Figure 2.4. Second, on top of this there has been an active choice to decrease the allocation to Euro-denominated assets. As a matter of fact, the share of the US dollar has remained more or less constant

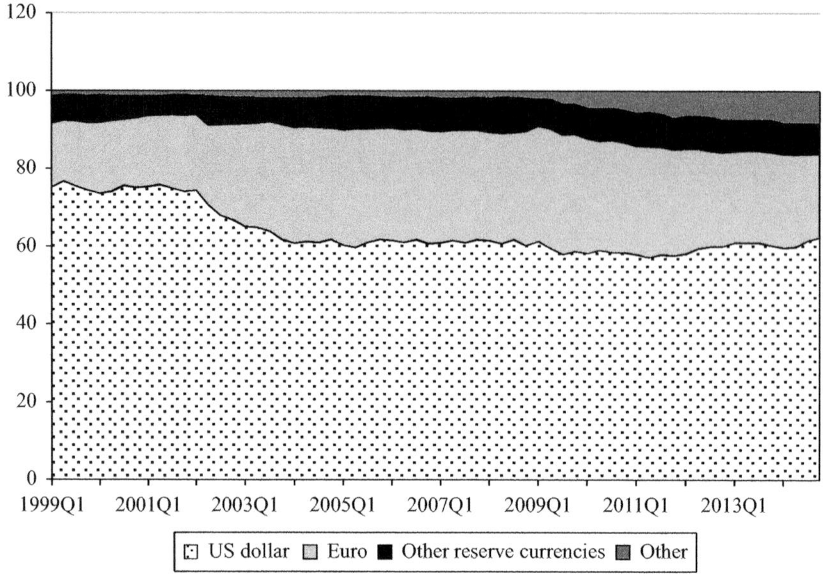

Figure 2.4 Emerging and developing economies reserves – currency shares, 1999–2013
Note: Other reserve currencies are Swiss Franc, British Pound Sterling and Japanese Yen
Source: Authors' calculation based on IMF COFER

in the same period, while that of the British Pound Sterling has also been decreasing but only by about 1 per cent from 5.9 per cent to about 5 per cent. In absolute terms, Euro reserves have remained constant from the first quarter of 2009 while Pound Sterling reserves increased by 25 USD billion.

This change implies that emerging and developing countries seems to take into account the stability of capital markets in the countries to which they allocate their reserves. In Europe, despite over two decades of work in creating an effective common capital market, the stigmatization of sovereign debt and the fears of a breakdown of the common currency have rendered markets in Euro-denominated assets unattractive. Caution in holding European assets is rational from the point of view of holders of foreign currency reserves since such reserves need to be easily disposable to allow for foreign exchange interventions. As a result they are held in liquid and stable securities. Indeed it is likely that within the Eurozone they are held in German and French government bonds (Pineau and Dorrucci, 2006). The increased riskiness of these assets results in a decreasing allocation by emerging and developing countries' Central Banks, just like any portfolio manager would behave.

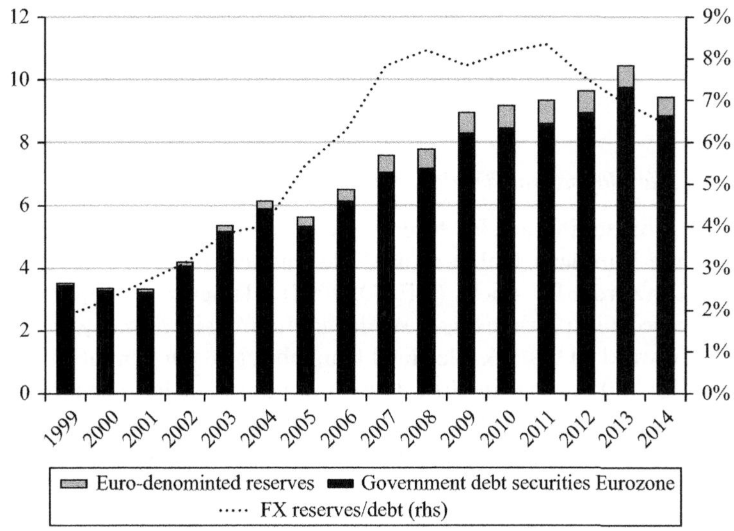

Figure 2.5 Government debt and reserves held by emerging and developing economies, 1999–2014, in trillions of USD

Source: Author's calculation based on IMF COFER, IMF Exchange Rate report and ECB statistical data warehouse

Given these trends, it would seem that foreign exchange reserves have provided less financing to Europe precisely when it was most needed, i.e. the sovereign debt turmoil. This seems to be largely confirmed by Figure 2.5. Foreign exchange reserves of emerging and developing countries increased from 2 per cent to about 8.5 per cent of total Eurozone outstanding government debt in the 1999–2010 period. Since then they have decreased to just above 6 per cent. This coincides precisely with the timing of the sovereign debt crisis, and in this sense reserve holders behaved exactly like most investors, shifting out of Euro-denominated government bonds when their perceived riskiness increased.

It would therefore seem that the Euro, while being a major currency, remains below the US dollar in the world hierarchy. While the long-run trend sees developing countries diversifying away from heavily dollar-based reserves portfolios, the Euro remains affected by macro-financial 'short-term' issues. The US remains the ultimate global safe asset issuer – indeed the dollar strengthens during crises (Obstfeld, 2010).

In sum, although most of emerging and developing countries' external assets are held as currency reserves, and a substantial part of them is in Euro, this is unlikely to be a major stabilizing force to the European government debt markets and therefore foster economic development through financial stability.

Direct investment to Europe

This section provides an overview of foreign direct investment to EU-member countries. It will look at total FDI, and then dissect by macro-regional aggregates, specific developing regions and sector of destinations.

FDI to Europe: developing and developed investors

Europe is a major destination for foreign direct investments (FDI). At the end of 2013, the European Union as a whole was the first world region in terms of total inward FDI stocks (OECD, 2014). However, its importance has declined, especially after the crisis. While maintaining its primacy, the EU share of total inward FDI stocks declined from about 38 per cent at the end of 2007 to around 30 per cent in 2014. Even more dramatic has been the fall in the FDI inflows share, from 40 per cent to about 17 per cent over the same period. As shown in the 2014 World Investment Report this meant that the EU from its top position in 2011 was overtaken by developing Asia and Latin America as a recipient of FDI inflows.

Despite these trends FDI inward positions steadily increased in the 2004–2012 period, more than doubling from around 4.8 trillion to over 10 trillion EUR as shown in Figure 2.6. Flows presented a more volatile picture, increasing steadily in the 2004–2007 peaking at about 1.1 trillion EUR, but then decreasing every year, except 2011, to about 450–550 billion EUR as shown in Figure 2.7. The global financial crisis therefore heavily hit direct investments into EU companies, which is still very far from its pre-crisis levels.

Most of EU members' inwards FDI is intra-EU, which constituted about 63 per cent of FDI inflows to the EU on average in the 2004–2012 period according to UNCTAD (2014, p. 79). Eurostat data seem to broadly confirm this fact, as intra-EU 27 FDI constitutes more than 66 percent of FDI inward positions throughout the whole period, and about 58.8 per cent of FDI inflows, slightly less than the UNCTAD figure.

However, the importance of intra-EU FDI has declined over the same period. As shown in Figure 2.8 in only four years since 2008, FDI inward positions declined from 66.6 per cent to 62.3 per cent. FDI inflows, as Figure 2.9 shows, declined even more substantially: splitting up the period into two four-year sub-periods gives an average of 70.6 per cent for 2004–2007, and 44.9 per cent for 2008–2012. This highlights how the global financial crisis and the Eurozone troubles had a sizeable impact mostly on intra-EU direct investment, which therefore account for most of the EU inward FDI decline. It also reflects a trend towards registering ownership of multinational corporations in off-shore financial centres, rather than within European fiscal jurisdictions.

Both non-European developed countries and developing and emerging countries have contributed to an increasing proportion of inward direct investments. Inflows from other advanced countries increased from 14.3 per cent in 2004 to about 45.8 per cent of total 2012 FDI inflows, whereas

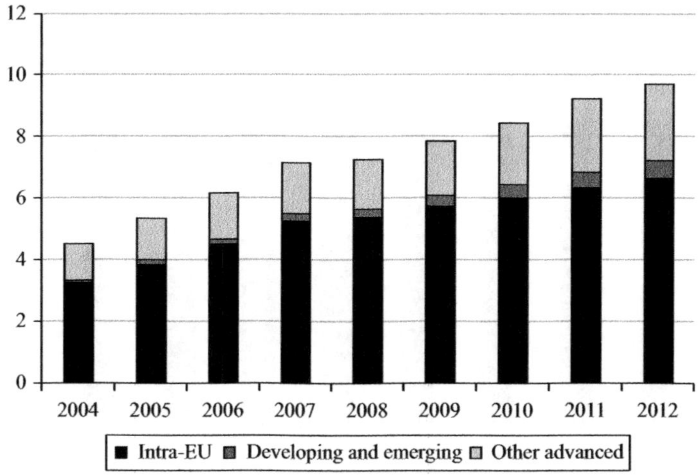

Figure 2.6 EU-27 FDI inward positions, 2004–2012, in trillions of EUR

Note: While data for 2013 exist, they are likely to be still incomplete, as they show sizeable declines in both FDI flows and positions, which is at odds with the evidence of other sources (e.g. OECD, 2014). For this reason the analysis will be conducted using data only up to 2012. Emerging and developing countries is the sum of Africa, Asia (excl. Japan), Latin America and Russia. Other Advanced countries are Northern America, European Free-Trade Agreement countries and Japan.

Source: Authors' calculations based on Eurostat

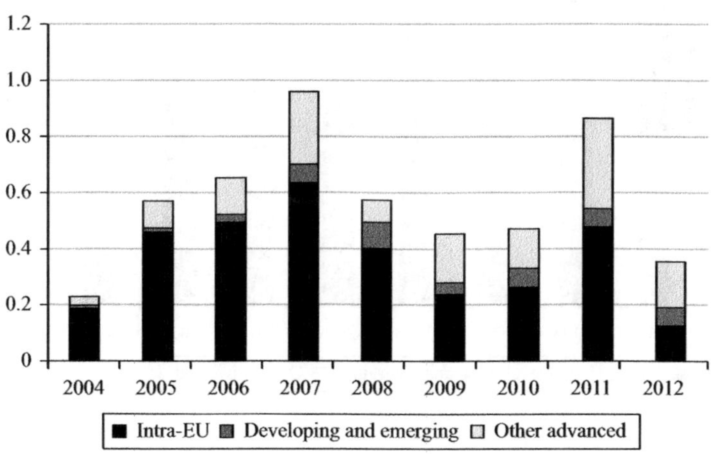

Figure 2.7 EU-27 FDI inward flows, 2004–2012, in trillions of EUR

Source: Authors' calculations based on Eurostat

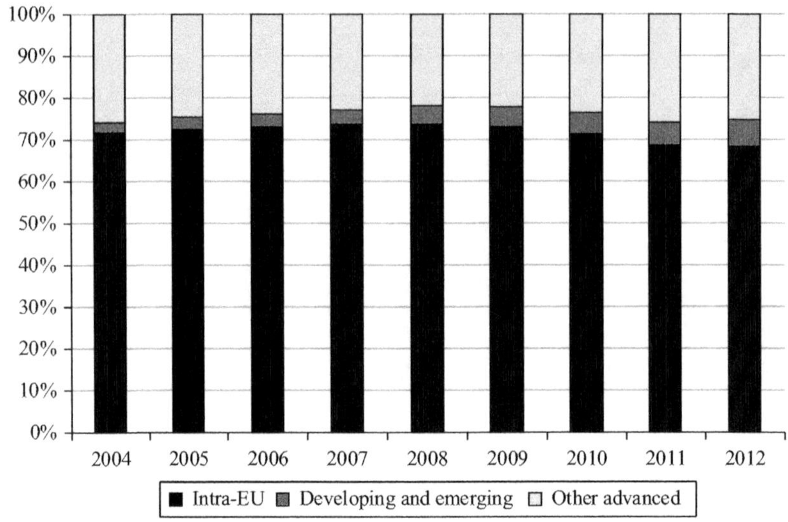

Figure 2.8 EU-27 FDI inward positions shares, 2004–2012
Source: Authors' calculations based on Eurostat

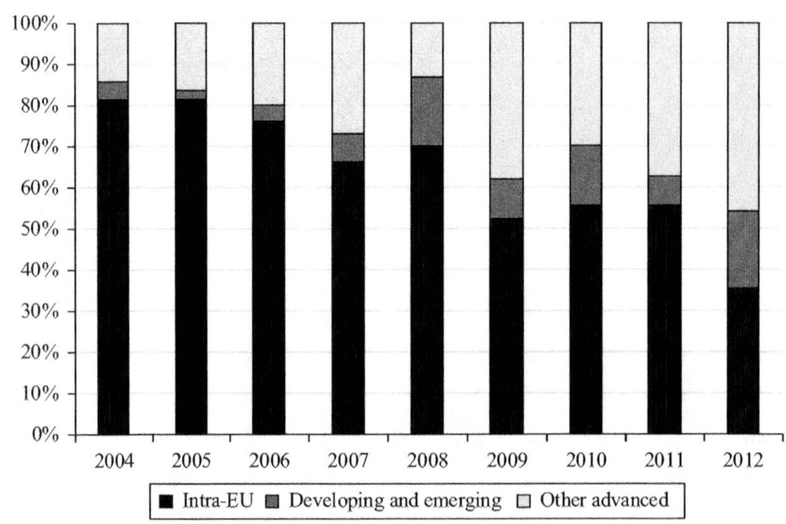

Figure 2.9 EU-27 FDI inward flows shares, 2004–2012
Source: Authors' calculations based on Eurostat

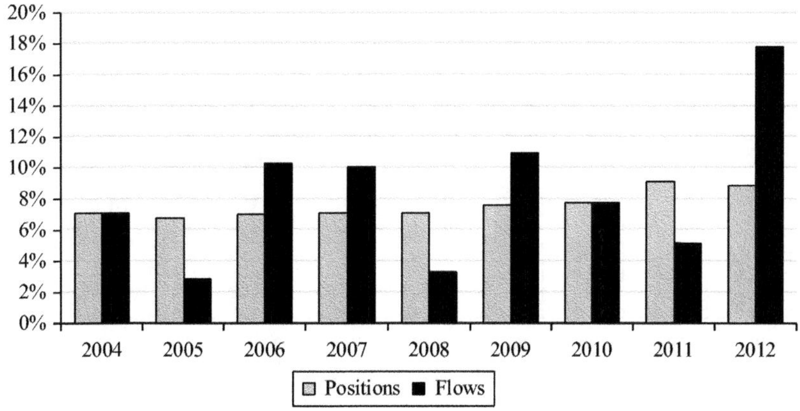

Figure 2.10 Offshore financial centres, 2004–2012, % of total FDI
Source: Authors' calculations based on Eurostat

inflows from developing and emerging countries increased from 4.3 per cent to 18.8 per cent over the same period. Inflows from emerging and developing countries however increased much more substantially: in absolute terms the average inflows more than doubled in the 2008–2012 period, compared to the 2004–2007 period, while inflows from other advanced countries only increased by 30 per cent.

Similarly, the share of FDI inward stocks from non-EU advanced countries at the end of 2012 was very close to the levels of 2004 at 23–24 per cent, decreasing in the first four years and increasing since 2008. Meanwhile the share of developing and emerging countries increased steadily throughout the period from 2.3 per cent to 5.7 per cent.

As shown in Figure 2.10, offshore financial centres count for about 8.3 per cent of inwards FDI flows and 7.5 per cent of inward stocks over the whole period. Without further details, it is impossible to tell which proportion of offshore financial centres intermediates FDI comes from developing and emerging countries. However, these numbers are more or less in line with the global figures (UNCTAD, 2014, p. 3) and furthermore, offshore financial centers in Asia (e.g. Hong Kong or Singapore)[2] would be included in the count. It is therefore not implausible to assume that this would not result in substantial changes of the proportion of FDI from emerging and developing countries.

FDI from developing and emerging countries by region

To get a sense of the importance of FDI to Europe for each of the developing regions, Figure 2.11 scales FDI positions by GDP. This proportion grew for

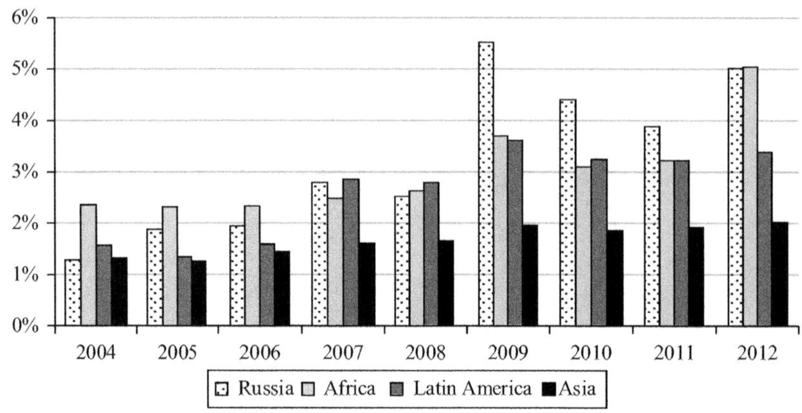

Figure 2.11 FDI to EU, 2004–2012, % GDP

Source: Author's calculations based on Eurostat, Economist Intelligence Unit and IMF Exchange Rate Report

all the regions, in line with the growing foreign investments from the developing world as a whole – shown in Figure 2.11. Asia however has a lower share than the other developing regions. Partially, this might be the result of their very high growth rates, thus inflating the denominator of the ratios. However, it is likely that this indicates regional proximity, as well as cultural and/or political ties to Europe resulting in a higher proportion of FDI allocated to European countries.

This is confirmed in Figure 2.12, where FDI to the EU is shown as a proportion to total external FDI holdings. Latin America and Africa invest in the EU a much higher proportion of their FDI than Asia.[3] Over time however these proportions have grown in Latin America, from 20 per cent to about 40 per cent of total outward FDI and Russia from 8 per cent to 25 per cent, whereas in Asia and Africa they have not substantially changed since 2004.

FDI by sector of destination

The breakdown of inward FDI by sector, as Figures 2.13 and 2.14 show, of destinations reveals the dominance of the services sector, and the financial sector in particular. On average in the 2004–2011 period, slightly above 70 per cent of total inflows and inward positions are allocated to the services sector. More than two-thirds of this is allocated to the financial sector, which alone constitutes about 42 per cent of total inward positions and 45 per cent of total inflows on average over the period. By contrast manufacturing constitutes a declining share of inwards FDI, accounting for about 16–17 per cent of the total.

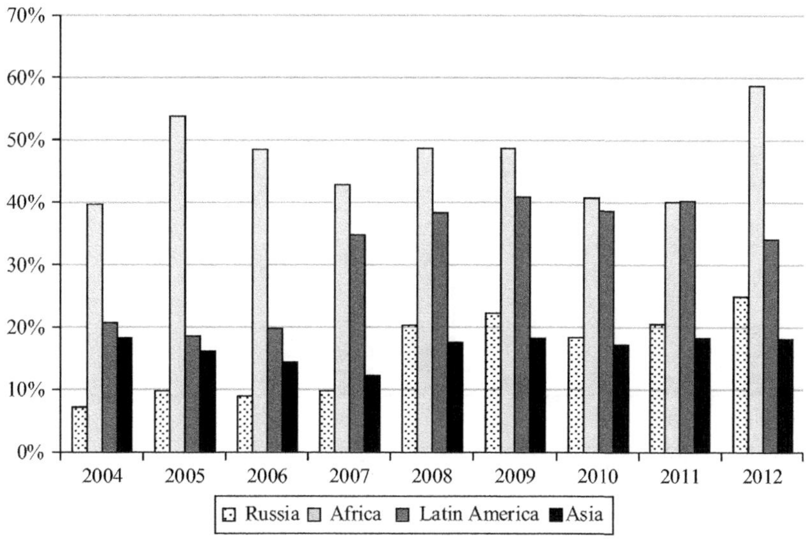

Figure 2.12 FDI to EU, 2004–2012, % of total FDI

Source: Authors' calculations based on Eurostat, UNCTAD and IMF Exchange Rate Report

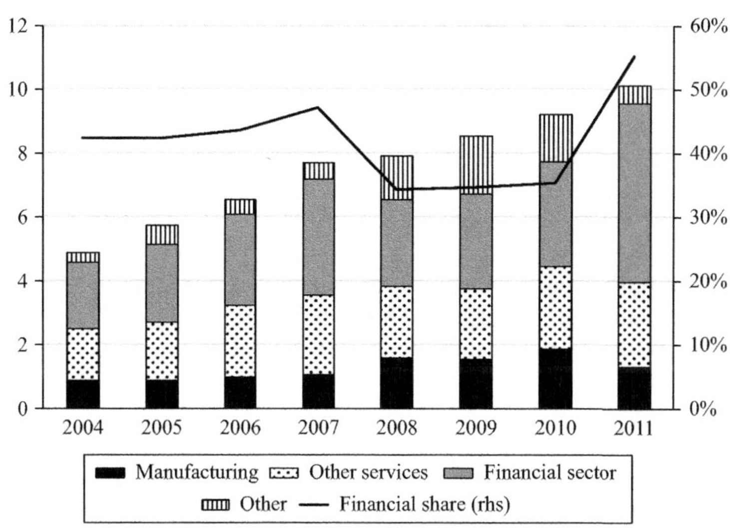

Figure 2.13 FDI inwards positions by sector, 2004–2011, in trillions of EUR

Note: Other includes: agriculture, mining, electricity and gas provision, and unallocated FDI

Source: Authors' calculations based on Eurostat

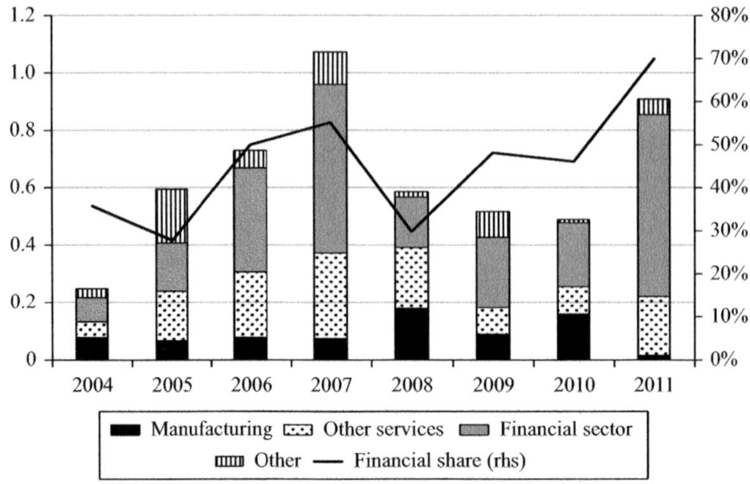

Figure 2.14 FDI inflows by sector, 2004–2011, in trillions of EUR
Source: Authors' calculations based on Eurostat

Summary

In sum, FDI to Europe has been declining since the crisis, mostly due to a fall in intra-EU FDI. On the other hand FDI from developing countries has been increasing, so that their importance as a source has been increasing. This seems to be mostly the result of their increasing outward orientation and their fast economic growth, as the overall picture does not show a growing allocation to Europe as a destination for direct investments.

Insofar as emerging and developing economies grow faster compared to developed and especially European countries, these trends are likely to continue. Therefore these countries could contribute to the economic development of Europe in the coming years. Much will however depend on the type of direct investment they undertake. This will be the purpose of the next section, focusing on major emerging economies, the BRIC countries.

The BRIC countries

FDI from Brazil, India, Russia and China has increased very quickly over the past 15 years. According to UNCTAD data, FDI outward stocks increased about fourfold between 2004 and 2013 in Brazil, China[4] and Russia, and by more than 15 times in India, which started from a much lower level.

FDI from BRIC: overview

As Figure 2.15 shows, FDI to Europe has experienced an even more dramatic rise. Between 2004 and 2013 Chinese positions increased over fivefold,

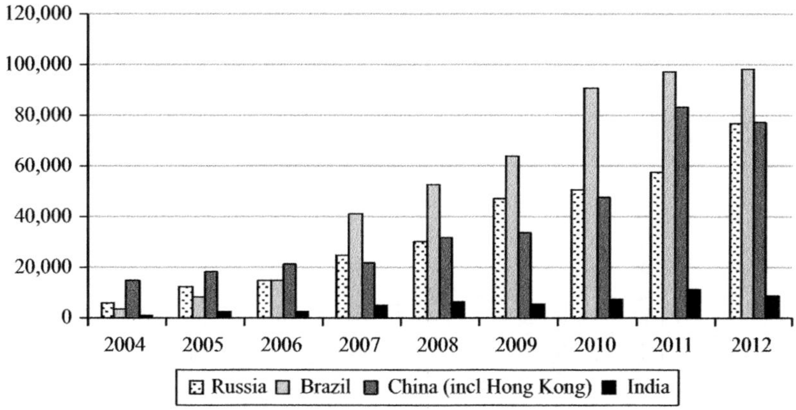

Figure 2.15 FDI positions from BRIC countries to EU-27, 2004–2012, in millions of EUR

Source: Authors' calculations based on Eurostat

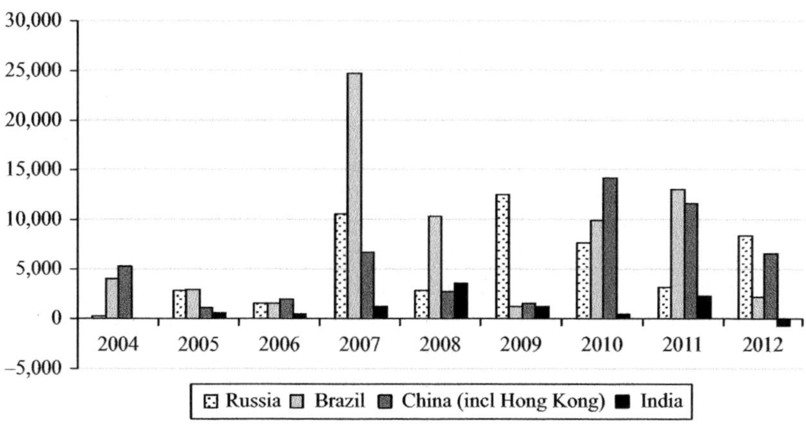

Figure 2.16 FDI flows from BRIC countries to EU-27, 2004–2012, in millions of EUR

Source: Authors' calculations based on Eurostat

Russian by 13 times, Indian by 15 times and Brazilian positions by almost 30 times. Brazil has been the top investing country since 2007, with Russia and China as close seconds, whereas India's FDI is considerably smaller. As Figure 2.16 shows, in line with the results of the previous sections, FDI from the BRIC countries has not yet reached their pre-crisis levels of 2007.

Also in line with the previous section is the observation, as shown in Figure 2.17, that FDI to Europe has been a relatively stable proportion of total outward FDI: Russia and especially Brazil have invested a growing proportion of their FDI to Europe,[5] whereas the proportions for China and India

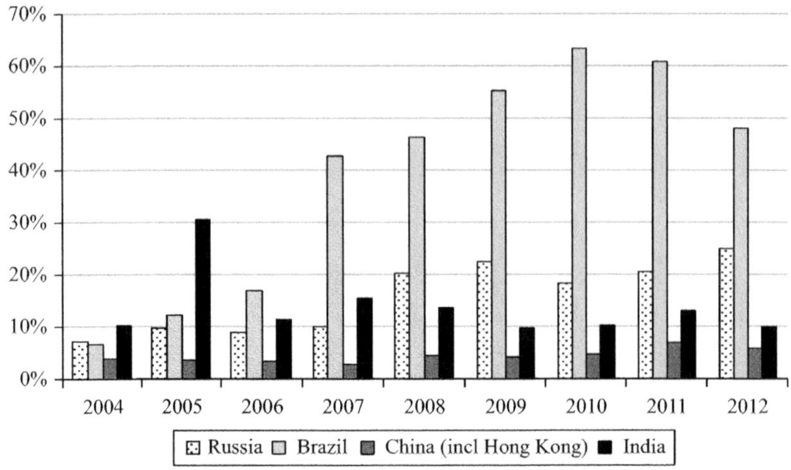

Figure 2.17 FDI positions from BRIC countries to EU-27, 2004–2012, share of total outward FDI

Source: Authors' calculations based on Eurostat, UNCTAD and IMF Exchange Rate Report

have not significantly changed since 2004. As these figures are remarkably similar to those shown in Figure 2.14, it is likely that the BRIC countries are systemically important within their respective regions, therefore driving the regional trends. And indeed, BRIC countries account for a sizeable and increasing proportion of developing and emerging countries outward FDI to Europe. The proportion of positions has grown steadily from about 20 per cent in 2004 to almost half of the total in 2011, while flows oscillated around an average of about 47 per cent. Focusing on the BRIC countries therefore allows capture of an important and potentially representative snapshot of developing and emerging countries' direct investment activities.

FDI from BRICs characteristics

Aside from balance of payments figures, it is useful to look at Eurostat Structural Business Statistics, which have indicators for non-financial firms operating in the EU. As shown in Table 2.1.[6] BRIC countries, like all foreign investors, tend to invest in bigger and more productive firms than those domestically owned by the recipient countries.

However, the results present some elements of difference compared to the previous section. India, which is by far the smallest investor in monetary terms, controls firms that at the aggregate level have the highest value added, and value added per enterprise. Brazil on the other hand, while being the top

Table 2.1 Business statistics, 2009–2010

	No. of enterprises		*No. of employees*		*Value added (EUR m)*	
	2009	*2010*	*2009*	*2010*	*2009*	*2010*
Russia		1,777	50,195	45,973	1,625.58	2,100.30
Brazil	151	245	19,729	21,056		600
China	2,446	3,064	87,508	99,208	5,680.93	6,531.60
India	820		107,908	121,170	5,323.70	8,894.00
Reporting country	18,189,279	20,063,436	109,067,062	111,154,451	4,291,639	4,554,237
Total	18,425,453	20,307,663	126,941,664	129,467,943	5,468,372	5,893,366
Total foreign	236,174	244,227	17,874,602	18,313,492	1,176,732	1,339,129
	Av. employees per enterprise		*Av. value added per enterprise*		*Value added/FDI positions*	
	2009	*2010*	*2009*	*2010*	*2010*	
Russia		25.87		1.18	0.042	
Brazil	130.66	85.94		2.45	0.0007	
China	35.78	32.38	2.32	2.13	0.14	
India	131.6		6.49		1.22	
Reporting country	6	5.54	0.24	0.23		
Total	6.89	6.38	0.3	0.29		
Total foreign	75.68	74.99	4.98	5.48	0.15	

Source: Authors' calculations based on Eurostat

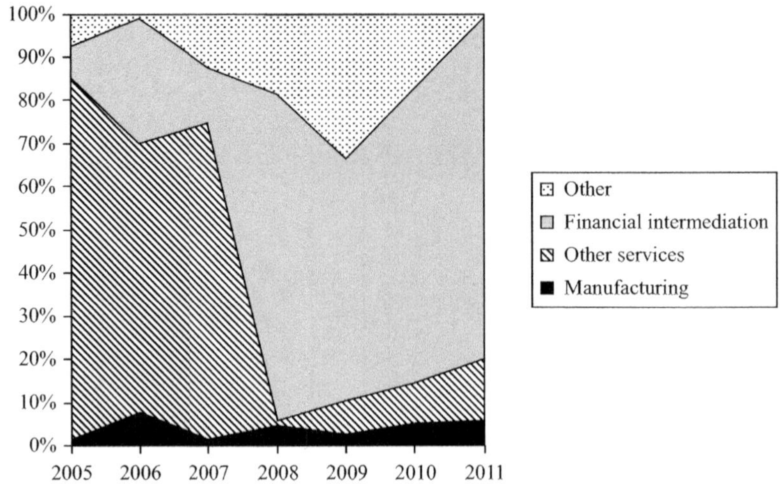

Figure 2.18 FDI positions from Brazil to EU-27, 2005–2011, % by sector
Source: Authors' calculations based on Eurostat

investor in monetary terms, controls very few enterprises in Europe producing on aggregate much less value added. Finally, Russia controls relatively smaller and less productive firms than the other four countries.

It would therefore seem that the FDI from Brazil and Russia is less conductive to generate value added in Europe. As shown in the last column of the table, scaled by FDI positions value added differs dramatically across the BRIC: while India and China added value for 0.14 – in line with the global average – and 1.22 Euros per Euro of inward investment positions, for Russia the ratio goes down to 0.042 and for Brazil to even less at 0.0007.

Figure 2.18 helps in rationalizing these facts. The majority of Brazilian FDI to Europe is allocated to financial sector activities. In 2011 these account for about 80 per cent of total FDI positions, while manufacturing only accounts for about 6 per cent. Indeed, this explains why the number of Brazilian controlled firms is so small compared to their direct investment and their value added so low.

Compared to Brazil, Russia has had over the period a higher proportion of 'other' FDI holdings, partially reflecting data classification issues, but also a higher proportion dedicated to electricity and gas provision companies as presented in Figure 2.19. Financial intermediation still represented a key sector, at about over 30 per cent of total holdings since 2005 (except in 2008), reaching 68 per cent in 2011.Once again this explains the relatively low value added figures for Russian FDI shown by Table 2.1.

As Figure 2.20 shows, China invests between 20 and 40 per cent into financial sector companies, much less than Brazil and Russia but also less than the total FDI to EU, as was shown in Figure 2.15.

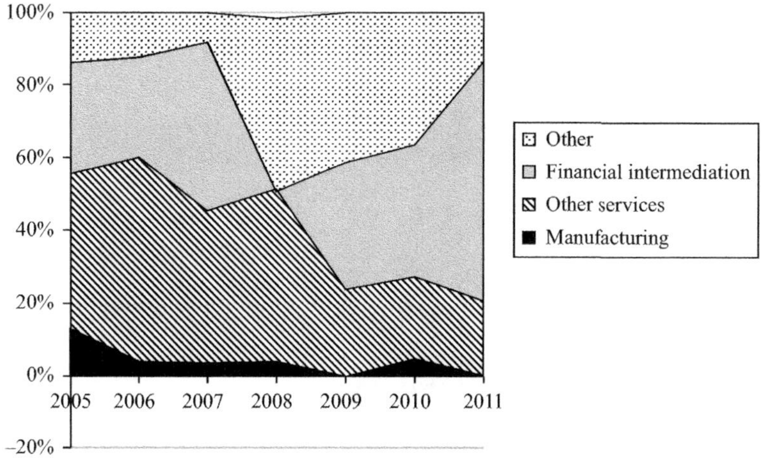

Figure 2.19 FDI positions from Russia to EU-27, 2005–2011, % by sector
Source: Authors' calculations based on Eurostat

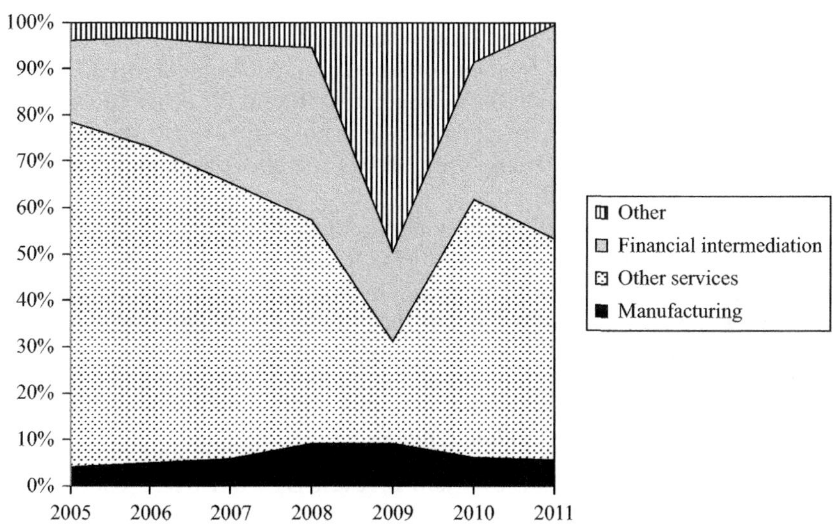

Figure 2.20 FDI positions from China to EU-27, 2005–2011, % by sector
Source: Author's calculations based on Eurostat

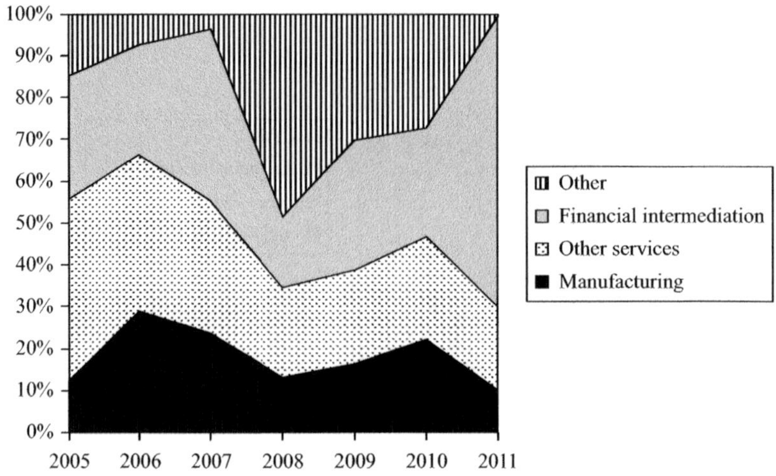

Figure 2.21 FDI positions from India to EU-27, 2005–2011, % by sector
Source: Authors' calculations based on Eurostat

India, as Figure 2.21 shows, is the only BRIC that invests a sizeable portion of its FDI into manufacturing, and in general has a balanced EU-FDI portfolio across sectors. Although the weight of the financial sector has been on the rise since the global financial crisis, manufacturing remains as high as 15 per cent, much higher than the average for FDI and the other BRIC countries. Nevertheless, given these allocations it is not surprising to see that India has the highest value added across the BRICs and above average value added per enterprise on their FDI.

Despite the important differences highlighted thus far, clearly the importance of the financial sector within the BRICs' FDI to Europe is on the rise for all these countries. The rise presented in Figure 2.22 has been remarkable, such that financial sector FDI flows in 2011 totalled 20 billion Euros, up from 400 million Euros in 2005.

BRICs' FDI to Europe: concluding remarks

This section has provided an overview of the FDI from BRIC countries to Europe. BRICs are key sources of FDI within the developing and emerging countries category, representing almost half of the total in recent years. Within the group there are however differences. Brazil and Russia have similar investing patterns. They allocate a high proportion (and growing) of their FDI in Europe – also similar in absolute monetary terms. They also both invest a very large proportion to the financial sector, thus making their FDI concentrated in low value added firms. At the opposite end is India, investing a declining proportion of its FDI to Europe, with a relatively high proportion

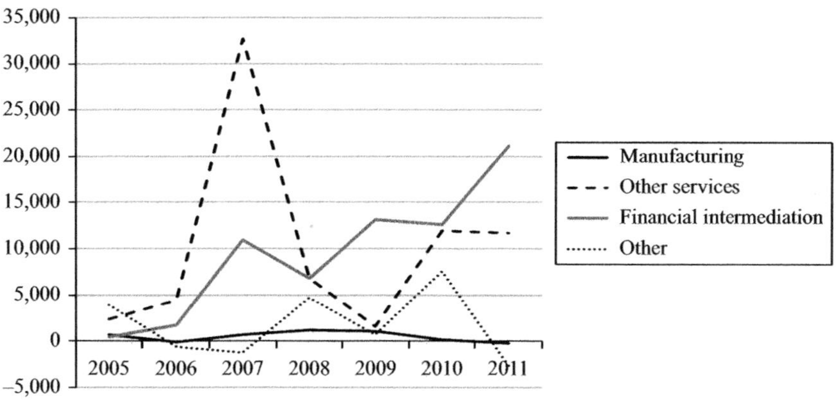

Figure 2.22 FDI inflows, 2005–2011, % of total
Source: Authors' calculations based on Eurostat

to manufacturing, and high value added. China has the lowest allocation to Europe across the BRICs, and the sectoral allocation and structural features of its FDI are very much in line with the global FDI to EU figures.

It would therefore seem that there is a negative correlation[7] between the importance of the financial sector as a target sector and the value added performance of the BRICs' FDI. Moreover Brazil and Russia, which have higher allocations to Europe, invest more into the financial sector than India and China. Given this and the increasing trend in allocation to financial sector activities over time by all countries, it would seem that BRIC FDI may not substantially contribute to provide finance to high value adding firms. Insofar as the BRICs are representative for the developing and emerging countries group, this would imply that, despite their growing importance as investor countries, the scope for generating economic development from FDI to the EU from the developing world is likely to be small.

This is consistent with the idea that BRIC countries invest abroad for reasons other than generating high value added. Indeed, emerging countries should ideally have greater opportunities domestically to invest in high value added activities. Moreover, the existing literature suggest that BRIC based companies mostly invest abroad to access European markets and therefore open up new channels through which to sell their products (Clegg and Voss, 2012; Holtbrügge and Kreppel, 2012). Given these trends, it is not surprising that their focus is on the services sector, and the financial sector in particular, which may facilitate their access to the European markets more than manufacturing activities.

These results can also be interpreted through the lenses of financialization. Controlling financial sector companies in advanced economies may be a strategic goal for the emerging world. The role of finance has become so pervasive at the global level that such a strategy appears rational, even if it foregoes potentially more productive investment opportunities.

Conclusion

An aspect of financialization is the greater financial integration across countries. In this chapter we explored a particular subset of such integration: foreign exchange reserves and direct investment from the developing world to European countries. It was shown that such investments are unlikely to bring benefits to Europe. Allocation to Euro-denominated reserves do not appear be a stabilizing force in European bond markets, and FDI is for the most part allocated to low value added, and in particular financial sector, activities.

This shows how financialization permeates all international financial relations. Emerging and developing countries act in a world where finance is prominent by following its rules. Reserves are managed as any private portfolio would be managed, divesting from assets when risks appear to be higher, and controlling advanced countries' financial companies becomes a strategic goal. As such, international financialization is as likely to be potentially disruptive to the developing world as it is unlikely to be beneficial to the advanced world.

Notes

1 Due to their political sensitiveness, countries do not fully disclose the currency composition of their reserves. In the IMF composition of official foreign exchange reserves database (COFER), about half of the reserves – the figure as of 2014 is two-thirds of emerging and developing countries and about 12 per cent of advanced economies – are 'unallocated', i.e. with unknown currency composition. The considerations made in this section therefore refer to the 'allocated' part of reserves.

2 These countries are kept within the developing and emerging markets group because they are closely linked to their neighbouring developing and emerging countries. Hong Kong for example is the top destination of Chinese outward FDI, but it is likely that an important part of this only goes through the country to other destinations across the world (Salidjanova, 2011).

3 Russia is a peculiar case, as data from Eurostat give a very different indication than data from Russian sources and UNCTAD. This will be further explored in the next section.

4 All figures for China include Hong Kong as in the previous section. This is because a great deal of Chinese outward direct investment goes through Hong Kong, as discussed.

5 Using bilateral data from UNCTAD, which in turn derive from data from the Russian Central Bank, results in substantially upward figures for Russia: in 2012 almost 68 per cent of FDI would be allocated to EU countries, almost half of which would go to Cyprus. Eurostat data are preferred for two reasons. First, they ensure the consistency of data sources. Second, the very high figure for Russia may actually reveal the 'round-trip' FDI that goes from Russia to Russia through Cyprus (Ledyaeva *et al.*, 2013) for tax and other purposes.

6 2009 and 2010 are the only two years for which data for these countries are reliable and reasonably complete.
7 With these few observations it is impossible to meaningfully prove the statistical significance of such a correlation.

References

Chinn, M. and Frankel, J., 2005. *Will the Euro Eventually Surpass the Dollar as Leading International Reserve Currency?* Cambridge, MA: Working Paper, National Bureau of Economic Research.

Clegg, J. and Voss, H., 2012. *Chinese Overseas Direct Investment in the European Union.* London: Europe China Research and Advice Technology.

ECB, 2014. *The International Role of the Euro.* Frankfurt: European Central Bank.

Economist, 2011. Climbing Greenback Mountain. *The Economist*, 24 September.

Gammeltoft, P., 2008. Emerging Multinationals: Outward FDI from the BRICS Countries. *International Journal of Technology and Globalisation*, 4(1), pp. 5–22.

Gournichas, P. O. and Rey, H., 2005. *From World Banker to World Venture Capitalist: US External Adjustment and the Exorbitant Privilege.* Cambridge, MA: Working Paper, National Bureau of Economic Research.

Habib, M. M., 2010. *Excess Returns on Net Foreign Assets: The Exorbitant Privilege from a Global Perspective.* Frankfurt: Working Paper Series, European Central Bank.

Holtbrügge, D. and Kreppel, H., 2012. Determinants of Outward Foreign Direct Investment from BRIC Countries: An Explorative Study. *International Journal of Emerging Markets*, 7(1), pp. 4–30.

Lane, P. R. and Milesi-Ferretti, G. M., 2007. The External Wealth of Nations Mark II: Revised and Extended Estimates of Foreign Assets and Liabilities, 1970–2004. *Journal of International Economics*, 73, pp. 223–250.

Ledyaeva, S., Karhunen, P. and Whalley, J., 2013. *Offshore Jurisdictions (including Cyprus), Corruption Money Laundering and Russian Round-Trip Investment.* Cambridge, MA: Working Paper, National Bureau of Economic Research.

Obstfeld, M., 2010. Expanding Gross Asset Positions and the International Monetary System. In: *Proceedings – Economic Policy Symposium.* Jackson Hole: Federal Reserve Bank of Kansas City, pp. 463–478.

OECD, 2014. *FDI in Figures, 2014.* Paris: Organisation for Economic Co-operation and Development.

Papaioannou, E. and Portes, R., 2008. *The International Role of the Euro: A Status Report.* European Commission: European Economy – Economic Paper, Directorate General Economic and Financial Affairs (DG ECFIN).

Pineau, G. and Dorrucci, E., 2006. *The Accumulation of Foreign Reserves.* Frankfurt: Occassional Paper Series, European Central Bank.

Salidjanova, N., 2011. *Going Out: An Overview of China's Outward Foreign Direct Investment*, s.l.: USCC Staff Research Report, US–China Economic and Security Review Commission.

Sauvant, K. P., 2005. New Sources of FDI: The BRICs – Outward FDI from Brazil, Russia, India and China. *Journal of World Investment & Trade*, 6(5), p. 639.

UNCTAD, 2014. *Investing in the SDGs: An Action Plan.* New York, Geneva: World Investment Report, United Nation Conference on Trade and Development.

3 Does sustainable global prosperity require global financial governance?

Gary A. Dymski

Introduction

This chapter considers whether attaining sustainable global prosperity at the present historical moment will require global financial governance. Of course, many elements must be in place for sustainability and for prosperity on a global scale. We focus here on finance. We take as a premise of this argument that productive finance will be needed to support a global green transition. This transition requires both mitigation and adaptation measures. The former involves, for example, technological transitions on a global scale; the latter involves measures ranging from the protection of low-lying human settlements, such as cities exposed to global ice-pack melt, and cities in areas being stripped of forest cover. Time is running out. Financing the technological investments needed to support these measures will require financing: both because some investments are large-scale and involve near-term mismatches between short-term and long-term income and debt flows; and because some of the places that require climate-related investments have national income levels that will require international transfers. The point of the analysis undertaken here is not to specify what and where these investments are, but rather to consider whether the current global structure of finance is capable of providing finance where and when it is needed. We argue here that it is not. Global finance has evolved in ways that have compromised its functionality for the economy as a whole, in favour of an emphasis on zero-sum speculation and on position-taking within the shadow-banking megaplex.

The first section summarizes the history of post-War finance, considering whether the immense changes observed are evidence of gradual evolution or of coercive, self-undermining shifts? The next section considers the argument that the post-regulation evolution of financial structure since the 1980s is not problematic, a view embedded in the finance/growth literature. This view underlies much post-crisis debate about needed reforms in finance, which asserts that the megabank-centred structure of finance should be made safer, without questioning its functionality. The fourth section summarizes evidence suggesting that financial markets are not self-adjusting, and instead can generate crises with unpredictable – and adverse – consequences for the normal functioning of national macroeconomies. On the basis of this evidence, the final section considers what reforms in financial structure are needed to renew the economic functionality of finance. Two approaches are considered. One calls for 'reforms from below' based on opting out and crowd-funding strategies. The other advocates 'reforms from above'. One possibility would be effective global regulation; another, national regulation in the context of effective capital controls.

The puzzle of post-War financial history: gradualist change or punctuated-equilibrium?

If aliens were to visit the financial system of the late 1950s, they would find that loans originated by banks were generally held to maturity on those same banks' books, and that money markets were used to re-allocate reserves as needed between the more expansionary and the more cautious banks. Depository institutions – defined as financial firms that can accept deposits, and thus that can create deposits in making loans – satisfied the great majority of credit needs within the economy. Non-bank financial intermediaries, in turn, had very specialized roles within the broader architecture of financial services – they offered trusts, insurance, money transfers and so on. Regulators' primary concern, in this context, was with maintaining the viability and solvency of depository institutions. Keeping the financial sector safe and sound, as a hand-maiden to overall economic growth, permitted the central banks to shift the pace of economic activity up or down by altering short-term interest rates.

To revisit that same financial system in the mid-2010s is to traverse an altered landscape. Whilst banks originate loans, these are sold off to investors. Money markets, in turn, have been turned into leveraged mechanisms for supporting market-based financial positions, including credit contracts that bypass banks completely. The roles of banks and non-banks within the financial system are continually shifting. And these firms and their balance-sheet positions are, in any event, so intertwined that central banks and regulators – now often one and the same – must focus jointly on the triple goals of insuring the solvency and viability of depository institutions, maintaining stability in financial markets and guiding the macroeconomy.

How did these radical shifts occur, and how should they be understood? Throughout the post-War era, financial systems operated in almost completely fixed ways. This immutability was due, in the first instance, to the twin legacies of the Depression and World War II. Bank failures and financial-market collapse in most nations led to restrictions on financial competition and to the functional separation of banking functions (the US case), tightened control of large, strategically important financial firms (France), or both (the UK). Then, in World War II, the nations involved had nationalized or controlled their financial systems so as to effectively marshall all available savings – and all money-generating capacity – to maintain their war efforts and domestic fronts. After the War, financial channels were shifted and underwritten in many nations to permit the spread of home-ownership. Activist macroeconomic stabilization policies under the Bretton Woods system maintained growth rates and price inflation within boundaries consistent with the regulatory muzzles placed on finance.

Step by step, this landscape has been remade in the past 40 years. Widening tensions between highly regulated institutions and deteriorating macroeconomic fundamentals resulted in disintermediation (loss of savings and of credit customers) from regulated intermediaries, destabilizing their balance sheets and performance of established financial activities. Deregulatory momentum then built, starting at the end of the 1970s in the US, then carrying on to the UK, to France and other nations. The era was accompanied by an increasing pace of financial crises throughout the globe (Dymski, 2010; Reinhart and Rogoff, 2010). The first wave of crises, the 1980s savings and loan crisis in the US and the 1982 Latin American debt crisis, was triggered by factors exogenous to finance per se – US monetary policy under Paul Volcker, commodities-market crash, and (in the view of some) moral-hazard design flaws in prevailing debt contracts. So financial change was evidently not to blame; to the contrary, it arguably made the system more resilient. As deregulation continued and new financial practices emerged, crises mounted throughout the 1990s, culminating in the 2007–2008 subprime crisis and the 2010 Eurozone crisis. This suggested that out-of-control financial growth and deregulation underlay these increasingly deep crisis episodes (Farlow, 2013).

Endogenous financial evolution and equifinality in the finance-growth approach

How did the build-up of financial innovations and changes affect the real economy: was this fundamentally a process of gradual change along an unaltered continuum, or instead did these shifts result in disjunctures and crises that may have shifted the terrain of the financial sector relationship onto new coordinates? The mere appearance of crises at different points in the trajectory from 1980 forward does not imply the superiority of the latter interpretation: for it could be argued that what should have been a smooth transition from one set of institutional arrangements and practices to a more advanced one was disrupted by exogenous shocks for which market participants are not responsible.

In considering how economists have addressed this question, it is helpful to recall a key moment in the history of science. In 1972, Niles Eldredge and Stephen J. Gould (Eldredge and Gould, 1972) challenged the dominant account of how evolutionary processes work in nature: change, they argued, did not occur gradually and smoothly, but instead involved fluctuations between long periods of stasis and then short periods in which such equilibria were punctuated; in the latter, species would rapidly change, often in ways that altered their relationship to the changed environments that may have triggered those shifts.[1]

Economists' views on the matter line up according to these two views. In this section, we consider the theoretical and empirical approaches of economists who see financial evolution and economic growth as fundamentally smooth; in the final section, we turn to those whose views are more consistent with a 'punctuated equilibrium' approach, to use the Eldredge and Gould metaphor.

Raymond Goldsmith (1969) launched an entire literature premised on a gradualist approach to the relationship between the evolution of financial structures and the level of economic activity. Its core assertion was that financial development enhances economic activity. Ross Levine, in a 1997 *Journal of Economic Literature* (JEL) review article, wrote that 'the preponderance of theoretical reasoning and empirical evidence suggests a positive, first-order relationship between financial development and economic growth' (Levine, 1997, p. 688). It follows that financial system evolution is economically functional: it directly or indirectly generates either increased economic output, or more options for insuring against adverse outcomes at either the microeconomic or macroeconomic scale. Financial development in this literature is defined as an enhanced set of options, adopted by participants in financial markets (and subject to market discipline), for 'the trading of risk, allocating capital, monitoring managers, mobilizing savings, and easing the trading of goods, services, and financial contracts ... basic functions [that] remain constant through time and across countries' (Levine, 1997, p. 689).

The core theoretical idea of symbiotic finance in a productive circuit of capital is simply expressed. The finance/development approach posits that output Y will vary positively with injections of labour N, capital K and financial services F, such that Y = f(N, K, F). The core assertion of this approach, 'through time and across countries', as noted, is that more finance, ΔF, will lead to more growth, ΔY. Suppose we place finance in real-time trajectories of capitalist accumulation as envisioned by Marx, such as M – C (MP, LP) ...C' – M', where M equals the money capital pledged and M' the money capital earned, where C(MP, LP) equals the use of this capital to purchase means of production (MP) and labour power (LP), and where C' equals the output generated through combining MP and LP in production. We can readily see that roles for productive finance: equity and working-capital finance are needed to support the transition from enterprise capital M to production (C(MP, LP)); trade credit and risk-management services are needed to support the distribution of produced output to sales outlets C'; consumption credit is needed to support the purchase of C' by those with money to buy, M'; and expansion finance is needed at the end of the cycle to augment M' for the next round of production. In this depiction, finance has productive spillovers, as it augments the pace of the accumulation and circulation of capital. It is also bounded in size, as F – given any state of technology – is limited by the scale of accumulation and its activities by the needs of accumulation. Here, then, we have symbiotic finance–credit relations supporting – and bounded by – real-sector activity.

In the Spring of 1997, the same year in which Levine's JEL paper was published, the East Asian crisis hit: currency crises emerged in Malaysia, Thailand and Indonesia, and roared up from the south-east coasts of Asia, plunging Korea into a crisis that resulted in that nation's newly elected president, Kim Dae Jung, signing an IMF agreement on 24 December 1997, the day of his inauguration into office. These events, striking the heart of a portion of the developing world that had been regarded as undertaking 'best practices', led the IMF to construct a broad-based database of financial crises so as to try to understand what forces were at work empirically. This database contained comprehensive financial and macroeconomic indicators from 1960 to the present (Beck *et al.*, 2000).[2]

This database has been used primarily as the source of two types of reduced-form studies: first, 'signalling models' of currency and banking crises, as pioneered by Kaminsky and Reinhart (1999); second, multivariate logit models of the probability of banking crises, following Demirgüç-Kunt and Detragiache (1998).[3] Generally, these models are built by collecting data from different countries, for periods just before and just after key events (e.g. a banking crisis); then a dynamic panel is analysed empirically for this custom-built event-centred cross-section.[4]

The finance-growth literature reached an apotheosis in 2004, when Demirgüç-Kunt and Ross Levine (2004) reported econometric evidence confirming Goldsmith's hypothesis. The subprime crisis that occurred three years after that volume's publication undercut this result; but even the studies demonstrating that financial structure growth may adversely affect economic growth[5] have taken the gradualist approach characteristic of the field.

Certainly, disturbances in the smooth progress of financial activity and income growth can be attributed to governmental interference with market forces.[6] But more broadly, the idea of conceptualizing the finance-growth link as a smoothly evolving trend, whether in a positive or negative relationship at any point in time, stems from the peculiar relationship of this literature with economic theory. In an era in which many fields of economics demand that every modelling feature be assigned a specific analytical role – be 'micro-founded' – micro-founding has been set aside in the finance-growth approach. Merton and Bodie (2005), in a paper on the design of financial systems, explained this seeming anomaly as follows:

> The neoclassical model … offers important, but incomplete, guidance to decision makers seeking to understand and manage the process of institutional change. In accomplishing this task, the neo-institutional and behavioral perspectives can be very useful. In this proposed synthesis …, institutional structure is endogenous. When particular transaction costs or behavioral patterns produce large departures from the predictions of the ideal frictionless neoclassical equilibrium for a given institutional

> structure, new institutions tend to develop that partially offset the resulting inefficiencies. In the longer run, after institutional structures have had time to fully develop, the predictions of the neoclassical model will be approximately valid for asset prices and resource allocations.
>
> (p. 1)

A 2009 IMF study on finance and growth reinforces this perspective, setting forth a 'framework consistent with the functional view of financial system design, [which] is anchored in studying the incentives facing the key players in financial markets – borrowers, lenders, liquidity providers, and regulators – whose actions determine whether and how markets develop' (Chami *et al.*, 2009, p. 1), And whilst Fohlin (2014) insists that history matters in financial evolution, she also writes, 'financial systems historically took on a wide and complex range of forms that are difficult to categorize narrowly, yet provided similar functions; thus arguing for a functional, rather than institutional, approach to financial system design and regulation'. And Kapadia (2013) argues that even 'hierarchy is an abstract, functional requirement' (p. 436).

The upshot of the gradualist approach to the finance-growth relationship is that whatever trends occur are by definition functional for the overall system; and whilst the institutional and historical forces underlying financial evolutionary processes are too differentiated to analyse across cases, these processes are equifinal: if the evolution is permitted to proceed, an end-state characterized by economic efficiency in allocation, conventionally defined, will be achieved.

Global finance and punctuated 'equilibrium' in financial evolution

The literature summarized in this section rests on two premises: first, a gradualist understanding of the links between financial development and economic activity; second, a view that banking resilience is symbiotic with the growth of the non-financial sector. Overturning these two premises suggests a very different conclusion: specifically, the possibility that banking can advance by punctuated equilibrium processes whose outcomes may be that banks' resilience has become independent of the health of non-financial sectors in the economy.

Could such changes happen, and how? First, could they? The answer is yes, as is readily shown with some simple analytics. The finance/development approach argues that in the production function $Y = f(N, K, F)$, $\Delta F \rightarrow \Delta Y$ through more efficient transactions and savings allocations. But this is not the only relationship that may be at work. What if ΔF also leads to $-\Delta K$, a slower pace of (real) capital growth, due to a shift away from loan-making to certain categories of firm (for example, small and medium enterprises), or even overall? And what if ΔF absorbs a part of public spending; and in moments of crisis, liquidity is not available to support non-financial firms that need bridge financing? In this case, $\Delta F \rightarrow -\Delta Y$, as ΔF has negative spillovers on the growth of the non-financial sector. If its activities are independent of those of the non-financial sector, then its size is limited only by its capacity to manage its leveraging, combined with the availability of liquidity. That is, ($F + \Delta F_1 + \Delta F_2 \ldots$) whilst K and N remain largely fixed. And what if this growth of F was accompanied by rising profits for financial firms, and by rising levels of financial incomes (interest and fees, in particular), then bank resilience can be seen as independent of what happens to non-financial sectors. These logical possibilities suggest many ways in which finance can serves itself, not the non-financial economy, and is partially parasitic. Some testable hypotheses can readily be generated.

These sorts of hypotheses and results are based on homogenized or normalized data, of the type that is built into the IMF/World Bank database; see, for example, the variables listed in Table 1 on page 80 of Beck *et al.* (2010). During the industrial revolution and in many nations' developmental trajectories, financial systems have varied tremendously and served national needs in different ways, as shown by the comparative analyses of scholars such as Rondo Cameron (1967) and Alex Gerschenkron (1962).The formalization of efficient-market theory led some scholars, such as MacKinnon (1973), to assert that once barriers to market forces were removed, financial systems would converge to a uniform market-based model. Whilst Zysman (1983), among others, rebutted this assertion by pointing out that 'bank-based' systems such as those in Germany and Japan had been superior to 'capital-market-based' systems like that in the US and UK, in preparing these nations' industries for deepening global competition, MacKinnon (1973) was the most influential in shaping the finance-growth literature (Levine, 1997, p. 710). And in the 1980s and 1990s, history – aided in some cases by IMF-mandated system-opening – appeared to prove the gradualist-liberalization viewpoint right.

But a funny thing happened on the way to a gradualist evolution toward what Charles Sanford, then CEO of Bankers Trust, called the world of 'particle finance' (Sanford, 1994). The step-by-step dismantling of regulated financial systems and the insertion of market forces at many more points in the financial transmission mechanism brought about a punctuated-equilibrium transformation of finance. The period from the 1980s to the present has witnessed step changes so profound as to alter not only the structure, but the very functioning of the financial system.

Structural changes have been vast: shifts toward heavier reliance on financial activities in generating net income on the part of non-financial firms (Epstein, 2005); large-scale bank merger waves in the US (Dymski, 1999) and around the world (Dymski, 2002); and the pioneering of new savings instruments, new money-market funds and new investment vehicles, including asset-backed commercial paper, hedge funds, private equity funds, subprime mortgages and payday loans (Dymski, 2013).

Structural shifts in banking have altered its functional relationship with the real sector. But, as the finance-growth authors point out, it is function and not form that counts. So we now elaborate a set of four epochal changes that have,

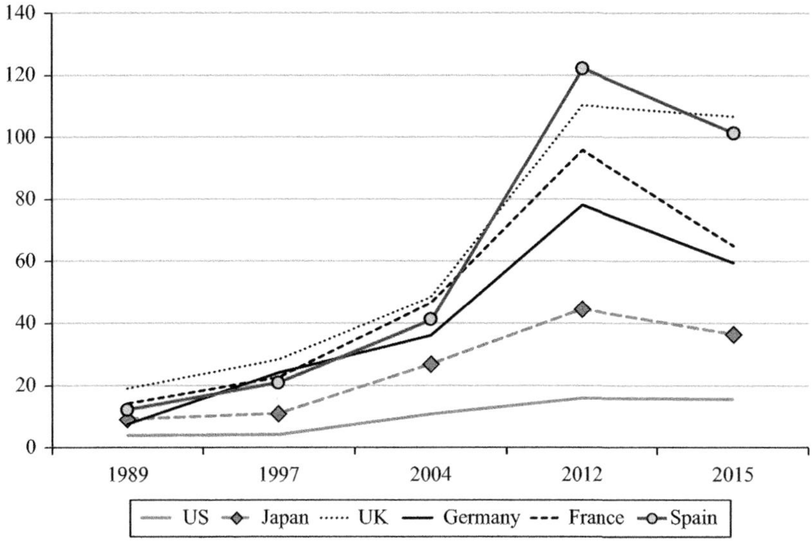

Figure 3.1 Assets of largest bank, selected countries, 1989, 1997, 2004, 2012 and 2015, % of GDP

Source: Author's calculation based on OECD, *Fortune* (2004, 2008, 2012, 2015), and *Business Week* (1989, 1997)

taken together, shifted the nature of finance's system functioning vis-à-vis other sectors in the economy. One shift is the opening up of financial markets to globalization – cross-border claims, ownership and institutional linkages. The fact that banks could grow in size so as to take on positions in the global market, not just serve the local/national market, implied that they could grow substantially larger than (in particular) whatever smaller nation-state served as their home base. This shift is demonstrated in Figure 3.1, which shows the asset size of the largest bank relative to that nation's GDP for a sample of countries. The largest bank-asset/GDP ratio is below 20 per cent in 1989, but by 2012 this ratio exceeds 75 per cent for four of the six banks shown. The two countries whose banks fall below this threshold are Japan and the US, both of whose economies are larger than the others. If Japan's economy equalled Germany's in size, its data would overlay those of Germany.

This leads to the second key shift – the super-sizing of the very largest banks. In many countries, this is related both to banks' physical expansion and to their taking on new activities, the latter often by merger. These very large banks' expansion often involved moving into more highly leveraged activities. This hyper-leveraging had multiple dimensions: it pertained to banks' willingness to support more off-balance sheet activity, to their willingness to expand their on-balance sheet activity (the difference often depended on whether these banks were operating under 'universal banking' mandates), to their willingness to offer loan products that relied on leveraging of household wealth (subprime mortgages) and household income (payday loans) to an unprecedented extent.

These first two shifts have resulted in the creation of 'megabanks' in several nations of the world. This term refers to banks that meet these criteria: they are an order-of-magnitude larger than other members of their banking systems; they have an organizational interest in market expansion to capture new revenues through geographic or product-line growth, and compete to introduce innovative products in the markets they serve (or hope to serve), so as to multiply revenue gains; and they are complexly interdependent on webs of contracts with other large financial entities, across a wide landscape of markets and products.

Megabanks are frequently 'systematically important', a term defined by the Financial Stability Board.[7] Megabanks' size, their hyper-leveraging and their centrality in financial market transactions – the impossibility of unwinding the thick knot of real-time contingent and spot payments commitments and contracts – makes them, at present, too big to fail in a double sense. For one thing, in failure they would generate capital losses and liabilities too large for their host nation-state to absorb; for another, their contractual commitments are simply too dense to cleanly cut. This is the third shift – the fact of too-big-to-fail (TBTF) protection for these entities. TBTF policy, by its very nature, cannot be officially declared; but since 1983 it has been the de facto policy of the US government for its largest banks, and after the subprime crisis it is clearly the de facto policy of many other governments as well.[8]

The fourth critical shift in finance stems from a feature unique to the neoliberal era: the dollar hegemony of the US, linked jointly to its centrality in global trade and financial flows, and to the US's 35-year-old structural current-account deficit. Both elements here are critical in establishing how structure, in this case, alters function (rather than vice versa, as the gradualist view contends).

First consider dollar hegemony, which actually has carried this aspect of US competitive advantage from the Bretton Woods era into the neoliberal era. Because the dollar is readily accepted in exchange anywhere, and is freely held as a store of value, the nation emitting it has a capacity denied any other to the same degree – the capacity to print liquidity without limit in the event of a financial meltdown. This 'lender of last resort' (LLR) capacity is not uniquely held by the Federal Reserve. However, the US central bank's capacity to backstop financial markets and institutions in crises – illustrated in the underwriting of the failed Continental Illinois Bank in 1983, in the 1987 stock-market crash, in the Long Term Management agreement in 1998, and then most definitively in the 2008 subprime crisis – far exceeds that of any other nation (Eichengreen, 2015).The fact that this sequence of LLR rescues demarcates the progress of the neoliberal era is no coincidence: nations that are financial hegemons permit more financial-firm risk-taking, as this is a source of competitive advantage and episodes of system crisis can be handled through reserve emission and other means (Dymski, 2009). Every nation with its own currency can have its central bank print currency; but this capacity is a matter of degree, not kind – something aptly demonstrated in crises. Whilst financial regulators in nations with limited LLR capacity must avoid the possibility of panic and failure in the markets they control, the US is at the other end of the risk-avoidance spectrum; its banks can play with fire whilst seeking to expand their footprint in global financial markets.

Next, the US's chronic capital-account inflow (trade deficit), which implies, of course, a capital-account inflow. This imbalance has persisted over decades. It has been made permissible both by the scale of the US economy relative to others, the prominence of US firms in global finance and by oil-exporters' use of dollars. Dollar hegemony has, in turn, been reinforced insofar as chronic crises elsewhere have accentuated the US's 'global safe haven' status. This steady inflow of financial savings seeking assets to buy has underpinned the growth of loan securitization. Indeed, it can also be observed that chronic US governmental deficits have provided a ready supply of Treasuries, which in turn play a critical role (as collateral) in underpinning the highly leveraged ('rehypothecated') money markets that have grown up in the neoliberal era. It might be mentioned, without further elaboration here, that this structural circumstance encouraged the shift toward increasingly risky loan-making – especially different forms of predatory lending, from subprime mortgages to payday loans – and the growth of shadow banks, for which holding and distributing repackaged securities has been a central enterprise.

These shifts, taken together, have facilitated the escape of finance from a primary role of servicing the real sector (a symbiotic relationship) to an independent role in the economy as a whole. This role centres on the creation and circulation of new financial instruments, the opening of new financial markets and the multiplication of leverage in the money, securities and derivatives markets. The layers on layers of intertwined contracts are impenetrable by regulators and incomprehensible to megabanks' top managers. So growth-enabling finance has been swallowed up in these interlinked shifts, leading among other things to the nearly universal growth in the financial share of value added in GDP.

Large, multi-market, financial firms – especially megabanks – have become autonomous by finding ways to create value (capture surplus) through extending transaction chains. One pathway is through event-contingent risk-shifting: the specialties of London and Paris – either exchange-traded or over-the-counter (custom) derivatives. Another pathway is through originating and placing credit via securitization: originating risk, but not bearing it. Shadow banking has emerged as so central to these new pathways because it permits the geographic rebasing of the huge risks and hyper-leveraging often required to achieve small-margin gains.

This shift in the financial/real sector relationship is seen in the withdrawal of banks from lending for SMEs and for working capital in the UK and in

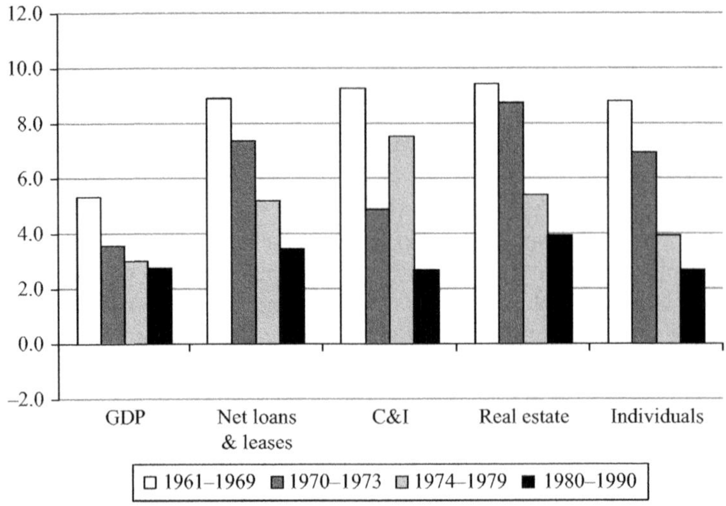

Figure 3.2 Trough-to-peak GDP and loan growth, US commercial banks, five-year time spans, 1961–1990, average annual % change

Note: All figures are calculated on the basis of constant 2009 prices. GDP is gross domestic product. Net loans and leases denotes all loans and leases by all US banks registered with the Federal Deposit Insurance Corporation; C&I.

Source: Author's calculation based on US Federal Deposit Insurance Corporation – Historical Statistics on Banking, Table CB-11, and US Bureau of Economic Analysis

Europe in the post-2008 crisis period is well known. However, evidence from the US suggests this shift is much longer in the making. Figures 3.2 and 3.3 contrast the average annual percentage change in loans, overall and by loan category, with the average annual GDP growth in different business-cycle periods from the 1960s forward. For every cycle, the trough year of that cycle is taken as year one, with up to five years' subsequent experience counted (unless the recovery in question fell short of five years). It is readily seen that whereas prior to the 1990s, loan growth across the categories of credit – commercial and industrial (C&I) loans, real-estate-based loans and loans to individuals – exceeded the pace of GDP growth. From 1991 onward, over three successive business cycles, this relationship has evaporated. These data are drawn from aggregate figures for the Federal Deposit Insurance Fund – that is, for all banks. However, it should be noted that overall loan volumes are increasingly dominated by megabanks; in data not shown here, this trend has intensified from the mid-2000s onward, after which period the 'big four' US commercial banks (JP Morgan Chase, Citibank, BankAmerica and Wells Fargo) have begun to account for more than half of all lending in most credit categories.

Figure 3.3 makes clear that even banks' credit growth no longer helps economies recover from periods of downturn; in recent years it has primarily financed real-estate and consumption-related activity, not investment.

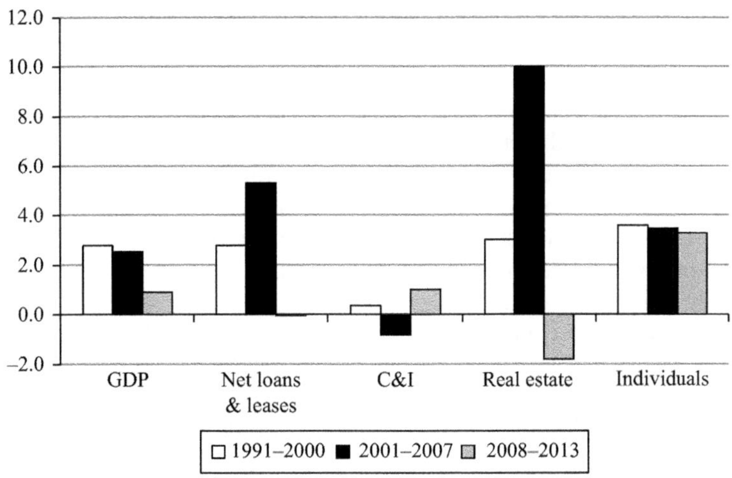

Figure 3.3 Trough-to-peak GDP and loan growth, US commercial banks, five-year time spans, 1991 to present, average annual % change

Note: All figures are calculated on the basis of constant 2009 prices. GDP is gross domestic product. Net loans and leases denotes all loans and leases by all US banks registered with the Federal Deposit Insurance Corporation; C&I.

Source: Author's calculation based on US Federal Deposit Insurance Corporation – Historical Statistics on Banking, Table CB-11, and US Bureau of Economic Analysis

In general, megabanks are no longer lenders but instead orchestrators of networks of buying and selling relationships in interlinked markets, as well as speculators in zero-sum position-taking. This is the 'escape of finance'. Financial resilience for megabanks depends on their access to ever new markets for fee-earning and zero-sum speculation possibilities, combined with a TBTF backstop. Resilience depends less on the health of their region/nation of origin, as their income streams become delinked from localities; indeed, the subprime and payday-loan episodes illustrate that lenders may even prey on borrowers in their home region's economy to increase their cash-flows.

What we have done, then, is to set out an alternative to the gradualist view of financial evolution. We have argued that after a period of relative tranquillity in financial structure – the post-War 'Golden Age' years – a series of complementary changes to the shape of finance have interacted, with increasing velocity, to change its 'function' – its relationship to the rest of the economic ecosystem, so to speak. That is, the notion of 'punctuated equilibrium' better describes what has happened.[9] Further, as Eldredge and Gould conjectured for the case of biological evolution, the effect of this 'punctuation' was to change not just the entities within the field of finance, but the relationship between finance and its environment – the broader economy. It is not any one element of the post-shift system that can be singled out as the problematic element – hedge funds, perhaps, or the size of the megabanks themselves, as Johnson and Kwak (2010) insist (as important as size undoubtedly is in shaping this shift). It is the structural nexus taken as a whole: the size of the megabanks, for sure, but also the persistent US current-account deficit, the global privilege of the dollar, the asymmetry of LLR capacity, the decisive shift of megabanks toward securitized loan-making, the US capital-account/current-account imbalance, and the global competition among megabanks and – for that matter – between megabanks and shadow banks. All this together creates an environment of coercive competition and instability that has seen two profound crises of global economy since 2006 and that has not fundamentally changed its character.

Figure 3.4 illustrates this point about coercive competition. It reprises the data shown in Figure 3.1, which measured asset size relative to GDP for the largest banks in six nations. Here, these banks' asset size is shown in billions of US dollars (not inflation-adjusted). Two points should be made. First, the shrinkage notable in Figure 3.1 is not evident here; only Deutschebank has deleveraged significantly between 2012 and the present. Second, the battle for global pre-eminence is clearly seen.[10]

The five shifts highlighted in this section have, in effect, created a global network of finance that both feeds off the interconnectedness of markets

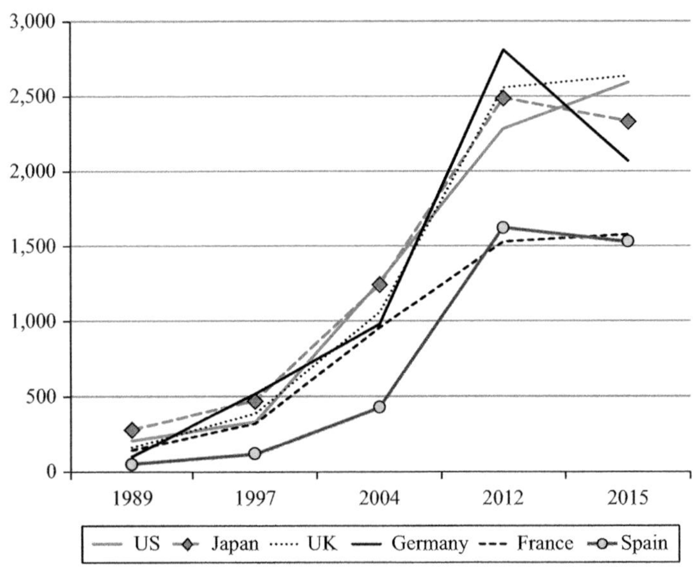

Figure 3.4 Assets of largest bank, in US$ billion, selected countries, 1989, 1997, 2004, 2012 and 2015

Source: Author's calculation based on OECD, *Fortune* (2004, 2008, 2012, 2015), and *Business Week* (1989, 1997)

for fees and customers, and at the same time competes for advantage within this network (Wójcik, 2012). The fee-taking exists side-by-side with zero-sum speculation, in an unstable mix. Indeed, considering the premium on speed in exploiting arbitrage in the context of other structural features of this system – the overlaid cross-border claims, the complexities of contingent and spot-market positions, and information asymmetries fanned by rumour mills – leads readily to the conclusion that the megabanks at the heart of this system are too big to manage (TBTM).[11] The existence of TBTF protection for this TBTM entity, however, leads to the further conclusion that megabank shareholders themselves know that the entity they own is unmanageable, but breaking it up will not generate more value, as market-forces advocates suppose, because the loss of TBTF underwriting may lead to a net loss in share value (Roe, 2013). Once the inability of national authorities or of global forums (such as the Bank for International Settlements) to fully control current risks or to derisk new practices and instruments is considered, the scope for another round of financial-system meltdown is evident. In this context, it is not idle to ask whether another round of TBTM-initiated TBTF will not tax the limits of even the Federal Reserve's crisis-management capacity. The US is, after all, a nation with a nearly four-decade current-account deficit – a structural weakness that has brought the wrath of the IMF down on many a smaller nation.

Two responses to the dysfunctionality of the 'new normal'

Two responses critical of the 'new normal' can be framed. One response, embodied in the peer-to-peer and positive-money ('democratic finance') initiatives of recent years, argues that those whose needs are not being met by megabank-dominated global finance should 'opt out': either by drawing boundary lines around those parts of the financial system that serve local communities and businesses; or by co-opting the machinery of modern finance by inventing portals for the participation of outsiders driven by community-building motives, not by the imperative of surplus extraction for its own sake.

These 'opt-out' approaches are subject to the critique that they ignore the coercive public-goods aspects of financial processes. As the work of Sheila Dow (1986) on regional aspects of monetary policy implies, the liquidity and credit flows generated by different configurations of financial institutions have public-goods characteristics. There are spillovers that adversely affect non-privileged regions (in the case she is discussing). If 'opt-out' financial proposals are implemented whilst an underregulated megabank complex remains in place, these spillover effects will be at work. The particular danger is that when crises arrive and megabanks need disproportionate access to liquidity, they will monopolize central-bank provisioning. Non-TBTF banks and whatever 'opt-out' non-bank alternatives exist will be subject to the double challenge of a stagnating real sector and liquidity starvation.

So the 'opt-out' option ends up being a non-option. A second response to the 'new normal' then comes into view. This response begins with the recognition that the problem is systemic, so the solution must be systemic as well. The megabank-dominated, regulation-resisting, tax-haven-seeking global financial system has, by embedding itself in the heart of modern economic systems, already required public subsidies in crises of its own making, imposing direct and indirect costs on the rest of the economy and reducing policy space. This system's coercive effect on regulatory restructuring makes future crises predictable. If this critique is right, then there is no alternative to confronting the dilemma: either financial governance is globalized, and somehow made to work, or means must be found to rein in the coercive and growth-undercutting aspects of globalized financial systems. A financial sector that again grows symbiotically with the real sector, and whose growth depends on robust real-sector growth, must be put in place.

The argument in support of this point has been set forth above, but might be briefly summarized.

The greater access of megabanks to liquidity and public subsidies, and the impact of this privileged access on smaller banks, worsens the effect of shocks from asset-bubble collapses or other causes. Subsidies paid to recapitalize (bail out) megabanks are paid by taxpayers in general, resulting in a transfer to megabank owners. Megabanks' ability to shift tax/'headquarter' locations ('inversion'), and/or to shift balance-sheet categories (bonuses to salary adjustments) is too great. Shadow banks' running to tax havens worsens the gap between those who give to the public fisc and those who take from it. The crisis-linked stagnation in local economies where these taxpayers live is then heightened as budget-cutback scenarios play out after reallocations of the public fisc in favour of the faltering financial system have squeezed 'policy space'. This adversely affects the smaller banks that do lend locally, causing their higher failure rate and leading to further negative consequences on locally based small and medium enterprises.

Since all economic units need fair access to financial services – and since the above dynamics generate arbitrarily unfair results – protective measures against excessive risk-taking, against tax-haven-hunting, and excessive leveraging, should be taken. Higher capital/asset ratios will not suffice. For megabanks and shadow banks, the margins to be earned from cutting-edge instruments or indices that open space for new fees and for new zero-sum speculation games are too attractive. The competition amongst the financial centres for capturing the spillover jobs and income flows from 'wins' is too great.

Further, the reality to be faced squarely is that the nation-states with the most 'advanced' financial structures have the least incentive and least capacity to control their dysfunctional – parasitic – behaviours. The capacity of US, UK and European legislators and executives to undo megabanks' reframing of 'banking' – and to successfully regulate it – is too limited.

There are two ways forward then in response to this systemic malfunctioning. One is to eliminate the sources of malfunction – excessive leveraging, subsidized zero-sum speculation, failure to make credit available to economically productive units, inability or unwillingness to create financial vehicles meeting longer-term sustainability/green-economy needs – by creating inescapable rules that cover the entire global economy. This 'Star Trek world' scenario would require regulators as incorruptible and clear-minded as Vulcans; and Vulcans are in short supply.

This leads to the global Plan B, which is for countries that lack financial hegemony to take protective action – to seal off their financial systems from coercive – and ultimately subsidy-generating – competition with countries that have financial hegemony. Since there are at most three to four countries in the latter category, and many in the former, it is worth summarizing the argument for this 'sealing off' strategy.

Financial centres and firms in those countries that have financial hegemony will protect their own financial firms in crises, monopolizing the flows of global liquidity. Post-crisis recovery scenarios will be asymmetric, with higher growth rates likely in financial-hegemonic nations. This result is evident in today's post-crisis scenario. So non-hegemonic nations should take action to protect the economically productive portions of their financial infrastructure and to insure that their own larger banks are more economically productive. The attraction of moving the opposite way – of becoming, say, the Wall Street of Latin America – should be resisted by non-hegemonic nations, for the booms available from such moves last only until the next currency crisis. This need to protect symbiotic flows of productive finance to non-financial firms – and to households – exists in every nation.

The re-establishment of symbiotic financial relations – by bringing megabanks under effective regulatory control and ensuring that the banking ecosystem in place meets real-sector needs in non-predatory ways – can be accomplished, in principle, in any spatial area that is able to control the entry/exit of megabanks and shadow banks across its borders. This will require sealing off the space of any reformed area from inversion risk, and/or tax-haven shifts, and definition risks; and it will require restricting competition of any financial centre within this space, with financial centres outside this space. Frankfurt cannot compete on equal terms with a Wall Street backed by dollar hegemony, nor can Mexico City or Sao Paulo. This in turn will require that this spatial area forego the attractions of opening borders to unregulated (or even less regulated) financial actors.

Maintaining such 'sealed off' space, via capital controls and effective regulation and other measures, will be very difficult in a world in which financial hegemonic nations are able to undertake asymmetric rescues in whatever financial crises are to come. Sealing off portions of the global economy from megabank/shadow-bank entry will, if it proceeds far enough, starve the beast. But in the end the way to avoid any escape anywhere is to draw a spatial area that includes the entire globe – so that the escape of finance becomes impossible. And in any case, what would be the overriding logic of a world in which parasitic finance has been eliminated, so that only symbiotic finance linked to goods/services production, distribution and exchange remains? Is that still a capitalist world, governed by capital accumulation and its contradictions? Does the reform of finance then ultimately mean the end of capitalism as we know it?

Notes

1 See: Gould and Eldredge (1977).
2 An updated database was subsequently released; see: Beck *et al.* (2010).
3 For a survey of this literature, see: Demirgüç-Kunt and Detragiache (2009).
4 These methods closely resemble those used to understand the determinants of the 'Solow residual' in aggregate growth models. Levine undertook empirical work on the Solow residual in the same period in which this database was first constructed (Easterly and Levine, 2001).
5 See, for example, Beck *et al.* (2014).
6 These views are summarized in Dymski (2013).
7 See: FSB (2014).
8 According to Chow and Surti (2011), 23 systematically important European financial institutions received financial assistance in 2008–2009, versus 5 systematically important US banks.
9 We pass over, here, the problematic concept of the term 'equilibrium' in economics.
10 An 11 October 2015 article in the *Financial Times* under banking editor Martin Arnold's by-line was entitled, 'Barclays chief says EU banking champion needed to compete with US'.
11 On ungovernability, see: Wójcik (2013). On the 'London whale' incident, which aptly illustrates the point made here, see Kregel (2013).

References

Beck, T., Demirgüç- Kunt, A. and Levine, R., 2000. A New Database on the Structure and Development of the Financial Sector. *The World Bank Economic Review*, 14(3), pp. 597–605.

Beck, T., Demirgüç-Kunt, A. and Levine, R., 2010. Financial Institutions and Markets across Countries and over Time: The Updated Financial Development and Structure Database. *The World Bank Economic Review*, 24(1), pp. 77–92.

Beck, T., Degryse, H. and Kneer, C., 2014. Is More Finance Better? Disentangling Intermediation and Size Effects of Financial Systems. *Journal of Financial Stability*, 10(C), pp. 50–64.

Cameron, R., 1967. *Banking in the Early Stages of Industrialization*. Oxford: Oxford University Press.

Chami, R., Fullenkamp, C. and Sharma, S., 2009. *A Framework for Financial Market Development*, Washington: IMF Working Paper WP/09/156.

Chow, J. T. and Surti, J., 2011. *Making Banks Safer: Can Volcker and Vickers Do It?*, Washington: IMF Working Paper WP/11/236.

Demirgüç-Kunt, A. and Detragiache, E., 1998. The Determinants of Banking Crises: Evidence from Developing and Developed Countries. *IMF Staff Papers*, Issue 45, pp. 81–109.

Demirgüç-Kunt, A. and Detragiache, E., 2009. *Cross-Country Empirical Studies of Systemic Bank Distress: A Survey*, Washington: IMF Working Paper WP/05/96.

Demirgüç-Kunt, A. and Levine, R., 2004. *Financial Structure and Economic Growth: A Cross-country Comparison of Banks, Markets and Development*. Cambridge, MA: MIT Press.

Dow, S., 1986. The Capital Account and Regional Balance of Payments Problems. *Urban Studies*, Issue 23, pp. 173–184.

Dymski, G. A., 1999. *The Bank Merger Wave: The Economic Causes and Social Consequences of Financial Consolidation in the United States*. Armonk, NY: M.E. Sharpe, Inc.

Dymski, G. A., 2002. The Global Bank Merger Wave: Implications for Developing Countries. *The Developing Economies*, 40(4), pp. 435–466.

Dymski, G. A., 2009. Financial Risk and Governance in the Neoliberal Era. In: G. L. Clark, A. D. Dixon and A. H. Monk, eds. *Managing Financial Risks: From Global to Local*. Oxford: Oxford University Press, pp. 48–68.

Dymski, G. A., 2010. The International Debt Crisis. In: J. Michie, ed. *Handbook of Globalisation*. Second Edition. Cheltenham: Edward Elgar Publishing, pp. 90–103.

Dymski, G. A., 2013. Understanding the Subprime Crisis: International Evolution and Theoretical Views. In: C. Rogers and J. Powell, eds. *Where Credit is Due: Bringing Equity to Credit and Housing After the Market Meltdown*. Lanham, MD: University Press of America, pp. 23–67.

Easterly, W. and Levine, R., 2001. It's Not Factor Accumulation: Stylized Facts and Growth Models. *The World Bank Economic Review*, 15(2), pp. 177–219.

Eichengreen, B., 2015. *Hall of Mirrors: The Great Depression, the Great Recession and the Uses and Misuses of History*. Oxford: Oxford University Press.

Eldredge, N. and Gould, S. J., 1972. Punctuated Equilibria: An Alternative to Phyletic Gradualism. In: T. J. M. Schopf, ed. *Models in Paleobiology*. San Francisco: Freeman Cooper, pp. 82–115.

Epstein, G., 2005. *Financialization and the World Economy*. Cheltenham: Edward Elgar Publishing.

Farlow, A., 2013. *Crash and Beyond: Causes and Consequences of the Global Financial Crisis*. Oxford: Oxford University Press.

Fohlin, C., 2014. *Financial Systems and Economic Development in Historical Perspective*. [Online] Available at: http://papers.ssrn.com/sol3/papers.cfm?abstract_id=2524109 [Accessed 12 October 2016].

FSB, 2014. *2014 Update of List of Global Systemically Important Banks (G-SIBs)*. [Online] Available at: www.financialstabilityboard.org/2014/11/2014-update-of-list-of-global-systemically-important-banks [Accessed 5 December 2016].

Gerschenkron, A., 1962. *Economic Backwardness in Comparative Perspective*. Cambridge, MA: Harvard University Press.

Goldsmith, R., 1969. *Financial Structure and Development*. New Haven, CT: Yale University Press.

Gould, S. J. and Eldredge, N., 1977. Punctuated Equilibria: The Tempo and Mode of Evolution Reconsidered. *Paleobiology*, 3(2), pp. 115–151.

Johnson, S. and Kwak, J., 2010. *The 13 Bankers*. New York: Pantheon.

Kaminsky, G. and Reinhart, C. N., 1999. The Twin Crises: The Causes of Banking and Balance of Payments Problems. *American Economic Review*, Issue 89, pp. 473–500.

Kapadia, A., 2013. Europe and the Logic of Hierarchy. *Journal of Comparative Economics*, Issue 41, pp. 436–446.

Kregel, J., 2013. More Swimming Lessons from the London Whale. *Public Policy Brief*, Issue 129.

Levine, R., 1997. Financial Development and Economic Growth: Views and Agenda. *Journal of Economic Literature*, Issue 35, pp. 688–726.

McKinnon, R. I., 1973. *Money and Capital in Economic Development*. Washington: Brookings Institution.

Merton, R. C. and Bodie, Z., 2005. The Design of Financial Systems: Towards a Synthesis of Function and Structure. *Journal of Investment Management*, 3(1), pp. 1–23.

Reinhart, C. and Rogoff, K., 2010. Growth in a Time of Debt. *American Economic Review*, 100(2), pp. 573–578.

Roe, M., 2013. London Whale is the Cost of Too Big to Fail. *Financial Times*, 24 March.

Sanford, C., 1994. Financial Markets in 2020. *Economic Review of the Federal Reserve Bank of Kansas City*, First Quarter, pp. 1–10.

Wójcik, D., 2012. Where Governance Fails: Advanced Business Services and the Offshore World. *Progress in Human Geography*, 37(3), pp. 330–347.

Wójcik, D., 2013. The Dark Side of NY-LON: Financial Centres and the Global Financial Crisis. *Urban Studies*, 50(13), pp. 2736–2752.

Zysman, J., 1983. *Governments, Markets and Growth: Financial Systems and the Politics of Industrial Change*. Ithaca, NY: Cornell University Press.

4 The macroeconomic determinants of financial literacy in the European Union (on the example of numeracy skills)

Tomasz Potocki and Krzysztof Opolski

Introduction

One of the major concerns in the EU is functional illiteracy and lack of numeracy which severely restrains the capabilities development and result in functionings failure (Arndt and Volkert, 2009, p. 8). In recent years, financial literacy has become 'an essential skill for individuals in all walks of life and a central public policy concern throughout the world' (Holzmann *et al.*, 2013, p. ix) and lack of financial literacy might play the dominant role in increasing vulnerability to social exclusion (OECD, 2005, 2009; EC, 2007). The costs of financial illiteracy might have far-reaching consequences (put at risk different capabilities, resulting in negative freedom) especially in the face of overwhelming financialization, which led to an enormous increase in the complexity of financial products, as well as to shifting responsibility for financial decisions from state (public goods) to free market (private goods). The financialization might lead to reflection irrationality as a result of a complex world.[1] Flejterski claims that 'in an advanced, modern economy welfare increase goes hand in hand with social risk increase, which gives rise to a new paradigm of the risk society' (Flejterski, 2007, p. 59). The high level of financial literacy can contribute to more effective allocation of financial resources, protecting the stability of the economy (Lusardi, 2008; Jappelli, 2010) and reducing the income inequalities (Ameriks *et al.*, 2003; Lusardi *et al.*, 2012).

In the face of the above-mentioned arguments, there is a growing need for macro cross-country evidence indicating the main determinants of financial literacy. Unfortunately, the greatest barrier is the access to international and long time series of financial literacy scores. In this chapter, the authors will use a mathematical score as a proxy to financial literacy and a large set of macroeconomic, financial development and education indicators between the 2003 and 2012 time series. The analysis covers all the European countries.

The aim of the chapter is to present empirical results verifying the following thesis: 'In the European Union numeracy skills are mainly determined by Education factors but the role of Financial Development factors are also noticeable.' This assumption is drawn from the conclusion that if well-educated, wealthy individuals with comprehensive knowledge and high educational achievements residing in rich countries are not able to make the right financial choices, then at some level of socio-economics there are some different factors (i.e. financial development) influencing the increase in financial literacy.

The results of the chapter might help:

- researchers in delivering conceptual framework for cross country indexes of financial literacy especially in the context of financialization;
- policy makers in establishing better forms of intervention (social and monetary policy), building cost-effective education solutions (national financial education strategies).

The emergence of financial literacy in the face of financialization

The last several years is the continuation of a tendency from the 1990s of the twentieth century, namely a dynamic financial development and financialization. According to Martin, 'financialization is a phenomenon that has led to the embedding of the financial world into people's everyday lives'.[2] Financial decisions, in Palley's opinion, are one of the three main transmission channels of financialization to economic outcomes (Palley, 2007, p. 15). Finlayson is of the opinion that it contributed to a 'change in individual relationships with finance, perhaps also in expectations and aspiration' and proved the need for creating the so-called 'finance rationality' (Finlayson, 2009, p. 402). Additionally, Froud *et al.* claimed that this influence is of great significance because 'the financial markets ... shape the behaviour of ... households' (Froud *et al.*, 2002, p. 120). Financialization has changed the relation between individuals and the financial market not only from an economic perspective, but also from psychological, social and cultural ones. Therefore, the level of development of financial markets and offered services has a significant influence on financial decisions taken by households.

Financialization led to a transfer of responsibility for financial decisions from the state to individuals and households (the shift from defined benefit (DB) to defined contribution (DC)) which, especially in post-communist countries, they were not prepared for, particularly in the context of financial literacy. One should pay attention to the fact that the lack of financial literacy might significantly influence the rationality of financial decisions of individuals and households, leading to an imbalance of a household budget (Ameriks *et al.*, 2003), excessive exposure to debts (Jappelli *et al.*, 2008), increasing the vulnerability to poverty (Anand and Lea, 2011). In the light of the above-mentioned arguments: 'As it was impossible to live and operate efficiently in the past without being literate, i.e., knowing how to read and write, so it is very hard to live and operate efficiently today without being financially literate' (Lusardi, 2008, pp. 15–16).

The last financial crisis exposed the lack of financial literacy, which led to poor financial decisions. At the same time, it showed the growing importance of risk connected with financial decisions and financial welfare. Gigerenzer explicitly asserted that by saying 'risk-savvy citizens are indispensable pillars of a society ... being risk savvy requires a basic knowledge of our intuitive psychology as well as an understanding of statistical information. Only with both skills ..., will we be able to take our lives in our own hands' (Gigerenzer, 2015, p. 16).

Macroeconomic evidence on financial literacy – dilemmas and challenges

There is a limited number of papers dedicated to macroeconomic evidence on financial literacy. There are two important limitations. First, there is the lack of consistency in defining and measuring financial literacy. As mentioned by Hung *et al.* and Huston, researchers very often assess the level of financial literacy without defining what in fact the financial literacy is, and if they do deliver it, in the majority of cases the definition and the measurement framework are conceptually different – the same is true with interpretation of the results (Hung *et al.*, 2009, pp. 3–9; Huston, 2010, pp. 298–305). Moreover, the definition of financial literacy frequently combines the number of different components, like in Atkinson and Messy: 'financial literacy: a combination of awareness, knowledge, skills, attitude and behaviours necessary to make sound financial decisions and ultimately achieve individual financial wellbeing' (Atkinson and Messy, 2012, p. 4). In the opinion of the authors of this chapter, such an approach to defining financial literacy considerably reduces the chance to measure it correctly.

Second, the access to international databases with financial literacy score is scare. The most common scientific approach is adding financial literacy tests to national longitudinal surveys. It allows the analysis of financial literacy determinants but only at an individual level within the country. Additionally, it rarely covers series of data (more than one wave of panel data) and, therefore, limits the longitudinal advantage of surveys.[3] The second most common approach is to assess financial literacy in several countries.[4] The advantage of this approach is coherent methodology of financial literacy assessment. Unfortunately, there are some disadvantages including the lack of time series and a limited number of countries.

The perfect solution to the above-mentioned limitation might be inclusion of a financial literacy module in 2012 PISA studies, which could serve as a confirmation of this new international trend (OECD, 2014, p. 13). It also seems that 'PISA has taken the position that financial literacy is now recognized as an essential skill to be able to operate in today's economy' (Lusardi and Mitchell, 2013, p. 13). It significantly reduces the lack of consistency in defining and measuring financial literacy in a longitudinal survey at a country level. Jappelli said clearly that 'the ideal dataset would include an assessment of financial knowledge and skills, such as is provided by OECD-PISA for 15-year olds for math or science' (Jappelli, 2010, p. 2). Unfortunately, the financial literacy module is available for the 2012 wave only and the number of pilot countries is only 13. Therefore, to do a comparative analysis of financial literacy, which also allows us to assess the macroeconomic determinants of financial literacy in the longer perspective, it seems reasonable to use the PISA database and make some simplifying assumptions. The second possible approach is to use a comparable database, especially in terms of consistency in measuring financial literacy with a large number of participating countries and a long enough time series of financial literacy score.

Jappelli used the second approach but as the independent variable he used economic literacy scores of business leaders which come from the IMD World Competitiveness Yearbook. Thanks to that, he was able to use a database of 55 countries and a 13-year time series (between 1995 and 2008).[5] The authors of this chapter used the first approach. They used PISA scores in mathematical literacy as a proxy for financial literacy. This approach has its justification in related research literature. In a number of financial literacy research papers, it is repeatedly indicated that numeracy plays a significant role in building financial literacy, and both concepts are interrelated.[6] Additionally, it is partly consistent with the OECD-PISA 2012 estimation of expected performance in financial literacy with mathematical performance (numeracy skills). On the basis of the results, it appears that performance between the 25th and 75th percentiles in financial literacy and mathematical performance are very similar (OECD, 2014, p. 78). Moreover, the application of the 50th percentile of mathematical performance (numeracy skills) as a proxy for financial literacy opens lots of possibilities in terms of comparative and macro analysis. The authors of the chapter are aware of the limitations of such presumptions, especially when studying the level of financial literacy in the adult population. It is easy to imagine a situation in which an adult individual represents the low level of numeracy skills but thanks to several years of experience in using financial products and services he or she was able to acquire some basic level of financial literacy. However, it seems that in the case of pupils assessed in the PISA study the expected variance should be much lower. This argument is in line with Lusardi and Mitchell who say 'it may be difficult to enhance numeracy in the older adult population, whereas it may be easier to boost knowledge of a few financial concepts fundamental for making financial decisions' (Lusardi and Mitchell, 2011, p. 5). What is more, as stated by Jappelli, PISA test scores and economic literacy are positively correlated (Jappelli, 2010), which means that it might constitute a valuable source of knowledge about cognitive abilities especially in the financial literacy context.[7]

Regression analysis[8]

To verify the stated thesis of the study, the authors used three sets of variables which at macro level might have a substantial impact on numeracy skills. First, the most popular set of 16 socio-economics variables was used by the authors. This is due to the fact that, in the authors' opinion, including only basic variables such as inflation rate, GDP growth rate, unemployment rate or GINI index might be far from enough to sufficiently analyse the impact of these sets of variables. Inclusion of household final consumption expenditure, gross domestic savings, final consumption expenditure variables might have higher importance in explaining the variability of numeracy skills. Second, the authors included a set of 20 education variables which, in general, explain the inputs to education system (i.e. teacher salaries, expenditure on education), as well as the outputs of education process (i.e. school life expectancy, transition rates, enrolment rates). Third, the authors added to the analysis a set of financial development variables. These indicators come from the World Bank Financial Development Matrix and describe the level of depth, access, efficiency, stability of financial system for two different institutional models: market model and financial institution model.[9] Fourth, in the initial analysis the authors used three dummy variables, namely the National Financial Education Strategy dummy variable,[10] the banking crisis dummy[11] and the post-communist countries dummy. The authors have reason to believe that implementation of the National Financial Education Strategy may serve as a proof of institutional and political support for treating financial literacy as the highest policy priority, as well as the start of the financial literacy building process in the population. Inclusion of a financial crisis dummy arises from a clear link between financial crisis and demand for financial literacy, and the post-communist countries dummy – from different institutional processes of financial literacy creation and development. To sum up, these four sets of variables in the authors' study are far more complex and rich than the ones included by Jappelli in the comparative study.[12]

The analysis covers 26 countries of the European Union excluding Malta and Cyprus. The reason for that is the lack of the majority of time series for these two countries. The time series covers 12 years (between 2000 and 2012) and includes five waves of PISA surveys, which are: 2000, 2003, 2006, 2009, 2012. The lack of data was removed case by case.

In the first stage of the analysis, correlation coefficients among independent variables and between dependent and independent variables were investigated. For further analysis only independent variables insignificantly correlated with each other and significantly correlated between dependent and independent variables were included.

From among 16 economic factors to regression analysis 11 were included, in the case of 20 education factors 7 were included, from dummy variables only the post-communist country dummy was included, while from 18 financial development factors there was not even one. At this stage of the analysis, it is clear that numeracy skills variability is barely explained by the financial development set of factors and it is dominated by the socio-economic and education sets of factors. Moreover, the inclusion of the post-communist country dummy seems interesting as it might serve as a precondition (needed further statistical verification) for a different historical experience concerning numeracy skills between old and CEE countries.

At the second stage of the analysis, the authors (on the basis of plots analysis) carried out the transformation of data (logarithmic) for dependent and independent variables. The aim of that stage was to answer the following questions: 'Does the logarithmic transformation help to better explain the variability of numeracy skills and independent variables?' and 'Does the non-linear regression model better explain and predict the analysed data?'. The following tasks have indicated that only for one variable Gross domestic savings (% of GDP) was such an improvement achieved. As a result, a new variable Log (Gross domestic savings (% of GDP)) was added to the independent variables. What is more, the new variable is significantly correlated with the non-transformed variable (r = 0.96). That way, the regression was run including only the Log (Gross domestic savings (% of GDP)), as shown in Table 4.1. Moreover, this task has proven that linear regression is the most adequate statistical model for this study.

At the third stage of the analysis, the authors analysed the descriptive statistics for independent variables which were incorporated in both regression models.

Descriptive statistics show the highest volatility for Household final consumption expenditure, etc. (% of GDP), Self-employed, total (% of total employed), Researchers in R&D (per million people), School life expectancy, primary to tertiary, both sexes (years), and the lowest for Primary to secondary general education transition rate, both sexes (%) as well as for Log (Gross domestic savings (% of GDP)). It demonstrates that there is practically no difference between the EU countries for Primary to secondary general education transition rate, both sexes (%) (range 3.24%), but differences are quite large for School life expectancy, primary to tertiary, both sexes (years) (range 7.26 years), Self-employed, total (% of total employed) (range 38.2%) as well as for Household final consumption expenditure, etc. (% of GDP) (range 77.89%).

At the fourth stage of the analysis, the authors ran two multiple regression models, back and forward with the assumption that only between three and five variables will be added to the model. In the case of the forward regression model, three variables were incorporated into the model: three from the education set: Primary to secondary general education transition rate, both sexes (%), School life expectancy, primary to tertiary, both sexes (years), and Researchers in R&D (per million people) and one socio-economic variable: Log (Gross domestic savings (% of GDP).

These four variables explain quite well the volatility of the independent variable which is Numeracy skills (Ad. R-squared = 0.64237824). All of the variables are stimulants (positive Beta) and the variable which has the highest impact on independent variable is Log (Gross domestic savings (% of GDP) (the highest Beta). Nevertheless, it is difficult to specify if correlation means causation in this case (better Numeracy skills leverage on the level of Gross domestic savings or maybe the higher the Gross domestic savings the more resources are directed to develop and increase Numeracy skills). In the case

Table 4.1 List of candidate variables

	Dependent variables
PISA-OECD	**PISA: Distribution of Mathematics Scores: 50th Percentile Score** **Mathematical Literacy**: the capacity to identify, to understand and to engage in mathematics and make well-founded judgements about the role of mathematics, needed in current and future private life, occupational life, social life with peers and relatives, and life as a constructive, concerned and reflective citizen
	Independent variables
Financial development	none
Education	School life expectancy, pre-primary, both sexes (years) Cumulative drop-out rate to the last grade of primary education, both sexes (%) Primary to secondary general education transition rate, both sexes (%) School life expectancy, primary to tertiary, both sexes (years) Labour force with tertiary education (% of total) Expenditure on education as % of total government expenditure (%) Government expenditure on education as % of GDP (%)
Socio-economic development	Employment in services (% of total employment) Final consumption expenditure, etc. (% of GDP) Gross domestic savings (% of GDP) Household final consumption expenditure, etc. (% of GDP) Internet users (per 100 people) Long-term unemployment (% of total unemployment) Researchers in R&D (per million people) Self-employed, total (% of total employed) Urban population (% of total) Unemployment, total (% of total labour force) (national estimate) Log (Gross domestic savings (% of GDP))
Dummy variables	Old – 0/ Post communism country – 1

Source: Authors' description

of the back regression model, three variables were incorporated: two from the education set: Primary to secondary general education transition rate, both sexes (%) and School life expectancy, primary to tertiary, both sexes (years), and two socio-economic variables: Household final consumption expenditure, etc. (% of GDP), Self-employed, total (% of total employed).

These four variables explain slightly worse the variability of independent variable (Ad. R-squared = 0.58721062). Two of the education variables are stimulants (positive Beta) and both of the socio-economic variables are distimulants (negative Beta). The variable which has the highest impact on

Table 4.2 Descriptive statistics

	AA	*Median*	*Min*	*Max*	*Range*	*SD*	*CV*	*Skewness*
Primary to secondary general education transition rate, both sexes (%)	0.9945552	0.9963000	0.9676000	0.10000	0.324000	0.064140	0.064491	−0.241929
School life expectancy, primary to tertiary, both sexes (years)	0.1568769	0.1581500	0.1166000	0.1892	0.726000	0.148964	0.949557	−0.010557
Household final consumption expenditure, etc. (% of GDP)	0.5266436	0.5508000	0.000000	0.7789	0.7789000	0.1531430	0.2907906	−0.192584
Self-employed, total (% of total employed)	0.1765402	0.1480000	0.790000	0.4610	0.3820000	0.920047	0.5211547	0.137821
Researchers in R&D (per million people)	0.2683353	0.2463860	0.000000	0.80035	0.8003510	0.1821770	0.6789154	0.088379
Log (Gross domestic savings)	0.3181	0.3195	0.207317	0.4037	0.1964	0.0369	0.1159608	0.006364
PISA: Distribution of Mathematics Scores: 50th Percentile Score	0.4912504	0.4952050	0.4134500	0.54836	0.1349100	0.2805325	0.5710581	−0.0725726

Source: Authors' calculations

Table 4.3 Results for forward multiple regression

R = 0.81879607 R-squared = 0.67042700 S Ad.. R-squared = 0.64237824
F(4.47) = 23.902 p <0.0000 SD: 17.949

	BETA	*SE. – BETA*	*B*	*SE. – B*	*t(47)*	*P level*
Constant			−0.832329	0.4816859	−0.172795	0.0090563
School life expectancy, primary to tertiary, both sexes (years)	0.0342548	0.0106676	0.6948	0.21637	0.321109	0.0002387
Log (Gross domestic savings)	0.0343061	0.0096013	0.33621	0.94095	0.357306	0.0000828
Researchers in R&D (per million people)	0.0254142	0.0105034	0.0003	0.00014	0.241962	0.0019459
Primary to secondary general education transition rate, both sexes (%)	0.0212483	0.0094454	0.11033	0.49042	0.224960	0.0029198

Source: Authors' calculations

independent variable is School life expectancy, primary to tertiary, both sexes (years) (the highest Beta) and the one with the lowest impact is Self-employed, total (% of total employed) (the lowest Beta). In the first case, the negative correlation between numeracy skills and household final consumption expenditure, etc. (% of GDP) is intuitively justified. The lower the level of Numeracy skills, the higher the level of Household final consumption expenditure, etc. (% of GDP) especially when controlled for high socio-economic development of the EU. However, also in that case further exploration is needed, which is outside the scope of this study. Similarly, in the second case, the negative correlation between Numeracy skills and Self-employed, total (% of total employed) might reveal some differences in institutional conditions (factors promoting full/part-employment agreements between employers and employees rather than self-employed managerial agreements) in the first place, and some different cognitive abilities than mathematical skills influencing entrepreneurship in the second place.

Table 4.4 Results for back multiple regression

R = 0.78713802 R-squared = 0.61958625 Ad. R-squared = 0.58721062 F(4.47) = 19.137 p < 0.00000 SE: 19.284

	BETA	*SE. – BETA*	*B*	*SE. – B*	*t(47)*	*P level*
Constant			−0.112310	0.5036436	−0.222995	0.0030565
Primary to secondary general education transition rate, both sexes (%)	0.0295239	0.0096046	0.1533	0.49869	0.307393	0.0003512
School life expectancy, primary to tertiary, both sexes (years)	0.0422609	0.0107154	0.857	0.21734	0.394395	0.0000266
Household final consumption expenditure, etc. (% of GDP)	−0.0263969	0.0110143	−0.061	0.02538	−0.239659	0.0020579
Self-employed, total (% of total employed)	−0.0223562	0.0099311	−0.078	0.03445	−0.225112	0.0029094

Source: Authors' calculations

Conclusion

The results of the study deliver some interesting conclusions. First of all, the study shows a negative correlation between Numeracy skills and Household final consumption expenditure, as well as a positive correlation with Gross Domestic Savings. It seems that in the EU in general, the higher the score in Numeracy skills, the better household budget management is and the higher the level of savings. Second of all, the higher the score in Numeracy skills, the larger the number of Researchers in R&D and the lower the percentage of Self-employed in population. It appears that the development of Numeracy skills supports R&D attitudes but not entrepreneurial skills. However, to conclude these two arguments, we need to bear in mind that the variability among the EU countries is quite large and this is a simplifying argument which should be explored in further studies.

The emergence of financial literacy skills in the general population, especially in the context of financialization, should be a part of border policy and academic discussion. Financialization has become the source of rising uncertainty of decisions' environment resulting in a significant increase in susceptibility to decision biases. Thus, financial literacy may play a role of 'effective decision buffer' reducing the negative role of financialization. It also may reduce the growing polarization of financial knowledge between financial institutions and population in general and, what is even more hazardous, between financial institutions and financial authorities. Deaton says 'the heavy recruitment of the best minds into financial engineering is the loss to the rest of the economy, likely reducing innovation and growth elsewhere' (Deaton, 2015, p. 209). Sen showed on a number of occasions that literacy and numeracy 'make a direct contribution to the extension of human capabilities and the quality of life' (Sen, 1999, p. 144). Jappelli added 'economic literacy also contributes to the good workings of markets and policies' (Jappelli, 2010, p. 6). We cannot build confidence and experience in financial matters in nations just by giving people access to financial markets, without producing internal opportunity (financial literacy skills). If we still do so, the financial literacy gap will become even larger and consequently income inequality.

Notes

1 Compare with Sen (2002, pp. 229–240).
2 Martin (2002) cited in: French *et al.*, 2011, p. 805).
3 See: Lusardi and Mitchell (2006).
4 See: OECD (2005); Atkinson and Messy (2012).
5 See: Jappelli (2010).
6 Compare with Lusardi and Mitchell (2007), Hung *et al.* (2009) and Christelis *et al.* (2010).
7 Compare with Hanushek and Woessmann (2008).
8 Acknowledgements: the authors are very grateful for constructive and useful suggestions from Dr Marek Cierpiał-Wolan, as well as support in conducting

statistical analysis received from the Mathematical Statistics Department in the Statistical Office in Rzeszów.
9 See: Čihák *et al.* (2012).
10 Taken from Atkinson and Messy (2012).
11 Taken from World Bank Database.
12 See: Jappelli (2010).

References

Ameriks, J., Caplin, A. and Leahy, J., 2003. Wealth Accumulation and the Propensity to Plan. *Quarterly Journal of Economics*, Issue 118, pp. 1007–1047.

Anand, P. and Lea, S., 2011. The Psychology and Behavioural Economics of Poverty. *Journal of Economic Psychology*, Issue 32, pp. 284–293.

Arndt, C. and Volkert, J., 2009. Poverty and Wealth Reporting of the German Government: Approach, Lessons and Critique. *IAW Discussion Paper*, Issue 51.

Atkinson, A. and Messy, F., 2012. Measuring Financial Literacy: Results of the OECD/ International Network on Financial Education (INFE) Pilot Study. *OECD Working Papers on Finance, Insurance and Private Pensions*, Issue 15.

Christelis, D., Jappelli, T. and Padula, M., 2010. Cognitive Abilities and Portfolio Choice. *European Economic Review*, Issue 54, pp. 18–39.

Čihák, M., Demirgüç-Kunt, A., Feyen, E. and Levine, R., 2012. *Benchmarking Financial Development Around the World.* Washington: World Bank, Policy Research Paper 6175.

Deaton, A., 2015. *The Great Escape. Health, Wealth and the Origins of Inequality.* Princeton, NY: Princeton University Press.

EC, 2007. *Komunikat Komisji Europejskiej w Sprawie Edukacji Finansowej, KOM (2007) 808.* [Online] Available at: http://eur-lex.europa.eu/legal-content/EN/TXT/?uri=CELEX:52007DC0808 [Accessed 1 December 2014].

Finlayson, A., 2009. Financialisation, Financial Literacy and Asset-Based Welfare. *The British Journal of Politics and International Relations*, Issue 11, pp. 400–421.

Flejterski, S., 2007. *Metodologia Finansów. Podręcznik Akademicki.* Warszawa: Wydawnictwo Naukowe PWN.

French, S., Leyshon, A. and Wainwright, T., 2011. Financializing Space, Spacing Financialization. *Progress in Human Geography*, Issue 35, pp. 798–819.

Froud, J., Johal, S. and Williams, K., 2002. Financialisation and the Coupon Pool. *Capital and Class*, Issue 78, pp. 119–151.

Gigerenzer, G., 2015. *Risk Savvy: How to Make Good Decisions.* New York: Viking Adult.

Hanushek, E. and Woessmann, L., 2008. The Role of Cognitive Skills in Economic Development. *Journal of Economic Literature*, Issue 46, pp. 607–668.

Holzmann, R., Mulaj, F. and Perotti, V., 2013. *Financial Capability in Low- and Middle-Income Countries: Measurement and Evaluation.* Washington: The World Bank.

Hung, A., Parker, A. and Yoong, J., 2009. *Defining and Measuring Financial Literacy*, s.l.: Rand Working Paper WR-708.

Huston, S., 2010. Measuring Financial Literacy. *The Journal of Consumer Affairs*, 44(2), pp. 296–316.

Jappelli, T., 2010. *Economic Literacy: An International Comparison.* Frankfurt am Main: CFS Working Paper 2010/16.

Jappelli, T., Pagano, M. and di Maggio, M., 2008. *Households' Indebtedness and Financial Fragility.* Naples: CSEF Working Paper 208.

Lusardi, A., 2008. *Financial Literacy: An Essential Tool for Informed Consumer Choice?* Cambridge, MA: NBER Working Paper 14084.

Lusardi, A. and Mitchell, O. S., 2006. *Financial Literacy and Planning: Implications for Retirement Wellbeing*. Cambridge, MA: NBER Working Paper 17078.

Lusardi, A. and Mitchell, O. S., 2007. Baby Boomer Retirement Security: The Role of Planning Financial Literacy, and Housing Wealth. *Journal of Monetary Economics*, Issue 54, pp. 205–224.

Lusardi, A. and Mitchell, O. S., 2011. *Financial Literacy Around the World. An Overview*. Cambridge, MA: NBER Working Paper 17107.

Lusardi, A. and Mitchell, O. S., 2013. *The Economic Importance of Financial Literacy – Theory and Evidence*. Cambridge, MA: NBER Working Paper 18952.

Lusardi, A., Michaud, P. and Mitchell, O. S., 2012. *Optimal Financial Knowledge and Wealth Inequality*. Cambridge: NBER Working Paper 18669.

Martin, R., 2002. *Financialization of Daily Life*. Philadelphia: Temple University Press.

OECD, 2005. *Improving Financial Literacy: Analysis of Issues and Policies.* [Online] Available at: www.oecd.org/finance/financial-education/37742200.pdf [Accessed 1 December 2014].

OECD, 2009. *Financial Literacy and Consumer Protection. Overlooked Aspects of the Crisis.* [Online] Available at: www.oecd.org/finance/financial-markets/43138294.pdf [Accessed 1 December 2014].

OECD, 2014. *PISA 2012 Results: Students and Money: Financial Literacy Skills for the 21st Century (Volume VI)*. Pisa: OECD Publishing.

Palley, T., 2007. *Financialization: What It Is and Why It Matters*. Washington: The Levy Economics Institute of Bard College, Working Papers 525.

Sen, A., 1999. *Development as Freedom*. Oxford: Oxford University Press.

Sen, A., 2002. *Rationality and Freedom*. Cambridge, MA: Belknap Press of Harvard University Press.

Part II

Financialization: impact on financial institutions and financial markets

5 Bank failures and their implications for payment intermediation in conditions of financialization

Anna Iwańczuk-Kaliska

Introduction

In the last decades, the financial sphere has become one of the most crucial factors affecting the operation of developed economies. This phenomenon has been accompanied by an increase in financial flows carried out through payment systems. Thus, the role of individual payment intermediaries, mainly banks, has become more and more important. In recent years, the banking sector has become increasingly exposed to the risk of instability. Bank failures may have great influence on the situation of their counterparties and may cause systemic risk in the whole financial system. They may also disrupt payment intermediation at the national or international level. This study therefore combines the issues of financialization, bank failures and payment intermediation.

The aim of this chapter is to examine general implications of bank failures for payment intermediation and make some recommendations for authorities regarding bank resolution strategies. The research is focused on the consequences arising especially from banks' role as payment services providers and settlement agents. It is based on the assumption that payment systems operate nowadays in conditions of financialization.

The study starts with explanation of the phenomenon of financialization and its implications for some roles of banks in the economy. The second part covers the issue of banks identified by supervision authorities as weak or threatened with bankruptcy. This part mentions also the guiding principles for supervision authorities concerning the problem of potential bank failures. The third part of the chapter includes the consequences of bank failures arising especially from banks' role in payment intermediation and the assessment of the solutions which may be used to protect payment functions of a failed bank under the resolution mechanism.

Financialization and its consequences for some roles of banks in the economy

Nowadays one of the most significant factors affecting the functioning of developed economies is the growing importance of the financial sphere.

This phenomenon is called financialization. The concept of financialization appears in discussions and debates around the nature and dynamics of contemporary capitalism. In the literature there are different definitions of financialization. Some authors use this term interchangeably with the term 'financially dominated capitalism' (Hein, 2013, p. 2). According to Krippner (2005, p. 181) following Arrighi (1994) financialization is a pattern of accumulation in which more and more revenues are generated through financial channels rather than through trade and industrial production. Dore (2002, p. 116) defines this process as a growing dominance of the financial sector in economic activity. It means that financial operations are carried out without reference to the real economy. Furthermore, financialization covers almost every domain of social and cultural activities, limiting them to the money calculation and subjecting them to the dictates of financial markets and institutions. According to Phillips (2006, p. 268) financial services have taken over the dominant economic, cultural and political role in the national economy. In the opinion of Epstein (2005, p. 3) financialization means the increasing role of financial motives, financial markets, their participants and financial institutions in the operation of national and international economies.

Ratajczak (2012) distinguishes the term 'financialization' in a narrow and a broad sense. In a narrow sense it is identified primarily with the growing importance of financial activity of non-financial economic entities. We may observe a change in streams of income. An increasing share of companies' incomes is generated by financial activities rather than operational and investment ones. Consequently the financial sphere becomes superior over real economy in terms of size of income generated (Janc *et al.*, 2015, p. 12). In a broad sense, financialization is the process of, so called, autonomization of the financial sphere in relation to the real economy. It means that financial markets and financial elites gain increasing influence on economic policy, both at the microeconomic and macroeconomic level and on the effects of economic activity (Ratajczak, 2012, p. 282). Moreover, financial institutions become independent of the supervisory and monetary authorities (Marszałek, 2014, p. 139).

Financialization transforms the functioning of the economic system. It also contributes to increased income inequality and wage stagnation (Palley, 2007, p. 2). On the one hand, the phenomenon of financialization is combined with economic growth, on the other it is considered to be a source of financial instability. Many authors emphasize that the operation of the financial sphere, not real economy, is the source of contemporary financial crises (Ratajczak, 2012, p. 281). Moreover, the vulnerability of the economy to financial crises, due to the growing scale of risks and uncertainties, as well as severe contagion processes, is dependent on the degree of financialization of individual economy (Marszałek, 2013, p. 239).

The phenomenon of financialization in the world economy is reflected by different economic data. They include increases in financial transactions, real interest rates, the profitability of financial institutions, and the shares of national income accruing to the holders of financial assets (Epstein, 2005, p. 4). According to Palley (2007, p. 10)

> the era of financialisation has been marked by a slight shift in income toward capital, a change in the composition of payments to capital that has increased the interest share, and an increase in the financial sector's share of total profits.

It is worth noting, that these tendencies may be the result of different phenomena: globalization, liberalization or integration. These considerations are beyond the scope of this study.

One of the symptoms of financialization, defined as above or referred just to the growing dominance of capital market financial systems over bank-based financial systems (Epstein, 2005, p. 3), is the value of wholesale payment transactions. Table 5.1 presents the value of transactions in 13 large-value payment systems operating in 11 countries, based on the data from the reports of Bank for International Settlements. It shows that the value of payment transactions carried out through the majority of analysed payment systems has significantly risen for the last 10 years. Figure 5.1 considers three years from the period of the last 20 years, namely 1994, 2004 and 2014. These data support the tendency of the increase of the value of payment transactions in most countries. This is particularly evident in the case of the United States, Germany, Netherlands and United Kingdom.

Precise analysis of the statistical data requires the reference of the value of payment transactions to GDP. It is presented in Figure 5.2. The conclusions arising from the chart are not so evident. The relationship between values of payment transactions and GDP does not show a clear upward trend in this period. That may be the result of a too short period considered in the analysis. The phenomenon of financialization has been observed for several decades, not years. In western countries the biggest wave of financialization took place in the period 1970–1990. Moreover, payment transactions may be carried out through different mechanisms not included in calculations (e.g. CLS system, correspondent banking). This area requires further research and access to detailed data.

The membership in large-value payment systems is usually restricted to banks since the settlement of the payment leg takes place across the books of the central bank. This solution ensures safe transfer of money and enables delivery versus payment (DVP) settlement of securities, and also payment versus payment (PVP) settlement of currency exchange.[1] As shown in Table 5.1, higher volumes transferred through payment systems reflect growing significance of bank intermediation in the area of wholesale payments. At the same time banks gradually lose a leading position in retail payments in favour of other payment services providers (Sullivan and Wang, 2007; Bradford *et al.*, 2009). However, their role in payment intermediation remains crucial for the economy, especially when the transfer of money is considered.

Table 5.1 Value of transactions carried out through large-value payment systems in 11 countries, 2004–2014, in billions of USD

Country	*System*	*Value of transactions*											
		2004	*2005*	*2006*	*2007*	*2008*	*2009*	*2010*	*2011*	*2012*	*2013*	*2014*	*2014/ 2004*
Belgium	ELLIPS/ TARGET2-BE	18, 233	21, 448	24, 373	36, 453	39, 683	28, 980	26, 724	30, 816	24, 026	21, 477	21, 551	**1.18**
Canada	LVTS	25, 378	30, 321	36, 816	42, 928	43, 036	33, 885	36, 562	40, 003	38, 187	36, 517	34, 997	**1.38**
France	TARGET2-BDF	134, 697	151, 425	169, 587	198, 527	149, 131	130, 406	124, 456	142, 241	141, 546	116, 252	115, 099	**0.85**
Germany	TARGET2-BBk	157, 005	172, 023	189, 140	317, 934	323, 884	238, 260	342, 119	351, 659	353, 929	297, 821	322, 058	**2.05**
Italy	BI-REL/ TARGET2-BDI	34, 883	40, 840	47, 372	57, 635	60, 171	44, 844	43,727	45, 956	41, 938	49, 739	54, 938	**1.57**
Japan	BOJ-NET	188, 838	196, 452	218, 128	250, 381	285, 589	291, 305	291, 496	311, 549	341, 479	292, 331	288, 490	**1.53**
Japan	FXYCS	39, 782	36, 514	38, 015	47, 826	50, 080	33, 957	32, 859	35, 399	30, 848	29, 840	28, 871	**0.73**
Netherlands	TOP/ TARGET2-NL	36, 878	38,126	40, 146	53, 434	86, 153	88, 577	102, 476	110, 129	135, 881	91, 841	78, 165	**2.12**
Sweden	RIX	14,633	14, 867	16, 905	18, 181	20, 736	22, 835	19, 063	19, 206	18,364	17, 189	17, 125	**1.17**
Switzerland	SIC	33, 814	32, 845	35, 867	43, 570	53, 595	39, 453	37, 912	42, 716	32, 219	34, 450	32, 497	**0.96**
United Kingdom	CHAPS Sterling	94, 864	94, 299	107, 297	135, 836	132, 225	92, 892	87, 561	102, 393	113, 607	109, 637	111, 894	**1.18**
United States	CHIPS	345, 793	349, 871	394, 567	485, 624	508, 759	364, 355	365, 096	403, 349	364, 819	379, 985	390, 695	**1.13**
United States	Fedwire	478, 947	518, 547	572, 646	670, 665	754, 975	631, 127	608, 326	663, 838	599, 201	713, 310	884, 552	**1.85**

Source: Author's calculations based on the reports of Bank for International Settlements (Committee on Payments and Market Infrastructures)

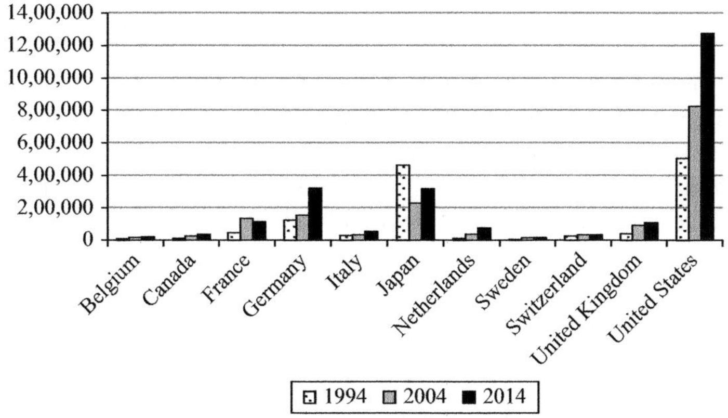

Figure 5.1 Value of transactions carried out through large-value payment systems, 1994, 2004 and 2014, in billions of USD

Source: Author's calculations based on the reports of Bank for International Settlements (Committee on Payments and Market Infrastructures)

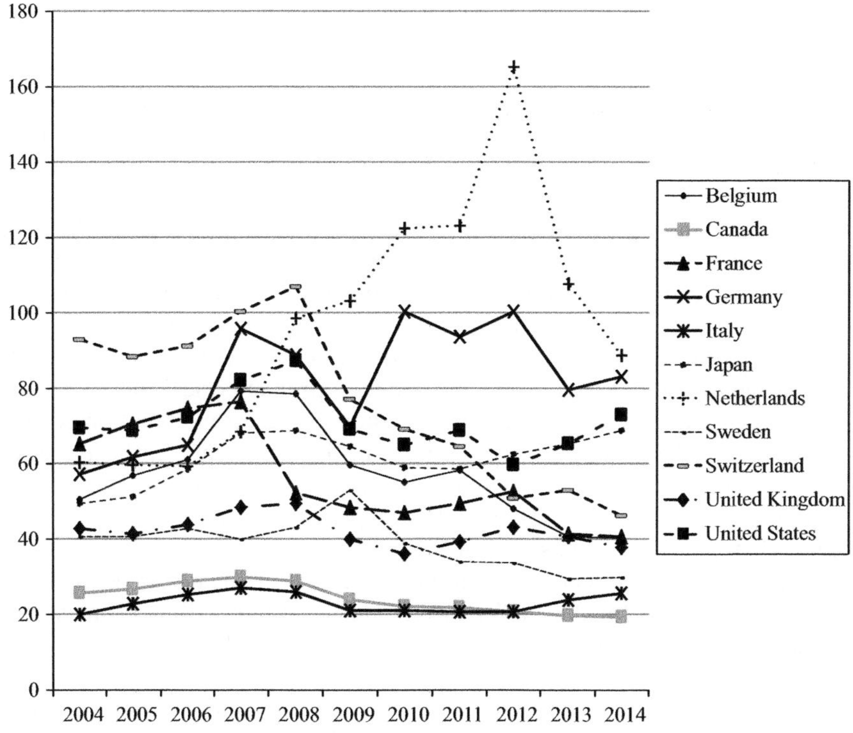

Figure 5.2 Value of transactions carried out through large-value payment systems in relation to GDP, 2004–2014

Source: Author's calculations based on the reports of Bank for International Settlements (Committee on Payments and Market Infrastructures)

Dealing with banks identified as weak or threatened with bankruptcy

The situation in the banking sector raises public policy concerns. This is due to crucial functions of banks in the financial system and increasing significance of the financial sphere in the economy. The financial crisis that afflicted the global economy in the years 2007–2009 revealed increased financial fragility. It resulted in changes to regulatory expectations and practices regarding early intervention, resolution frameworks, recovery and resolution planning, stress testing and macroprudential oversight (BIS, 2015, p. 3). The crisis highlighted the need for early identification of problems arising in banking institutions which may lead to insolvency or bankruptcy. Nowadays it is expected that bank supervisors will be prepared to minimize the incidence of weak banks and also to deal with them.

A weak bank may be defined in various ways. Bank for International Settlements (BIS, 2015, p. 6) gives the following definition: a weak bank

> is one whose liquidity or solvency is impaired or will soon be impaired unless there is a major improvement in its financial resources, risk profile, business model, risk management systems and controls, and/or quality of governance and management in a timely manner.

In the event that a bank is inevitably or likely to be no longer viable, the authorities should resolve the institution fulfilling several conditions. First of all the resolution should not induce severe systemic disruption in the financial sector. There are some financial firms that are systemically important or critical in failure. They are called SIFIS (systematically important financial institutions) or more commonly 'too important to fail'. Regarding the issue of payment intermediation some of them are just 'too interconnected to fail'. It may be evident during the crisis, since some institutions' interconnectedness in payment systems[2] may complicate the resolution procedure.

The resolution of such institutions requires a special approach to prevent escalation of the problem. The key issue is to protect critical functions of a bank. It concerns among others the continuity of access to execution of payments, especially in the case of a large bank. It is necessary in the aspect of stability and confidence in the financial system. Banks cannot enter normal bankruptcy proceedings and suddenly stop performing their special and critical role in payment systems (EC, 2014).

Dealing with weak banks was initially a subject of the report of the Basel Committee released in 2002 (BIS, 2002). The latest international supervisory guidance indicates that

> in dealing with weak banks, the objective of reducing the risk of loss to depositors and other creditors translates into supervisory actions aimed at preserving the value of the bank's assets with minimal disruption to its operations, subject to minimising any resolution costs and systemic impact.
> (BIS, 2015, p. 6)

The guiding principles for a supervisor when dealing with weak banks set out by BIS include (BIS, 2015, pp. 6–7):

- early identification of weak banks based on risk assessment;
- early but reasonable intervention;
- effectiveness of actions including the costs related to instability of the financial system;
- flexibility, meaning the early reaction to the results of prior recovery measures;
- clear internal governance processes of supervision activities;
- consistency of supervisory actions minimizing confusion and uncertainty in times of crisis;
- transparency of intended actions;
- avoiding potential systemic problems arising not only with large banks;
- early preparation for intervention in a crisis situation in a supervised bank.

All these guiding principles have important significance considering banks' role in payments as services providers, clearing and settlement agents, members of payment systems and other forms of participation in payment intermediation.

Consequences of bank failures for payment intermediation

The phenomenon of financialization combined with possible bad standing of banking institutions raise a number of important questions. They concern their implications for the economy and financial market. The consequences depend on the characteristics of a country's financial system, its economic and competitive landscape, and the range of functions individual banks provide.

In some circumstances, especially in case of a threat of systemic crisis, and when a private sector solution cannot be used, avoiding or dealing with bank failure entails the use of public funds. It imposes a cost on taxpayers. Thus, public funds should be used in resolution only as a last resort and should be subject to strict conditions that minimize the risk of moral hazard (BIS, 2015, p. 45). Bank failure has also the impact on competition in the market for banking services, especially when it entails a change in the market structure.

As mentioned earlier, banks provide some critical functions to the real economy and financial markets. A bank closure may disrupt the intermediation of funds between lenders and borrowers, with potential negative effects on the real economy. Borrowers may find it difficult to establish a relationship with a new bank. They also may have problems with completion of projects if expected bank loans are not forthcoming (BIS, 2015, p. 44). Taking into account deposit-taking activity a failure entails the cost of payout or transfer of insured deposits, in the event that there are no other resolution tools. As there are limits of the deposit insurance, some depositors, especially big companies, may lose their liquid funds.

Critical functions are defined by the Financial Stability Board as

> activities performed for third parties where failure would lead to the disruption of services that are vital for the functioning of the real economy and for financial stability due to the banking group's size or market share, external and internal interconnectedness, complexity and cross-border activities.
>
> (FSB, 2013, p. 7)

Examples of these functions include payments, which systemic relevance should be assessed differently than other functions. This is due to, among others:

- high frequency of payments;
- the importance of timely execution;
- the role that each payment intermediary plays in creating linkages between market participants.

The role of individual payment intermediaries in the functioning of the financial markets is varied. An institution may provide payment, clearing and settlement services as an intermediary between its own clients or as an intermediary between a client and other participants of the financial market. In some cases the institution may also be a provider of payment, clearing and settlement services as a part of financial market infrastructure (operator of a payment system) or may provide access to this infrastructure to other banks that are not clearing members.

The consequences of bank failure for payment intermediation depend on different individual and environmental factors. The Financial Stability Board (FSB, 2013, p. 21) calls them drivers of criticality. Referring to the individual factors the following elements should be considered:

- type of counterparties serviced by particular provider – they may be retail, corporate, financial or institutional;
- market share of a provider in a particular market segment – since the failure of a large provider affects more counterparties;
- the role in wholesale payment services market – a significant service provider may influence the liquidity of certain asset classes and the financial market as a whole;
- scope of operation – payment, clearing and settlement services to a larger geographic area or involving high volumes or high values, are deemed to be more critical;
- role as a settlement agent for other financial institutions (in two-tiered payment systems) – an interruption of the service may affect the liquidity position of them;

- the integration of payment services with transactions – the link to those related transactions might reduce substitutability;
- complexity of interfaces – since it requires more time to migrate to alternative services;
- other business activities of the bank embedded with payment, clearing and settlement services.

Some drivers of criticality are related to the environment, namely the characteristics of the payment services market. They include among others:

- segmentation of the payment services market – by asset classes, transaction characteristics (size, volume), region or counterparty type;
- market concentration in payment services – high concentration results in internalization and netting of payment transactions;
- the availability of substitutes – it refers to availability of alternative channels to clients enhanced by the existence of high standardization and common products, rules, operational and technical procedures;
- structure of domestic payment system and its interconnection with systems of other countries or cross-border systems;
- links between financial market segments – since some transactions involve several legs that are settled through different channels; through these links, the disruption of a service in one segment can affect others;
- barriers to entry into the market for new service providers.

In payment intermediation area the consequences of bank failure are usually related to the risk of loss of access to payment services to a large number of customers. Nowadays it does not seem to pose a threat to financial stability, due to a large number of institutions operating in the payment services market. This is true, however, when we do not consider the situation of a loss of confidence in the payment system described by Hoggarth *et al.* (2002).

In respect of payment intermediation it is very important to distinguish deposits arising out of a commercial payment or service relationship (operational deposits on payment accounts) from deposits that represent a form of credit investment in a bank (funding deposits) (IIF, 2014, pp. 19–20). Operational deposits are transferred by companies and individuals on a daily basis and, from the payment system stability and liquidity of payments perspective, should be available in all circumstances. Otherwise bank failure could result in a widespread loss of confidence in the banking system and non-cash money.

Special attention should be paid to the issue of wholesale payments. Failure of one payment systems' member may lead to disruptions in the financial system. Large-value payment systems (systemically important payment systems) are a part of financial market infrastructure that facilitates clearing, settlement and recording of payment transactions. They serve the financial market participants and play a critical role in fostering financial stability. Payment systems can be major channels through which the shocks are transmitted across domestic and international financial markets (BIS, 2012, p. 5). The inability of one or more participants to perform properly, regardless the reason of that (financial or operational[3]), could cause other participants to be unable to meet their obligations when due.

However, the operation rules for systemically important payment systems include the probability of failure of participants of the system which help to avoid disruptions in the financial system, undermining public confidence in the safety, soundness and reliability of the financial infrastructure. They are based on international risk-management standards for payment systems, especially 'Core Principles for Systemically Important Payment Systems' prepared by Bank for International Settlements, which provided ten principles for safe and efficient design and operation of systemically important payment systems (BIS, 2001). The negative consequences of a bank's failure related to payment intermediation would therefore affect only the customers of the failed bank. In such situation they would not be able to transfer money, due to lack of access to payment services for some period of time. Thus, criticality of payment services depends greatly on the ability of the market to substitute the role of the failing payment provider (bank or other payment institution) within a reasonable timeframe.

Another problem concerns the participation of payment intermediaries in retail payment systems. In order to ensure that core functions of these systems are not impeded by resolution mechanism, it is necessary to include provisions providing protections for all payment systems as creditors. It requires the analyses of the connections between payment and banking systems.

Considering proper functioning of national and global economy it is important to avoid the situation that payment services would be discontinued or continued on a smaller scale if any bank became insolvent (Kaufman, 2015, p. 2). Resolution strategies in respect of the failed bank should therefore take into account the growing role of banks operating as payment infrastructures, leveraging their ability to offer wide reach to payment services (ECB, 2008, p. 18). The mechanisms which may be used should be analysed in respect of stability of the payment system and safety of its participants. The FSB states that an effective resolution regime should among others 'ensure continuity of systemically important financial services, and payment, clearing and settlement functions' (FSB, 2014, p. 3). Resolution authority should also take into account that some services of a bank (e.g. basic payment account) are so elemental that they will need to be preserved in all circumstances (FSB, 2013, p. 6).

The solutions used in the event of bank failure include a transfer of assets and liabilities, relating to viable operations to a private sector purchaser or to a bridge bank. Their aim is to take over functions, assets and liabilities of the bank subjected to the procedure of restructuring and orderly liquidation. This ensures business continuity of critical functions including payment transactions following customers' orders. However, in the case of a bridge bank it requires the access to financial market infrastructure arrangements (especially payment systems). Continuity of the payment intermediation in a short period of time could also be ensured through the appointment of an administrator who takes control of and manages the bank with the objective of restoring the bank, or parts of its business, to viability. The advantage of this solution is that it would ensure the same level of services and would not influence the concentration of payments. However, it cannot be a permanent solution.

The resolution strategy doesn't apply only to payment and settlement activities. However, a decision about the mechanism used should be based on the assessment of its impact on payment functions continuity including substitutability of payment services provided by a particular institution. In general, payment system stability and payment intermediation continuity would be ensured by actions that eliminate the risk of disruptive cessation of payment services to customers. From that point of view it might be worth considering separating payment activities and subjecting them to another resolution regime than the other business lines.

Conclusion

Payment intermediation is definitely a key function of banks. It supports other types of their operations as well as transactions carried out by other financial institutions and non-financial economic entities. The findings of empirical analysis show that the phenomena occurring nowadays in the world economy including the growing role of the financial sphere have resulted in an increase in the scale of cash flows carried out through payment institutions, using the infrastructure of payment systems. Contemporary payment systems offer real-time transmission and settlement of payment orders (Leon, 2012, p. 96). Payment intermediation becomes more and more complex and prone to financial and operational risk. During the crisis payment intermediaries (banks) suffer from liquidity shortage or solvency problems or may be threatened with bankruptcy. Financial or operational problems in banks may have far-reaching implications for smooth money transfer, nationally and globally. They may threaten the operation of payment systems and affect intraday liquidity of non-banking financial market participants.

Taking into account the above issues, supervision and resolution authorities should pay special attention to the consequences bank failures might cause to the payment intermediation. They should take early and decisive actions in response to arising problems or just anticipate them. The general conclusion of the study is that assessing the significance of the bank in the financial system and deciding on a resolution strategy requires considering its importance as a payment intermediary and a settlement agent. This is consistent with the 'too interconnected to fail' doctrine. The evaluation should be based on both an individual and market-specific basis. In this regard substitutability of payment services seems to be more appropriate than dominance in the payments market. The assessment of systemic relevance requires the supply side analysis covering, among others, the number and concentration of payment services providers, potential new market entrants, availability of readily substitutable services and also the speed, costs and barriers of substitution.

An original view on the issues related to bank failures, payment intermediation and financialization considered together, that is presented in this chapter, forms the basis for further research and analysis of the relationships in financial systems. Drawing attention to these relationships may also play an important role in the debate concerning the future directions of development and regulation of the financial sector and financial markets.

Notes

1 Currency exchange transactions are carried out by the global system of continuous linked settlement (CLS). The CLS system is based on the account relationships that CLS Bank has established with the central banks of CLS-eligible currencies to facilitate the funding process that supports the payment versus payment settlement of foreign exchange trades across the books of CLS Bank (BIS, 2008, p. 1).
2 Interdependencies among market participants, financial markets and market infrastructures increase the potential for problems in one institution or market segment to propagate. Some of them are direct, e.g. exposures through inter-bank loans, through counterparty credit exposures on derivatives and repos, through payment and settlement relationships (Lumpkin, 2008, p. 8). These interdependencies are compounded by phenomenon of financialization.
3 Possible operational failures include errors or delays in processing, system outages, insufficient capacity, fraud, and data loss and leakage.

References

Arrighi, G., 1994. *The Long Twentieth Century: Money, Power, and the Origins of Our Times*. London: Verso.

BIS, 2001. *Core Principles for Systematically Important Payment Systems*. Basel: Committee on Payment and Settlement Systems.

BIS, 2002. *Supervisory Guidance on Dealing with Weak Banks*. Basel: Committee on Banking Supervision.

BIS, 2008. *The Interdependencies of Payment and Settlement Systems*. Basel: Committee on Payment and Settlement Systems.

BIS, 2012. *Principles for Financial Market Infrastructures*. Basel: CPSS/IOSCO.

BIS, 2015. *Guidelines for Identifying and Dealing with Weak Banks*. Basel: Committee on Banking Supervision.

Bradford, T., Hayashi, F., Hung, C. *et al.*, 2009. Nonbanks and Risk in Retail Payments: EU and US. In: E. M. Johnson, ed. *Managing Information Risk and the Economics of Security*. Hanover, NH: Springer, pp. 17–53.

Dore, R., 2002. Stock Market Capitalism and its Diffusion. *New Political Economy*, Issue 7, pp. 115–121.

EC, 2014. *Impact Assessment Accompanying the Document Proposal for a Regulation of the European Parliament and of the Council on Structural Measures Improving the Resilience of EU Credit Institutions*. Brussels: Commission Staff Working Document.

ECB, 2008. *Payments and Monetary and Financial Stability*. Frankfurt am Main: EBC – Bank of England.

Epstein, G. A., 2005. *Financialization and the World Economy*. Cheltenham: Edward Elgar Publishing.

FSB, 2013. *Recovery and Resolution Planning for Systemically Important Financial Institutions: Guidance on Identification of Critical Functions and Critical Shared Services*. Basel: Financial Stability Board.

FSB, 2014. *Key Attributes of Effective Resolution Regimes for Financial Institutions*. Basel: Financial Stability Board.

Hein, E., 2013. *Finance-dominated Capitalism and Redistribution of Income: A Kaleckian Perspective*. New York: Levy Economics Institute, Working Paper 746.

Hoggarth, G., Reis, R. and Saporta, V., 2002. Costs of Banking System Instability: Some Empirical Evidence. *Journal of Banking and Finance*, May, pp. 825–855.

IIF, 2014. *Achieving Bank Resolution in Practice*. Washington: A Report of the Institute of International Finance Cross-border Resolution Working Group.

Janc, A., Jurek, M. and Marszałek, P., 2015. *Polish Financial System in the Age of Financialisation*. Warszawa: C.H. Beck.

Kaufman, G., 2015. Banking and Public Policy: Too Big to Fail. *Economic Inquiry*, 53(1), pp. 1–8.

Krippner, G. R., 2005. The Financialization of the American Economy. *Socio-Economic Review*, 3(2), pp. 173–208.

Leon, C., 2012. Estimating the Intraday Liquidity Risk of Financial Institutions: A Monte Carlo Simulation Approach. *Journal of Financial Market Infrastructures*, Issue 1, pp. 75–107.

Lumpkin, S., 2008. Resolution of Weak Institutions: Lessons Learned from Previous Crisis. *Financial Market Trends*, Issue 2.

Marszałek, P., 2013. Finansjalizacja w Polsce – ciekawostka teoretyczna czy realny problem? *Finanse Publiczne – Uniwersytet Ekonomiczny we Wrocławiu*, Issue 306, pp. 235–246.

Marszałek, P., 2014. *Systemy pieniężne wolnej bankowości. Koncepcje, cechy, zastosowanie*. Poznań: Wydawnictwo Uniwersytetu Ekonomicznego w Poznaniu.

Palley, T., 2007. *Financialisation: What It Is and Why It Matters*. Amherst: University of Massachusetts, Working Paper 153.

Phillips, K., 2006. *American Theocracy: The Peril and Politics of Radical Religion, Oil, and Borrowed Money in the 21st Century*. New York: Viking Penguin.

Ratajczak, M., 2012. Finansjalizacja gospodarki. *Ekonomista*, Issue 3, pp. 281–302.

Sullivan, R. and Wang, Z., 2007. Nonbanks in the Payments System: Innovation, Competition, and Risk – A Conference Summary. *Economic Review*, 2012(3), pp. 83–106.

6 The Franc Zone

Can the operations account mechanism survive the push for financial deepening?

Christina Laskaridis

Introduction

The growth of the financial sector during the era of financial liberalization is associated with the process of financialization, a process that has been extensively studied in recent years. Financialization is characterized by general tendencies associated with the growth in importance of financial markets, financial institutions and financial motives for domestic and international economies (Epstein, 2005). This chapter contributes to the growing literature on financialization in developing countries,[1] and specifically low income countries, by exploring the particularities of financial sector development in the Franc Zone.

The Franc Zone consists of a common currency area between two sub-regions in Sub Saharan Africa and France. Each sub-region has a multilateral central bank, with the West African sub-region's central bank located in Senegal, and the Central African sub-region's located in Cameroon.[2] The currency area emerged out of colonial monetary arrangements when France consolidated many of its colonies' currencies and initiated the new currency, the CFA franc.

This chapter identifies several key historical and institutional factors that have shaped the development of the financial sector in the Franc Zone. At the heart of the Franc Zone is the Operations Account mechanism held at the French Treasury. It is this that differentiates the nature of financial integration in the Franc Zone from other low income countries. Current literature on and policy practice in the Franc Zone contain a series of underlying tensions. From the stifling debt crisis during the 1970s and 1980s, the Franc Zone now neatly fits within the expanding financial development literature and policy practice which extols the benefits of finance with few reservations. During this period, the presentation of government borrowing has undergone a transformation: from negative due to crowding out arguments to more favourable views arising from the provision of good collateral supposed to promote domestic financial deepening. This chapter concludes, however, that the internal mechanism of the Franc Zone, the Operations Account, may prove too strict to accommodate the generalized credit boom which is currently under way.

The operation accounts at the French Treasury

Four main pillars constitute the core of the Franc Zone. The first pillar of the Franc Zone is that CFA francs are freely convertible into euros at a fixed exchange rate, which prior to 2002 were convertible into French francs. The parity has remained unchanged from 1948 with the exception of the historic devaluation in 1994. The second pillar is that the convertibility between CFA francs and hard currency is guaranteed by France and this is done through the Operations Account held at the French Treasury. The third pillar is that in exchange for the convertibility guarantee, the countries of the Franc Zone must maintain the majority of their foreign exchange reserves at the two subregional central banks of the Franc Zone. The fourth pillar is the requirement of capital mobility throughout the Franc Zone and between the Franc Zone and France (Boughton, 1991; Allechi and Niamkey, 1994).

This set of arrangements has severe macroeconomic implications for the members. Members supply the Operations Account with foreign exchange generated through trade surpluses. The reserve pooling arrangement implies that countries can credit and debit the Operations Account by drawing on and supplying each other with reserves. Countries needing foreign exchange debit the Operation Account whilst those supplying non-CFA currencies credit the account (Engberg, 1973). Members' balance of payments imbalances are financed through the Operations Account, either using the pooled reserves of other members that are obligatorily kept there or if these do not prove sufficient, through the guarantee by the French Treasury to supply necessary foreign exchange via an overdraft facility in the Operations Account. Therefore, the French Treasury steps in when the overall balance of the Operations Account is in deficit. The degree of fiscal intervention by France is regulated by the overall payment balance across each sub-region, rather than imbalances in individual countries. Intervention by the French Treasury is unnecessary if the net overall balance is positive even if there are diverging balance of payments needs between the countries. For example, in the 1980s Benin, Cote D'Ivoire and Senegal drew down the operations of other countries with surpluses in the Operations Account, such as Burkina Faso, Niger and Togo (Allechi and Niamkey, 1994).

Restrictions are in place in order to safeguard the unlimited guarantee that France provides to the Zone. These limitations placed on the Operations Account constrict the ability of countries to draw down the 'unlimited' overdraft facility provided by France, by in effect, making it quite a limited facility. Automatic measures make it more costly to run extended deficits in the Operations Account. For example, the regional central banks restrict the availability of credit by raising the cost of rediscounting and by limiting the amount of credit available to governments. Limitations are imposed on the overdraft facilities of the Operations Account in the French Treasury. These include minimum reserve ratios between the foreign exchange reserves in French francs and restrictions on the monetary financing of governments' deficits by each central bank. Disciplining mechanisms on members with imbalances are invariably also applied politically by France. Apart from the statutory regulation between the two central banks and France, political involvement in regulating overall credit policy has been instrumental in the monetary arrangements of the Franc Zone. The governance of the two central banks has included greater African participation since independence, but French officials maintain high representation in the Boards and veto power.

Beyond the aforementioned institutional constraints, the fiscal contribution by France into the Operation Account is structurally limited by the heterogeneous nature of the Franc Zone itself and specifically the asymmetric responses to external shocks. The main consequence of reserve pooling has been to reduce the need to rely on France's overdraft precisely because Franc Zone countries have distinct and diverse export structures, which respond in unsynchronized ways to changing global conditions. The consequence of this is that countries most frequently draw on each other's reserves rather than relying on France.

This is worth placing in the context of the literature whose examinations of the Franc Zone rest on providing economic rationales and theoretical justifications for its continuity by contextualizing the Franc Zone through the optimal currency area lens (Mundell, 1961; McKinnon, 1963; Fleming, 1971). Aside from the characteristics that, according to this theory, allow the benefits of membership of a currency area to exceed the costs, such as wage and price flexibility (Mougani, 2014) and high factor mobility (Boughton, 1991), the similarity in response to external shocks are frequently mentioned desirable traits that can minimize the relative price shifts among countries. This theory suggests that highly integrated countries are more likely to reap benefits from a common currency. Contrary to the optimal currency area literature, however, there is a small degree of intra-regional trade in the Franc Zone and considerable diversity in export structures. The West Africa sub-region has traditionally relied on the export of coffee and cocoa and the Central African sub-region has relied on minerals and oil exports. The prices of these commodities may move in different directions, which in combination with the changing exchange rate that the exports are priced in, lead to changes in competitiveness between the countries in the Franc Zone (Boughton, 1991). In light of the Operations Account mechanism, it is the presence of features which make the Franc Zone non-optimal in this respect that have allowed for its durability. Although a majority of the English-speaking literature on the Franc Zone has optimal currency area theory as its starting point, the majority of studies conclude the Franc Zone cannot be interpreted in these terms (Boughton, 1991; Fouda and Stasavage, 2000; Hallet, 2008). Conversely, there is a broad consensus that the durability of the Franc Zone is better explained on political grounds (Fouda and Stasavage, 2000; Bordo and Jonung, 2003; Stasavage, 2003; Lamine, 2006; Assoua, 2013; Couharde *et al.*, 2013).

To summarize, the original mechanism of the Franc Zone was budgetary in nature, supported by the French Treasury. The Operations Account has been described as resembling a 'discount window' at the French Treasury for the two central banks (Engberg, 1973). What this implies is that the French Treasury performs a central banking function to the two sub-regions to cover the region's reserve deficit. Had this arrangement been based in the French central bank, financing the overdraft would represent reserve creation by the Bank of France, whereas, currently, the overdraft is financed through the budget or by borrowing (Engberg, 1973).

Financial sector development

This section discusses historical and institutional changes that have been instrumental in shaping and restructuring the Franc Zone's financial sector. The main drivers that contributed to financial sector transformation in the Franc Zone were the conditionality programmes implemented by the International Financial Institutions (IFIs) and the institutional re-organization following the devaluation in 1994. This section reviews this trajectory emphasizing the recent remodelling of the Franc Zone along EU lines.

In the 1980s Franc Zone countries saw their export earnings collapse with the prices of primary commodities declining. The sharp appreciation of the French franc under President Mitterand's 'Franc Fort' policy led to deteriorating terms of trade. Access to the expanding international dollar markets grew and the majority of Franc Zone countries were embroiled in a severe debt crisis. The entire region went through structural adjustment programmes and several rounds of debt restructurings, both through the IFIs and the private Paris Club. A key component of the conditionalities attached to these programmes included financial sector liberalisation and specific reforms to encourage competition within the domestic banking sector. This practice has continued with recent conditionality programmes.[3]

The discussion on government borrowing and indebtedness became central during the crippling debt crisis. Up to that point few doubted that the main merits of the Franc Zone for its members were the disciplinary capacity enforced by the currency union. Indeed fiscal discipline and price stability were frequently cited as the main merits of the Franc Zone (Boughton, 1991). The rationale was that an exchange rate peg with full convertibility would act as a disciplinary mechanism for expansionary fiscal policies since direct monetary financing could force the peg to be abandoned. Yet this is not a universally held view, neither in theory nor practice. Hadjimichael and Galy (1997) argue that the Operation Account rules were not sufficient to instil fiscal discipline. Stasavage (1997) presents mounting evidence for even the strongest proponents of the Franc Zone to agree that fiscal discipline was not promoted through the currency and monetary arrangements of the

Franc Zone in the 1980s and early 1990s. The reasons he gives are the institutional flaws in the design of the union and political interests on behalf of French and African elites. The institutional constraints of the Zone were circumvented in a number of ways. Under the Operation Account rules direct financing of treasuries via the two central banks was limited to 20 per cent of government's past fiscal receipts. However, indirect financing of budget deficits via domestic commercial banks which were often government owned circumvented the fiscal borrowing rule of the Franc Zone's central banks. These loans could then be refinanced though the regional central banks at subsidized rates (Honohan, 1993). This practice was central to the worsening conditions of the late 1980s and was part and parcel of the banking crises that developed in almost every Franc Zone country at that time. According to Stasavage (1997), the governments absorbed the debts of failed banks, which were then refinanced by the central banks. The consequence of this practice meant that the central banks' positions were weakened. Government deficits were also funded from abroad and once access to external commercial borrowing dried up, official multilateral loans and donor aid funds were the main or sole source of external financing. The de facto practice of accumulating arrears with domestic suppliers and creditors also created the image of improved fiscal positions by leaving pensions and public sector employees unpaid (Stasavage, 1997). As in Stasavage (1997) these choices were highly politicized by the de facto importance of French officials in decision making.

A deteriorating balance of payments built pressure to proceed with currency devaluation in 1994, altering the parity between the CFA franc and the French franc for the first time since 1948. This prompted deep institutional and policy changes within the Franc Zone. The result was the extension of the monetary union to include broader elements of economic and financial integration, such as economic, legal and regulatory reforms. The previous institutional arrangements were replaced by new ones, and the Central African Economic and Monetary Union (CEMAC) and West African Economic and Monetary Union (WAEMU) were created. The changes that occurred after the devaluation were modelled explicitly on the EU's integration model, thus representing an explicit transfer of norms and institutional similarities to the EU (Claeys and Sindzingre, 2003).

As the European Monetary Union members headed towards the third stage of integration and the introduction of a single currency, a protracted discussion began about how the Franc Zone arrangement ought to be interpreted and treated under Maastricht Rules. At the time of the euro's adoption a new wave of literature emerged which sought to assess the impact that the switch of the peg from French franc to euro would have on the Franc Zone. France initially argued that given the budgetary nature of the arrangement it should be treated as a domestic affair as it was entirely compatible with Maastricht criteria (Berignan and Carré, 1997). However, it was agreed that exchange rate arrangements linked to the euro ought to come under European Council oversight, so the switch of the Franc Zone's peg to the euro mechanism was formalized with an EU Council Decision of November 1998 (see: (Hadjimichael and Galy, 1997; Lamine, 2006). The Operation Account mechanism was to remain intact under the strict understanding that the European Central Bank remains under no obligation to support the peg or the convertibility (Allen and Hagan, 2005). Certain oversight functions were moved to the EU level, with any decisions to change the parity with the euro now requiring EU approval.

The institutional replication along EU lines followed the devaluation. Two regional Commissions, Council of Ministers and Heads of State meetings have been created and common Treaty Law has been established (Lamine, 2006). Economic integration is directed through convergence criteria for the Franc Zone countries, which focus on fiscal consolidation relating to budget balances, debt levels, wage bills and tax revenues. Attempts to meet the criteria occur through corollary multilateral surveillance arrangements, constituted in a Treaty along the lines of the EU's Growth and Stability Pact. The responsible authorities for the implementation of these surveillance mechanisms are the regional Commissions and similar to the euro area, countries deviating from the convergence criteria define a 'corrective' programme with the regional Commission (Banque De France, 2014).

A broad set of institutional changes have taken place: a customs union has been set up, common external tariff introduced and duties on intra-regional trade removed, common business law has been adopted, and a Court of Justice in each Zone has been set up. Financial sector reform was pushed forward through setting up new institutions, such as regional Bourses and the regional banking commissions, which were responsible for much of the financial sector restructuring in the post-devaluation period. Central to this push for further economic integration has been a set of policies to 'deepen' the financial systems of countries in the Franc Zone (Cabrillac and Rocher, 2009). At the time these changes were taking place, it was argued that the economic benefits of a currency and monetary union would be better harnessed if only the Zone was better integrated (Hallet, 2008). Specifically, it was recognized that the governments in the Franc Zone needed more effective debt markets to avoid recourse to the French Treasury or the International Monetary Fund. The development of the financial sector was promoted in order to reduce the financial and economic dependence on France.

Recent trends in financial deepening

The global financial crisis was frequently attributed as an impetus in the development of Sub Saharan debt markets on several accounts. Global investors' hunt for yield has encouraged higher investment into African markets yields (Adelegan and Radzewicz-Bak, 2009). Regular aid funds were reduced as donors cut back on their spending, which necessitated a search for alternatives, particularly through developing domestic markets. Long-term domestic financing was presented as a solution to financing development by enhancing diversification.

With regards to scholarship, there has been a decisive shift within the literature as it tries to contend with the latest enthusiasm for securitized government debt and market based financial integration. Following the contours of the development finance literature (see Bonizzi, 2013 for a critique) one finds a plethora of studies that discuss the benefits that could come from the expansion of finance in the Franc Zone (Gulde, 2008; Adelegan and Radzewicz-Bak, 2009). Arguments in favour of local security markets propose that reliance on bank lending would be reduced and investment opportunities broadened. The benefits of countries moving away from official bilateral and multilateral, mostly concessional lending and towards a market based financing, according to this viewpoint, is that capital allocation would be enhanced, and the creation of a liquid government securities market would help monetary policy implementation.

The practical efforts of the private sector and the donor community to develop domestic bond markets have been considerable (Moyo, 2008; Dahou *et al.*, 2009). However, the efforts at furthering financial deepening have often been disparate and uncoordinated. To address this problem, the African Development Bank hosts the collaborations between the IFIs, the private sector and the major donors; the creation of the African Financial Markets Initiative has the sole goal of developing and deepening domestic financial markets in Africa.

Low income countries have had limited, if any, access to international capital markets. Due to the highly concessional external borrowing available to Sub Saharan African countries, local borrowing has generally been more expensive. Beaugrand *et al.* (2002, p. 3) argue that 'highly concessional external debt is usually superior to domestic debt in terms of financial costs and risks, even in face of probable devaluations'. Despite the higher costs associated with domestic debt, the promotion of market based financing has placed developing the domestic debt market at the heart of the financial deepening agenda. Local security markets have been institutionally promoted by the International Monetary Fund and the World Bank as part of a stepping stone in the overall process of financial development of low income countries. For example, the IMF has placed limits on the borrowing low income countries under IMF programmes can access at non-concessional rates. These limits have now been made looser allowing for a greater proportion of non-concessional borrowing for low income countries under IMF programmes (Allen and Hagan, 2005).

The arguments in favour of developing local government securities markets are not solely in terms of better financing for governments, but are also for the purpose of enhancing private sector security markets. 'Achieving rapid growth in private debt markets is generally the second key objective of a government securities issuance strategy' (Cabrillac and Rocher, 2009, p. 10). The development of the government securities market, alongside the institutional changes that facilitate it, are seen as prerequisites for the subsequent development of a private debt market. A key part of this process is the benchmark created from the government securities market from which private securities can be priced. 'Yields on government securities can serve as a pricing benchmark for long-term private debt issued by banks or enterprises' (Abbas and Christensen, 2010, p. 6). It is argued this would enhance corporate bond market development and put pressure for competition on the banking sector (Fabella and Madhur, 2003).

The specific experience of the Franc Zone amongst these broader developments is as follows. The development of the domestic debt market in the Franc Zone countries has lagged behind the development of the domestic debt market in non-Franc Zone Sub Saharan African countries which had begun from the 1980s (Christensen, 2004, p. 4). The recent promotion of government debt markets has been accompanied by changes in the Franc Zone rules about how governments finance themselves. In particular, domestic debt market development is linked to increased restriction of direct monetary financing by the regional central banks (Banque de France, 2006). The international financial community encouraged the WAEMU and CEMAC to move towards central bank independence thus limiting or phasing out the direct advances made by central banks to governments. This is evidenced in Figure 6.1 which indicates a steady increased reliance in market and bank based funding for governments in the West African sub-region and the steady decrease in reliance on central bank financing.

Under the previous rules the central banks of the Franc Zone could provide borrowing for member governments of up to 20 per cent of their budget. New rules further limit member states' fiscal deficits from being financed by the central banks thus prompting governments to turn to issuing securities, and encourage the development of local currency debt markets. As indicated

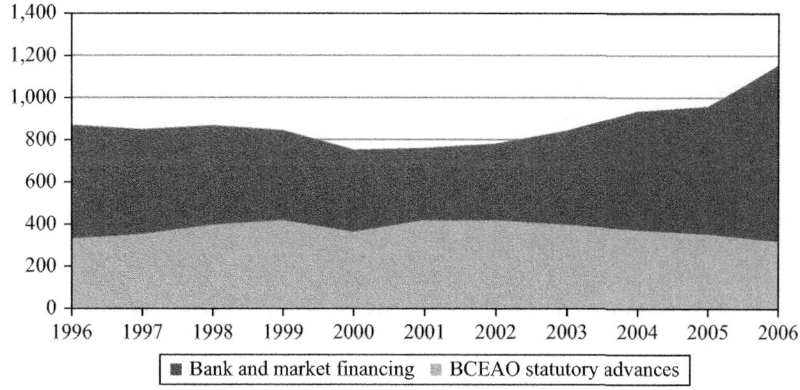

Figure 6.1 Changes in WAEMU government financing by source, 1996–2006, in billions of CFA francs

Source: Banque de France (2006)

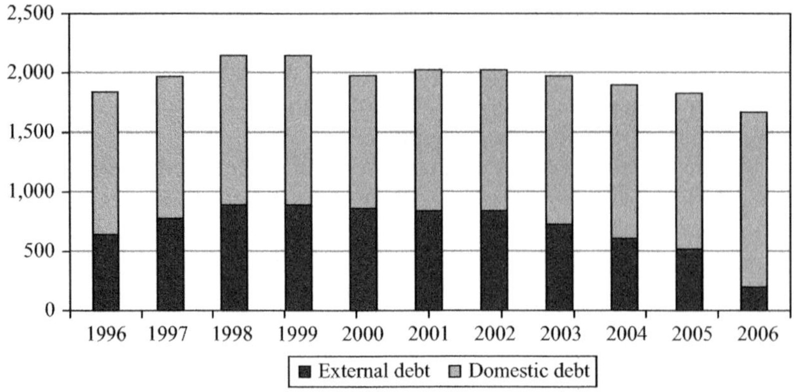

Figure 6.2 Changes in WAEMU government financing by type, 1996–2006, in billions of CFA francs

Source: Banque de France (2006)

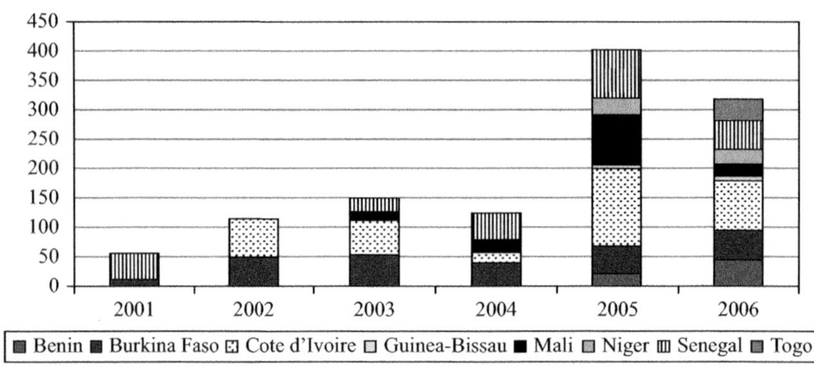

Figure 6.3 Government debt securities issuance, 2001–2006, in billions of CFA francs

Source: Banque de France (2006)

in Figure 6.2 domestic debt became an increasing component of government financing as opposed to external debt.

Other changes in the Franc Zone include a new credit rating system set up in 2006 to encourage bond issuance in the WAEMU region (Moyo, 2008). Institutional barriers were targeted and attempts were made to reduce transaction costs. A mortgage market and securitization programme began, spearheaded by the regional Bourse and the custodian agent of the regional central bank.

The issuance of debt securities has rapidly increased in the 2000s as shown in Figure 6.3 and Figure 6.4.

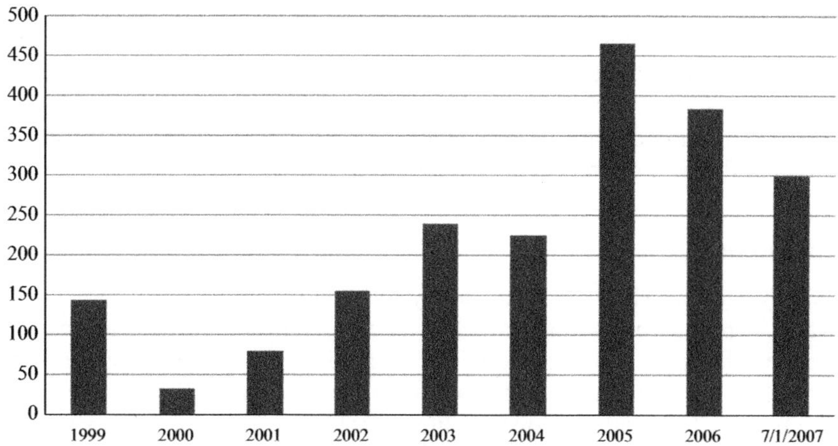

Figure 6.4 WAEMU total gross issuance of debt securities, 1999–2007, in billions of CFA francs

Source: Author's calculation based on Sy (2007)

Table 6.1 Credit growth extension in selected Franc Zone countries, 2000–2010

Credit growth 2000–2010 (% GDP)	
Benin	99.1%
Burkina Faso	52.8%
Burundi	15.6%
Cameroon	44.2%
Central African Republic	68.2%
Chad	47.0%
Comoros	47.0%
Cote d'Ivoire	13.8%
Mali	286.7%
Niger	174.4%
Senegal	48.5%

Source: Author's description based on Griffith-Jones and Karwowski (2014)

Certain countries in the Franc Zone have seen a rapid credit growth in the past decade. Recent research by Griffith-Jones and Karwowski (2014) shows that for a few of the Franc Zone countries, credit growth was close to or far above 100 per cent of their GDP. This is shown in Table 6.1.

The changes described above have set up the members of the Franc Zone for a new cycle of borrowing. Where the problem of the 1980s was interpreted as a problem of foreign currency borrowing, the solution that developed was to expand debt markets in domestic currency. The contribution of domestic debt markets to debt sustainability lies in the greater ease with which governments and companies may manage cash flows and borrowing in their own currency. However, the most serious challenge posed to the financial sector development agenda is the increasing attention drawn to the potential for yet another serious debt crisis in the region.[4] This highlights the serious tension as although the risks are recognized, the process is continuing rapidly.

Conclusion

This chapter has shown how the analytical and theoretical trajectory in the Franc Zone has been shaped on the one hand by the structural changes brought about by the conditionality attached to IFI programmes and the explicit modelling along EU lines, whilst on the other hand, the gradual application of the financial development literature has created a new policy agenda for the Franc Zone. The constraints of the replication of the EU model in the Franc Zone have been detailed by Claeys and Sindzingre (2003). To these concerns the on-going crisis of the EU can be added, which profoundly affects the feasibility as well as desirability of the model.

The institutional mechanism in the Franc Zone's centre, the Operations Accounts at the French Treasury, may come up against problems in light of the promoted credit boom. This is associated with the rise in domestic incomes that growth in private sector investment could lead to, which would increase the import bill and widen trade deficits. The Operations Account mechanism would frustrate this kind of private sector economic development. Furthermore, large calls on these accounts could materialize if national authorities (central banks or governments) are obliged to act as lenders of last resort in the event of a credit bubble. The main condition under which this may not happen is if export markets expand or export commodity prices rise. However, this is unlikely with slow economic growth in the major economies of the world.

The discussion about the Franc Zone has been almost entirely about the costs and benefits of a common currency, in terms of trade competitiveness and fiscal rectitude, to the neglect of the impact of the currency arrangement on the debt structures that build up over time. There are strong reasons to doubt that the Operations Account mechanism of the Zone, designed to sustain convertibility through overall trade equilibrium, could be effective with a build-up of cross-border debt in the private or public sectors of member countries.

The way financialization is experienced under a variety of monetary institutional settings is an under-researched area, particularly in developing countries. Such research is important to assess the impact that general trends of increased market access and security issuance currently under way in Sub Saharan Africa have on the Franc Zone. It is also necessary in order to distinguish the features that are particular to the Franc Zone countries. Given the recent warnings (UNCTAD, 2015) regarding potential vulnerabilities in the build-up of debt positions, this chapter has attempted to highlight some particular areas of concern.

Notes

1 See: Bonizzi (2013) for a review.
2 The West African zone consists of Benin, Burkina Faso, Cote D'Ivoire, Guinea Bissau, Mali, Niger, Togo and Senegal and the Central African region consists of Cameroon, Central African Republic, Chad, Republic of Congo, Equatorial Guinea and Gabon. The Comoros Islands are also part of the Franc Zone.
3 As an example see Cameroon's Poverty Reduction Strategy Paper (IMF, 2006).
4 See: UNCTAD (2015).

References

Abbas, S. M. A. and Christensen, J. E., 2010. The Role of Domestic Debt Markets in Economic Growth: An Empirical Investigation for Low-Income Countries and Emerging Markets. *IMF Staff Papers*, 57(1), pp. 209–255.

Adelegan, O. J. and Radzewicz-Bak, B., 2009. *What Determines Bond Market Development in Sub-Saharan Africa?* Washington: International Monetary Fund.

Allechi, M. and Niamkey, M. A., 1994. Evaluating the Net Gains from the CFA Franc Zone Membership: A Different Perspective. *World Development*, 22(8), pp. 1147–1160.

Allen, M. and Hagan, S., 2005. *Fund Surveillance Over Members of Currency Unions.* Washington: International Monetary Fund.

Assoua, K., 2013. *The Nexus Between Political Instability and Monetary Sustainability: The Case of a West African Monetary Union.* Cape Verde, Bonn: West Africa Institute, Center for European Integration Studies.

Banque de France, 2006. *Rapid Growth of Government Securities in Sub-Saharan Africa: The Case of WAEMU, Rapport Zone Franc 2006.* Paris: Banque de France.

Banque de France, 2014. *Rapport Zone Franc 2014.* Paris: Banque de France.

Beaugrand, P., Loko, B. and Mlachila, M., 2002. *The Choice Between External and Domestic Debt in Financing Budget Deficits: The Case of Central and West African Countries.* Washington: IMF Working Paper WP/02/79.

Berignan, J. and Carré, H., 1997. Exchange Arrangements with Eastern Europe, Mediterranean, and African Countries. In: P. Masson, T. Krueger and B. Turtelboom, eds. *EMU and the International Monetary System.* Washington: International Monetary Fund.

Bonizzi, B., 2013. Financialization in Developing and Emerging Countries. *International Journal of Political Economy*, 42(4), pp. 83–107.

Bordo, M. and Jonung, L., 2003. The Future of EMU: What Does the History of Monetary Unions Tell Us. In: F. Capie and G. Woods, eds. *Monetary Unions: Theory, History, Public Choice.* London: Routledge.

Boughton, J., 1991. *The CFA Franc Zone: Currency Union and Monetary Standard.* Washington: IMF Working Paper No. 91/133.

Cabrillac, B. and Rocher, E., 2009. Government Debt Markets in African Developing Countries: Recent Developments and Main Challenges. *Quarterly Selection of Articles – Bulletin de La Banque de France*, Issue 15, pp. 5–25.

Christensen, J., 2004. *Domestic Debt Markets in Sub-Saharan Africa*. Washington: IMF Working Paper WP/04/46.

Claeys, A. and Sindzingre, A., 2003. *Regional Integration as a Transfer of Rules: The Case of the Relationship Between the European Union and the West African Economic and Monetary Union (WAEMU)*. Glasgow: University of Strathclyde.

Couharde, C., Coulibaly, I., Guerreiro, D. and Mignon, V., 2013. Revisiting the Theory of Optimum Currency Areas: Is the CFA Franc Zone Sustainable? *Journal of Macroeconomics*, Issue 38, pp. 428–441.

Dahou, K., Omar, H. and Pfister, M., 2009. *Deepening African Financial Markets for Growth and Investment*, s.l.: (Ministerial Meeting and Expert Roundtable). NEPAD-OECD Africa Investment Initiative.

Engberg, H., 1973. The Operations Account System in French-Speaking Africa. *The Journal of Modern African Studies*, 11(4), pp. 537–545.

Epstein, G., 2005. *Financialization and the World Economy*. Cheltenham: Edward Elgar Publishing.

Fabella, R. and Madhur, S., 2003. *Bond Market Development in East Asia: Issues and Challenges*. Philippines: ERD Working Paper Series No. 35, Asian Development Bank.

Fleming, J., 1971. On Exchange Rate Unification. *Economic Journal*, 81(323), pp. 467–488.

Fouda, S. and Stasavage, D., 2000. The CFA Franc Zone After EMU: Status Quo, Reform or Dissolution? *World Economy*, 23(2), pp. 221–233.

Griffith-Jones, S. and Karwowski, E., 2014. *A Financial Sector to Support Development in Low Income Countries*. London: Overseas Development Institute (ODI).

Gulde, A., 2008. Overview, Chapter 1. In: *The CFA Franc Zone: Common Currency, Uncommon Challenges*. Washington: International Monetary Fund.

Hadjimichael, M. and Galy, M., 1997. *The CFA Franc Zone and the EMU*. Washington: IMF Working Paper No. 97/156.

Hallet, M., 2008. *The Role of the Euro in Sub-Saharan Africa and in the CFA Franc Zone*. Brussels: Office for Infrastructures and Logistics.

Honohan, P., 1993. Financial Sector Failures in Western Africa. *The Journal of Modern African Studies*, 31(1), pp. 49–65.

IMF, 2006. *Cameroon: Poverty Reduction Strategy Paper. Third Annual Progress Report*. Washington: IMF Country Report No. 06/260.

Lamine, B., 2006. *Monetary and Exchange Rate Agreements Between the European Community and Third Countries*. Brussels: European Commission, Directorate-General for Economic and Financial Affairs.

McKinnon, R., 1963. Optimum Currency Areas. *The American Economic Review*, 53(4), pp. 717–725.

Mougani, G., 2014. *Challenges Towards Regional Financial Integration and Monetary Coordination in the West African Monetary Zone and the East African Community*. Côte d'Ivoire: African Development Bank, Regional Integration Policy Paper.

Moyo, J., 2008. *Mapping of Current Ongoing Initiatives Related to Bond Market Development in Africa*. Côte d'Ivoire: The African Financial Markets Initiative, African Development Bank.

Mundell, R., 1961. A Theory of Optimum Currency Areas. *The America Economic Review*, 51(4), pp. 657–665.

Stasavage, D., 1997. The CFA Franc Zone and Fiscal Discipline. *Journal of African Economies*, 6(1), pp. 132–167.

Stasavage, D., 2003. *The Political Economy of a Common Currency: The CFA Franc Zone Since 1945*. Aldershot: Ashgate.

Sy, A., 2007. *Local Currency Debt Markets in the West African Economic and Monetary Union*. Washington: IMF Working Paper WP/07/256.

UNCTAD, 2015. *Revisiting Debt Sustainability in Africa, Trade and Development Board, 61st Executive Session*. Geneva: TD/B/EX(61)/3, United Nations.

7 Alternative investment funds under new financial and legislative reality and Russian specific

Oksana Martanus and Elena Merekina

Introduction: alternative investment funds' development as a part of financialization

The process of financialization is not just the globalization of finances, the growth of the importance of the field of finance both in the global and national economies. Financialization also implies the increase in the diversity of the financial institutes and tools. Alternative investment funds (AIFs) are a shining example of that. Their popularity is growing in the more developed countries as well as the developing countries.

The financial reality tends to change rapidly. It is not simple for investors not only to predict the quality of their future allocations, but even to assess the quality of their allocations – especially if they are dealing with the AIFs. Nevertheless, these funds attract investors worldwide. This trend towards alternatives successfully overcame even the financial crisis and followed tightening of regulation. Despite the increasing popularity of the AIFs, their correct classification does not exist. However, before discussing the methodology, it is important to evaluate the financial environment of these funds in the context of different countries.

The Russian fund industry is relatively young, especially compared to the European financial market. The long history of development of the European funds can now be combined with the Russian internal experience. As a result, it creates the unique environment where experience of foreign countries and the specifics of the domestic economy are both taken into account.

Historical context

The alternative investment market began to emerge not too long ago, in the 1970s. The popularity of fixed income instruments in the late 1960s led to the boosting of allocations in equities in the next decades (Sedlacek, 2014). Further development of complex financial instruments and lack of government regulation resulted in the global financial crisis of 2008. It was followed by a slow recovery and the subsequent tightening of rules regulating financial markets. Booming growth in private capital and increased demand for allocations determined a rising quantity of investment funds and their assets under management in the USA, EU and other developed countries. To meet the demand of all categories of investors, a wide range of investment fund types and investment strategies were developed. Since the alternative funds were constantly undergoing changes, the subject of alternative investments remains almost unexplored. The main difficulties encountered by researchers were the low level of transparency of such institutions and the absence of formal criteria for the classification of different investment vehicles and intermediaries.

Only a few years ago the large-scale studies were undertaken by regulatory bodies such as the European Commission and the European Securities and Markets Authority (ESMA) and the US Securities and Exchange Commission (SEC). They provided the basics of the legal regulation of AIFs' activities and major international organizations, such as Alternative Investment Management Association (AIMA) and European Fund and Asset Management Association (EFAMA).

To analyse the AIFs' activities and assess their investment attractivity first an adequate classification of funds must be implemented and alternative ones must be defined. Then we identify the factors that influence funds' investment attractivity. The basic model will include all the factors analysed by such authors as Beyer, 2014; Brown and Goetzmann, 2001; Ibbotson and Caplan, 2000; and Kat, 2004. Then we analyse factors that are specific for Russia and include them in the model.

Classification

The lack of theoretical researches and the complexity of analysis of the AIFs' activities make it difficult to implement a common classification of investment funds. We will use the European classification provided by the ESMA. Europe ranks as the second largest domicile for investment funds worldwide, holding 37 per cent of market share and nearly 19,000 of AIFs (EFAMA, 2014). The USA is the current leader in the AIF industry, however, there is no unique US classification of AIFs yet.

The EU classification is based on the availability of funds to different types of investors and by the basic principles of their investment portfolios creation. According to this classification, funds can be divided into two basic groups, namely 'traditional funds' and 'alternative investment funds'.

Funds, which fall into the first group, are known to invest in shares and bonds or combine these investments. In the USA they are known as 'mutual funds' and in the EU as 'UCITS' (Undertakings for the Collective Investment in Transferable Securities). They account for approximately 75 per cent of all collective investments in Europe and the majority of studies cover this type of fund (EC, 2016b). Traditional investment funds are regulated by UCITS Directive (2009/65/EC), as amended from time to time.

As stated in this Directive, UCITS is a collective investment vehicle that raises capital from the public markets and invests it according to specific restrictions on investments and diversification requirements. Specifically, their capital may be invested in liquid assets, which are generally transferable securities such as stocks and bonds, money market instruments, financial indices, and other open-ended undertakings.

Allocation requirements ensure that any asset type should not exceed a particular share in the investor's portfolio. For example, one of the rules ('5/10/40 rule') requests that maximum 10 per cent of net asset value may be invested in financial instruments issued by the same body. These restrictions help to reduce risks and increase diversification of the investments.

Along with the above stated, the UCITS funds by themselves are open-ended, which means that they are committed to redeem the investor's securities at any time at the investor's request. They are requested to ensure the absolute transparency of funds' activities to investors.

The UCITS Directive implements these strict rules on UCITS funds, its strategies and allocations to provide maximum protection of investors (Shamraev, 2014). These requirements have arisen, because the UCITS funds are available for any investors independent of their financial capability. It is recognized that not all investors may be able to assess the related risks properly.

The second type of fund is usually called 'alternative investment funds'. There are two ways of defining it. According to the EU legislation, any collective investment vehicle that does not qualify as a UCITS is designated as an AIF, while non-European researchers apply the following definition: 'Alternative investments collectively refer to the many asset classes that fall outside of the traditional definitions of stocks and bonds' (CFA Level 1 2012 – Schweser CFA Study Notes, 2011).

Hedge funds, private equity, venture capital and real estate funds are the most well-known allocation types. They arose before the others and today have a bigger share of assets under management among the alternatives (Sedlacek, 2014). The AIF category also includes exchange-traded funds, funds of managed futures, distressed securities, commodities and currencies, funds of funds, family offices, probably an infinite number of trust types and this list may be further extended (Schulaka, 2011). As it is, the AIFs are almost impossible to define, because they cover an infinite number of fund types with unique characteristics that require a different approach by the analyst.

Since 2011, the AIFs have been regulated by the AIFMD, or Alternative Investment Fund Managers Directive. According to the above, the definition of AIFs is 'collective investment undertakings, including investments compartments thereof, which raise capital from a number of investors, with a view to investing it in accordance with a defined investment policy for the benefit of those investors' (EC, 2016a).

While the UCITS Directive is more than 25 years old, the AIFMD appeared in 2011 only and came into force in 2013. The 2008 financial crisis determined a creation of governmental regulation for all of the investment funds, so the purpose of the AIFMD was to cover all types of funds that are not the traditional funds and to provide the most comprehensive definition of AIFs.

Similar to the UCITS Directive, the main aim of the AIFMD is to increase the investors' protection, reduce their risks and increase funds' transparency. However, the subject of the AIFMD is not an investment fund and its strategies but the fund's manager. This decision is based on a fact that the AIFs differ significantly depending on a fund type.

An overall goal of the AIFs is to provide correlation to the standard asset classes and serve as 'alternatives' especially during a financial crisis. For this purpose, they implement less liquid or illiquid strategies in comparison to the public markets, including short selling and arbitrage, commonly use leverage and invest in derivatives and other unconventional assets. Along with the above stated, the majority of AIFs are closed-end funds that issue a fixed number of shares, which are not redeemable from the fund before a particular time. Before the fund's expiration date, it normally does not inform investors about its activities and financial circumstances.

For all these reasons the AIFs are beneficial to qualified investors only, who are expected to assess their own risks properly. Depending on the national laws, 'qualified' or 'accredited' or 'sophisticated' investors are persons or entities with high annual individual income or net worth, have working experience or refer to the financial sector. This list includes high-net-worth individuals, banks, insurance companies and other financial intermediaries. In general, the AIFMD will not change these relations and limit funds' investment strategies. However, the Directive will require AIF managers to disclose certain information to investors prior to as well as after their investment allocations and inform them about any material changes. It also implies several reporting obligations to competent authorities. Furthermore, each manager has to set a limit on leverage and to comply with this limit on an ongoing basis. The competent authorities are entitled to limit this leverage if they consider it necessary. Consequently, the protection level of the investors significantly increases but the costs of the funds increase as well.

To sum it up, if we compare UCITS and AIFs the results will be the following: AIFs are less liquid and less transparent and face less governmental regulation. They are mostly close-end investment companies available for qualified investors only. Their investment strategies are not limited to only stocks and bonds but vary significantly among funds. Funds are allowed to assume risks and use leverage.

Though the USA does not have its own classification of AIFs and does not fall under AIFMD regulation, it was decided to strengthen regulation in this area by the example of the EU. The Dodd-Frank Act requires the registration of some AIFs with the Securities and Exchange Commission (SEC). The US AIFs' managers will be subject to regulatory and reporting requirements as well as the European ones.

Table 7.1 AIFs vs UCITS

Criteria	*UCITS*	*AIF*
Regulation issue		
Governing Directive	UCITS	AIFMD
Scope of regulation	UCITS fund (legal entity)	Manager of an AIF
Purpose	Reduce risks, protect investors	Reduce risks, protect investors
Implemented by:	Limit investment strategies and allocations	Increase managers' activities transparency
Fund issue		
Duration	Open-end	Closed-end
Investors	Any	Qualified
Strategies and financial instruments		
Common asset allocation	Shares and bonds	Depends on fund type
Liquidity	Only liquid assets	Depends on fund type
Diversification	Required	Depends on fund type
Leverage	Mostly not used	Depends on fund type
Transparency	Required to the full extent	Depends on fund type

Source: Authors' description

Investment attractivity of AIFs

The biggest challenge faced by investors by their allocations into AIFs is to assess the investment attractivity of the fund. As mentioned above, these allocations may be completely unique and therefore difficult to evaluate.

The common method for assessment of investments is the 'risk-return' rate. This principle suggests that potential return rises with an increase in risk. Low levels of uncertainty are associated with low potential returns, whereas high levels of uncertainty are associated with high potential returns.

The common method for assessment of the investments is the concept of the 'efficient frontier', implemented by economists Harry Markowitz and Bill Sharpe. Their modern portfolio theory attempts to construct portfolios to maximize the expected returns based on a given level of market risk, or, in opposite, to minimize risk for a given level of expected return by including correlated assets into a portfolio.

We can apply this method, because the AIFs diversify their allocations and include in their portfolio different types of assets in comparison to UCITS that invest in stocks and bonds only.

Analysis provided by Kenneth Hoffman (2013) indicates that if we build a portfolio that contains stocks and bonds only and then compare it to an 'alternative portfolio' we find out that the second one may both reduce risks and increase profitability. To prove this theory, he refers to the data that represents the performance of the traditional asset classes in the last decade and compares it to the alternative ones. The data indicate that the AIFs can perform well in strong equity markets and may also protect investors during a financial inefficiency or a crisis. For example, in 2008 the S&P 500 dropped by 37 per cent and an international index, EAFE (Europe, Asia, Far East) dropped by 43 per cent. At the same time the managed commodity index rose by 14.1 per cent, and the hedge fund index increased by 4.8 per cent. In the three worst performing years for the S&P 500 (2001, 2002 and 2008) the hedge fund and CTA indexes outperformed stocks each year.

However, during the S&P's three best years (2003, 2009 and 2012) when the stock market was growing, the AIFs did not perform as well as the traditional assets and show a higher yield. However, they had not been expected to reach the best results. Historically the main purpose of AIFs has been to provide correlation to the traditional assets and serve as 'alternatives' during financial uncertainty and crisis (Levaux, 2012). In contrast to the allocations into the UCITS that seek for returns, the AIFs are expected to hedge and to serve as counterweight to the performance of the traditional side of the portfolio.

The second factor of the assessment of investment attractivity of the AIFs is the costs. It is agreed and understood that taxes and costs may reduce the potential profits and therefore the investment attractivity. Allocations in UCITS do not require high charges. They implement only so called 'ongoing charges', which are used to pay for the running of the fund, and portfolio transaction costs. Both are a subject of regulation of the UCITS Directive and cannot exceed a particular level.

In comparison, allocations in AIFs vary in case of costs significantly. Some of them, for example exchange traded funds (ETFs), are similar to the UCITS and offer lower management fees than other investment solutions. Since they trade like stocks on an exchange, they may be subject to brokerage commissions. But the majority of alternatives have two fees: an annual administrative payment (usually 1–2 per cent of the investor's assets under management) and a percentage of profits (typically 20 per cent; subject to a high-water mark), which exceeds fees incurred by traditional funds. This is connected to the costs of the evaluation of alternative investments, which is significantly more difficult than evaluating the traditional assets and requires higher managers' remuneration. It is believed that the more competent the asset manager is, the higher the reward.

On the contrary, the majority of AIFs are situated in offshore jurisdictions, which reduce investors' taxes, which may compensate for high costs. Every fifth investor acknowledges that tax efficiency does matter for allocations (Stolz, 2011). Taking into account all these aforementioned facts, we came to the conclusion that by evaluating the investment attractivity of AIFs it is not enough to measure the returns. The basic model of assessment shall also include such factors as correlation with traditional markets, risks, fees and taxes.

The other way to assess the investment attractivity of an AIF is to measure the investors' satisfaction level. The empirical research conducted by the Financial Planning Association Research and Practice Institute (FPA) shows that nearly 88 per cent of AIFs investors report that they are either greatly or somewhat satisfied with their performance (Schulaka, 2011). These results are supported by the growth of the AIFs' assets under management (AuM) during the last decade. If the investors were not satisfied, they would have decreased allocations to AIFs.

Alternative investment funds in Russia

While the EU and the US investment markets have a long history of formation, contain a huge variety of funds and rely on the extensive legal framework, the Russian fund industry is still developing. The recent emergence of the Russian financial market and the limitations of regulation led to the fact that the definition 'traditional investments' refers to bank deposits only and any forms of collective investments are considered as alternatives. However, Russian investment funds differ in their characteristics. To clarify their classification, we are going to compare them with UCITS and AIFs.

The formation of the Russian financial market begins in the period of reforms in the 1990s. The first collective investment institutions appeared in 1991 and the definition of 'investment fund' was included in the legislative framework. In 1996 a presidential edict updated legislation and proposed a basic classification of collective investments in Russia. According to this edict, the collective investment undertakings in Russia include mutual funds (open-end, interval and closed-end), credit unions, joint-stock investment funds, investment banks and non-state pension funds.

Russian mutual funds are called 'PIFs', which stands for 'mutual investment funds'. PIFs are designed to accumulate and manage funds of retail investors, for which private asset management is too costly because of the small amounts of investments and expenses on asset management. As for investment strategies, they differ among fund types (Abramov, 2005).

Open-end PIFs are quite similar to the European UCITS and US mutual funds but their legal structure is different. They are required to invest in high-liquid assets only, such as stocks and bonds, and are available for all investors. Closed-end PIFs are available to qualified investors only. Russian law implements similar requirements to the accredited investors as the US law, as amended from time to time. Apart from investments in stocks and bonds, closed-end funds may invest in specific asset allocations, which are private equity, real estate and other (Abramov, 2005).

Interval PIFs combine features of open-ended and closed-ended schemes. In general they should be considered as AIFs because they involve more risks and less transparency to investors. Legally, transactions with derivatives are allowed only in order to reduce the risk of the fund's assets value reducing. The total value of these transactions may not exceed 10 per cent of the fund's assets (Abramov, 2005). Additionally, funds are not allowed to use leverage and high-risk investment strategies as short selling, arbitrage and other.

Based on these considerations, we came to a conclusion that the PIFs combine features of UCITS and AIFs. On the one hand, any PIFs are somewhat restricted in investment strategies, akin to UCITS. However, diversification is required mostly by investors, not by law. For this reason, open-end funds are almost mutual fund analogues as they invest in high liquid assets only. The characteristics of closed-end funds match with the characteristics of AIFs being applicable to the qualified investors only and investing to specific allocations. To be more precise, we will examine more parameters to determine more common features among PIFs and AIFs.

However, all types of PIFs are currently qualified as alternative investments. It means that we have to take into account open-ended PIFs as well as interval and closed-ended PIFs to conduct our research.

A sustainable growth in the mutual fund industry started from the beginning of the twenty-first century and continued until the world financial crisis in 2008. However, the total number of PIFs is still not comparable with the global or European funds' number (1,400 and 19,000 accordingly). Figure 7.1 represents the growth of funds industry in the last decade by the above mentioned fund types.

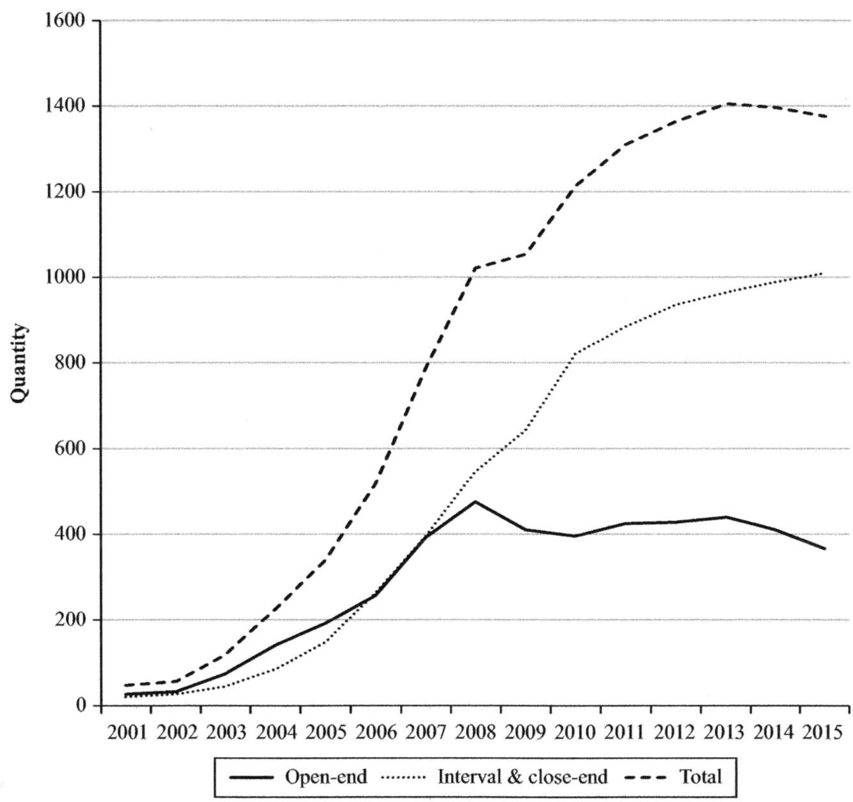

Figure 7.1 Quantity of PIFs, 2001–2015
Source: Authors' calculations based on Investfunds (2015)

Table 7.2 Quantity of PIFs by types and assets

Asset allocation	*Open-end*	*Interval*	*Closed-end*	*Total*
Stocks	127	14	25	166
Bonds	73	0	1	74
Stocks & bonds	79	14	33	126
Money market	10	0	0	10
Index	23	0	0	23
Fund of funds	51	2	0	53
Commodities		6	0	6
Hedge fund		11	17	28
Mortgage			6	6
Collectables			1	1
Venture fund			49	49
Real estate	*not allowed by law*		**577**	**577**
Private equity			110	110
Rent income			80	80
Debt income			63	63
Total:	363	47	962	1372

Source: Authors' calculations based on the National League of Management Companies (2010)

In our opinion, the quantity of funds could also represent the investment attractivity of funds. If there was no demand, the quantity would not have been rising. We can note that the quantity of open-end funds started to slightly decrease after 2008 and 2014 but the close-end funds continued on a growth path. The number of interval funds has been insufficient so they were packed with close-end funds.

In contrast to the European fund industry, the quantity of the closed-end funds in Russia exceeds the quantity of the open-end funds. If we analyse the industry by fund types and allocations, we may determine the key factors of this ratio and closed-end funds' growth. The table below discloses the current number of funds by types and asset allocations.

Table 7.2 indicates a significant quantity of the real estate investment funds. Currently, they reach nearly 60 per cent of closed-end funds and almost a half of the total quantity of funds. Their AuM has always composed nearly a third of funds' total AuM. During the crisis their share increased and constituted nearly a half of funds' total AuM. The current ratio is 37 per cent of closed-end funds AuM and 30 per cent of the total (Investfunds, 2015a).

Real estate is the most popular investment type in Russia. Empirical research shows that about half of Russians consider real estate the most sustainable investment (Edovina, 2014). The value of real estate has been steadily rising with a negligible drop during the crisis. Therefore, the high investment attractivity of real estate may have influenced the investment attractivity of the Russian real estate investment funds (REIFs).

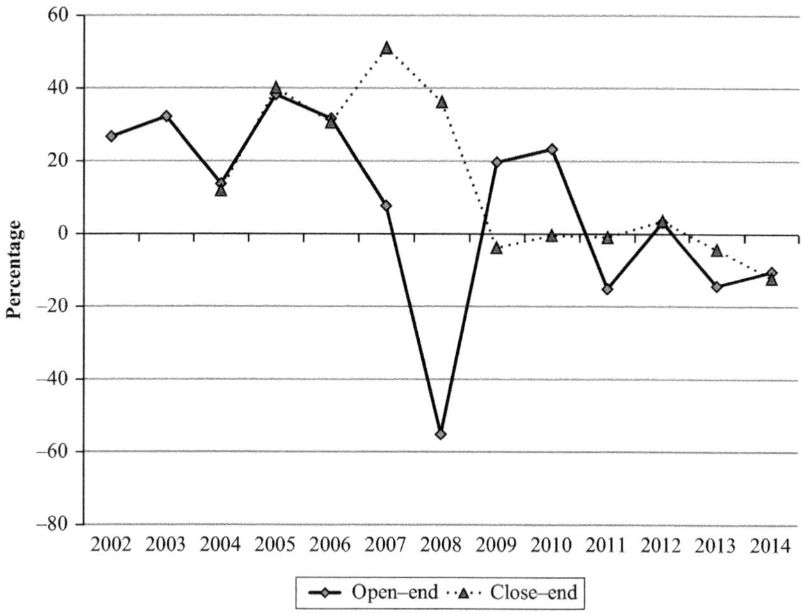

Figure 7.2 Annual average returns of PIFs, 2002–2014
Source: Authors' calculations based on Investfunds (2015)

To assess PIFs' investment attractivity, we provide the analysis of PIFs' risks and returns and their correlation to the traditional assets. We decided to exclude the interval funds from our study. First, their results show significant levels of similarity to the open-end funds. Second, their number has been rapidly reducing from 42 per cent of total funds quantity in 2001 to nearly 3 per cent in 2015 with nearly the same proportions in shortcuts of funds' AuM.

Figure 7.2 indicates that the closed-end funds have overcome the crisis more successfully than the open-end ones. However, we have to mention that the closed-end funds involve more risks. Their standard deviation varies significantly from year to year, so their risk-adjusted performance may deteriorate the results.

To assess the correlation we compare the returns of closed-end PIFs to the Russian stock market index MICEX. The closed-end funds appeared approximately in 2004, so we use the data starting from 2004. First we deteriorate annual average value of the index and its annual growth. Then we compare it to the funds' average returns.

The results indicate that open-end funds tend to reflect the dynamics of the index more than the closed-end ones. The dynamics of the closed-end PIFs during the crisis suggest that they are less volatile than the index and provide some correlation to the index and traditional assets.

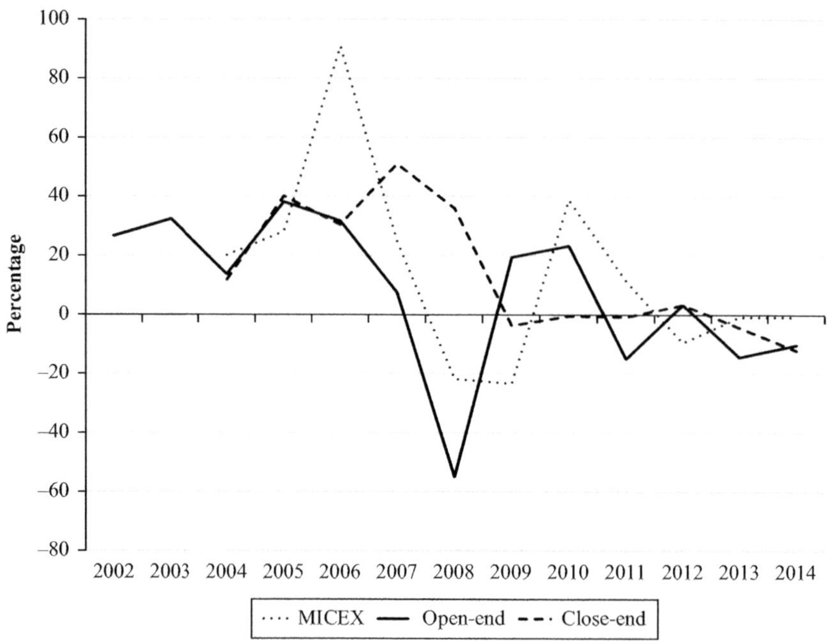

Figure 7.3 MICEX vs PIFs annual average returns dynamics, 2002–2014
Source: Authors' calculations based on Investfunds (2015) and Finam (2016)

To measure the correlation we build a regression based on ten investigations, which are the average annual returns of PIFs and annual growth of the MICEX index. The dependent variable (y) represents the fund returns and the independent variable (x) is the index growth rate.

The regression model indicates that the coefficient of determination R^2 is higher in the case of open-end funds (0.373 and 0.1127 respectively), which assumes the higher correlation between the open-end funds and index. It means that the returns of the open-end funds are more influenced by the index than the closed-end ones. On graphs this ratio is represented by the slope of the straight line, which is less steep than in the analysis of the open-end funds. In general, these findings support the view that the closed-end PIFs correlate with traditional assets and may be considered as alternatives.

Further development of the investment attractivity valuation model includes inflation as an additional factor. Inflation plays a crucial role in the determination of funds' investment attractivity. This factor is more important to the closed-end funds, which are long-term allocations by their nature. If a fund is able to achieve returns above zero or even higher returns than the stock market, it does not matter if it cannot exceed the inflation level.

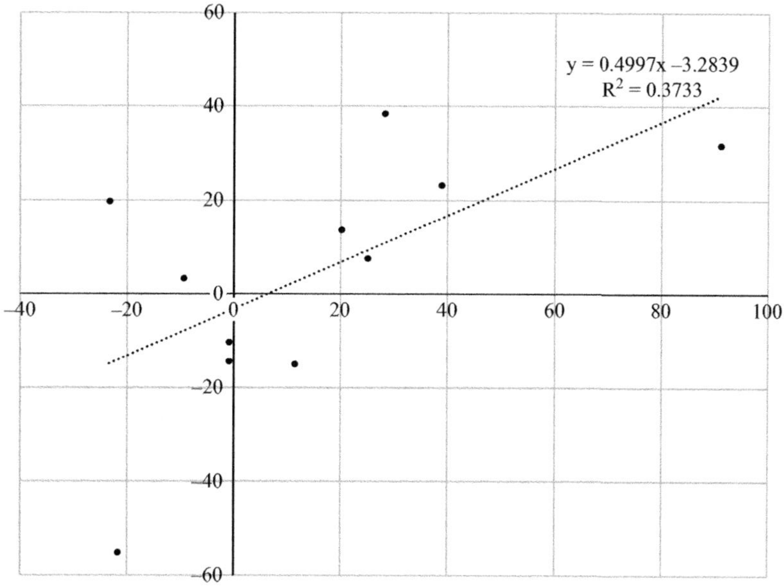

Figure 7.4 Regression based on annual average returns of open-end PIFs and MICEX
Source: Authors' calculations

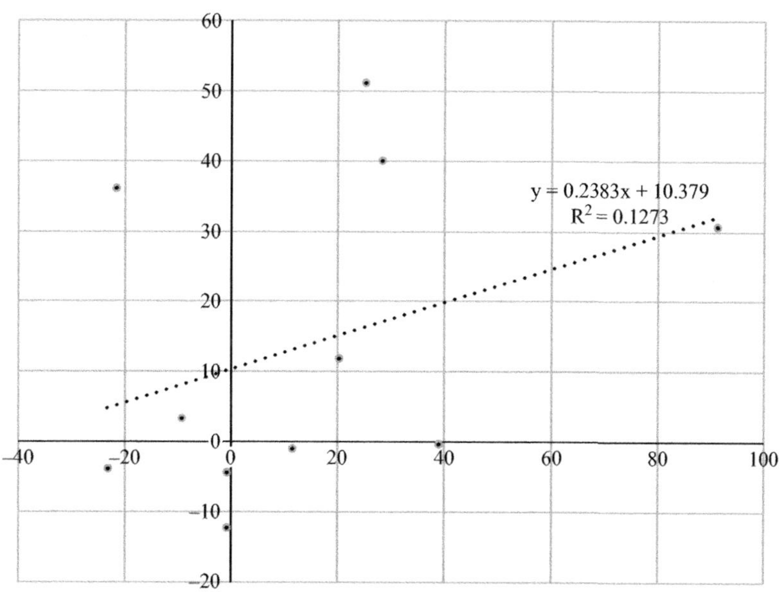

Figure 7.5 Regression based on annual average returns of closed-end PIFs and MICEX
Source: Authors' calculations based on Investfunds (2015) and Bank of Russia (2016)

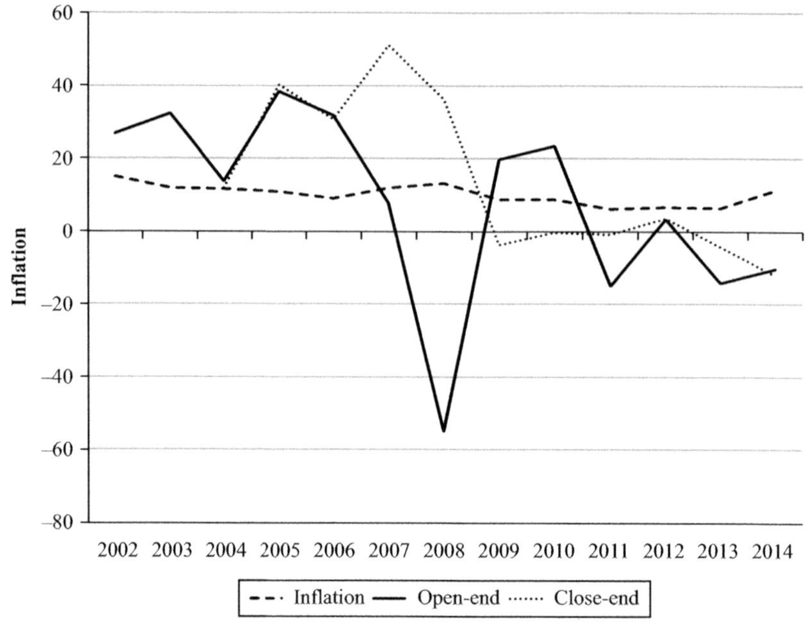

Figure 7.6 Annual average returns of PIFs vs inflation, 2002–2014
Source: Authors' calculations based on Investfunds (2015) and Bank of Russia (2016)

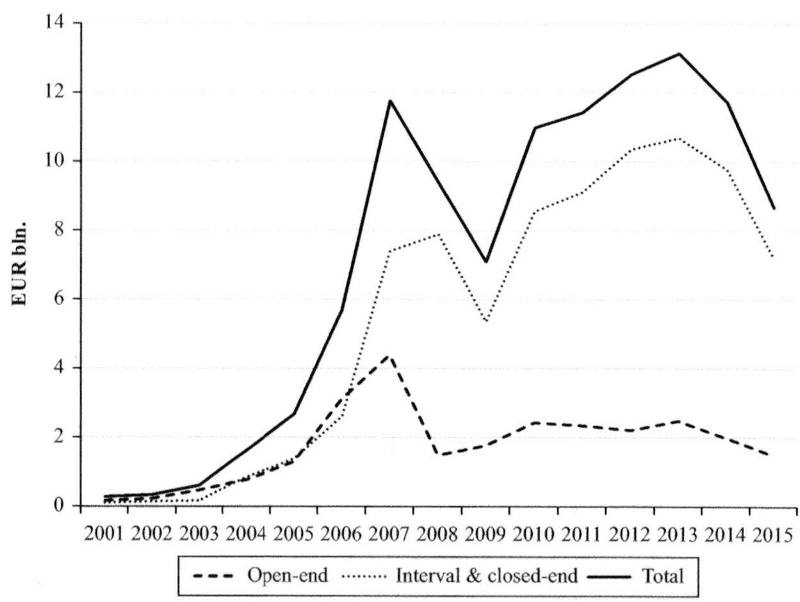

Figure 7.7 Assets under management of PIFs, 2001–2015, in billions of EUR
Source: Authors' calculations based on Investfunds (2015)

Historically, the inflation level in Europe has been low and therefore has been not influencing the funds' returns. In contrast to this, the inflation rate in Russia ranged from 6 to 19 per cent in the last decade. It provides additional challenge for the funds: its returns have to exceed the inflation level.

These findings indicate that the open-end funds have not been able to cope with inflation starting from 2007 as well as the closed-end funds starting from 2009, despite the fact that the inflation level at this period was at its lowest. It reduces the investment attractivity of the PIFs significantly.

Finally, we might consider AuM as an investment attractivity factor. If the PIFs were not attractive for investors, they would not allocate their assets into the funds. The data on the graph is in EUR billions to allow the comparison of the Russian and the European fund industries.

We can see that PIFs' total assets under management are many times lower than the European ones. However, the total AuM of interval and closed-end funds is higher than the open-end ones and they managed to overcome the crisis more successfully.

In conclusion, the Russian classification differs from the European one, but the funds share many similarities. The closed-end funds enable a sufficient correlation level to the stock market. They performed better during the crisis and therefore may offer investment opportunities for investors who do not avoid high risks. The evaluation of investment attractivity of the AIFs should not be based on the risk-return ratio only and should include additional factors. Taxes and costs play a crucial role in evaluation of a fund. In Russia the additional factor of assessment should be inflation.

References

Abramov, A., 2005. *Investments Funds: Return and Risk, Strategies, Portfolio Management, Investment Allocations in Russia*. s.l.: Alpina Business Books.

Bank of Russia, 2016. *Inflation in the Consumer Market*. [Online] Available at: www.cbr.ru/statistics/?PrtId=macro_sub [Accessed 24 November 2016].

Beyer, C., 2014. *Wealth Management Unwrapped*. New York: Rosetta Press.

Brown, S. and Goetzmann, W. N., 2001. *Hedge Funds with Style*. Cambridge, MA: NBER Working Paper Series.

CFA Level 1 2012 – Schweser CFA Study Notes, 2011. *Fixed Income, Derivatives and Alternative Investments*. Volume 5 ed. s.l.: Kaplan-Schweser.

EC, 2016a. *Alternative Investments*. [Online] Available at: http://ec.europa.eu/finance/investment/alternative_investments/index_en.htm [Accessed 24 October 2016].

EC, 2016b. *UCITS – Undertakings for the Collective Investment in Transferable Securities*. [Online] Available at: http://ec.europa.eu/finance/investment/ucits-directive/index_en.htm [Accessed 24 October 2016].

Edovina, T., 2014. *Save Up for a Rainy Day. Russians Still Conserve not for Profit, but "Just in Case"*. [Online] Available at: http://pif.investfunds.ru/news/39567 [Accessed 10 November 2016].

EFAMA, 2014. *Trends in European Investment Funds 2003–2013*. Brussels: European Fund and Asset Management Association.

Finam, 2016. *MICEX.* [Online] Available at: www.finam.ru/profile/moex-indeksy/micex/ [Accessed 24 November 2016].

Hoffman, K., 2013. The Role of Alternative for Taft-Hartley Plans. *Benefits Magazine*, 50(10), pp. 14–20.

Ibbotson, R. and Caplan, P. D., 2000. Does Asset Allocation Policy Explain 40, 90 or 100 Percent of Performance? *Financial Analysts Journal*, 56(1), pp. 26–33.

Investfunds, 2015. *Invest Funds*and *Mutual Funds* [Online] Available at: http://pif.investfunds.ru/funds/ [Accessed 10 November 2016].

Kat, H., 2004. Managed Futures and Hedge Funds: A Match Made in Heaven. *Journal of Investment Management*, 2(1), pp. 1–9.

Levaux, J., 2012. Alternatives Stay on Growth Path. *Research Magazine*, July, pp. 18–22.

National League of Management Companies, 2010. *Home.* [Online] Available at: www.nlu.ru/ [Accessed 24 November 2016].

Schulaka, C., 2011. Advisers Embrace Alternative Investments. *Journal of Financial Planning*, 24(9), pp. 30–33.

Sedlacek, V. O., 2014. *Alternatives Reality: What to Expect from Future Allocations.* Wilton, CT: Commonfund Institute.

Shamraev, A., 2014. *Mezhdunarodnoe i zarubezhnoe finansovoe regulirovanie: instituty. sdelki. infrastruktura.* Knorus: Moskovskij gosudarstvennyj institut mezhdunarodnyh otnoshenij universitetmid rossii.

Stolz, R., 2011. Investigating Alternative Investments. *Journal of Financial Planning*, Issue 9, pp. 22–28.

8 Financial risk and financialization

Andrzej Szopa

The essence of financial risk

Financial risk as we understand it is the phenomenon of variation between the actual and expected results of economic activity, with the result that an operator may incur losses. Currently in literature there are two basic concepts related to the nature and description of financial risk:

- The high-risk value (Value at Risk) (Szopa, 2012) is the maximum, expected and potential loss as a result of economic activity, resulting from the impact of a particular source of risk. The calculation value is partly dependent on assumptions arbitrarily derived from the properties of the normal distribution of the variable which is the source of financial risk (J. P. Morgan/Reuters, 1996).
- The black swan – for events occurring very rarely (with a low probability of occurrence), but generating large losses, difficult to forecast but at the same time easy to interpret.[1] This group includes, among others events: random events such as fires, earthquakes, floods. Here we may also include other phenomena bringing violent consequences: errors in management of enterprises, generating loss of liquidity, banking crises resulting in the 'run on the banks' phenomenon, currency crises causing the outflow of capital abroad, and errors in the use of financial engineering which resulted in a number of so-called financial disasters.[2]

The essence of the concept of black swans is based on the rejection of the traditional tools of classical analysis of financial risk. This is mainly due to the disbelief that the events of the past may forecast the future.

The losses generated by the phenomenon of financial risk enforce the necessity of managing it. This consists, on one hand, of securing the consequences of risk (losses), which means the appropriate disposition of the economic capital and on the other hand of closing open positions (so-called hedging).[3]

The size of economic capital is determined by the extent of expected loss and by definition it should provide full coverage of these losses. The easiest assumption would be that economic capital should be equal to the value of the risk.[4]

In other words, own funds smaller than the economic capital, failing to prevent losses, may expose the company to a loss of liquidity and as further consequence lead to its downfall.

Hedging, in turn, relies on a combination of opposing positions in instruments sensitive to the same source of financial risk. This in turn triggers the demand for financial instruments tailored to the sources of risk, experienced by companies in the course of their business. Combining opposing positions means closing open positions on the financial market.

Shaping the capital structure. These instruments allow the conversion of debt to equity or vice versa, thereby adjusting the size of own funds to the needs of financial risk management. The emergence of new risk sources enforces the search for instruments for closing open positions.

The easiest way to create contradictory positions is the combination of the position on the cash transactions market with futures instruments (derivatives).

Development on the derivatives market[5]

Derivatives are traded in financial markets in both forms:

- on the organized market – standardized instruments, transactions in such instruments are low cost;
- on the OTC market – allows adjusting the parameters of protection against risks to individual needs; this is a relatively expensive way, because it requires time-consuming commitment of both parties to the contract.

The most popular derivatives include:

- futures – forwards contracts are traded on the OTC market, while futures are traded on organized markets;
- option contracts – are traded on both types of market;
- swap contracts are traded only on the OTC market.

The belonging of a particular financial instrument to the particular market is conditioned by two basic factors:

- trading liquidity;
- possibility of standardization of transactions.

The use of derivatives in financial market management is conditional first and foremost to the realization of consequences.

Financialization

The financialization of the economy means the mutual influence of the financial sphere and the sphere of material production. This phenomenon takes place at the following levels:

- financing of business by the financial market;
- placement of financial surpluses by entities from the sphere of production on the financial market;
- exploitation of financial risk transfer instruments (Bailey, 2005);
- liquidity storage;
- treating the financial sphere as an alternative to property investments.

The investment of surplus funds by non-financial entities on the financial market is a form of speculation, since it relies on the conscious use of risk exposure in order to obtain additional income. The study will focus on the impact of financial risk on the deepening of financialization. The growing importance of financialization will be associated with a build-up of the phenomenon of financial risk. What is the source of this phenomenon? It manifests itself in the form of:

- deepening of the phenomenon of business co-operation, the production process becomes more complicated by including a growing number of others in the activities of the entity;
- opening of national economies – on one hand intensifies competition, and on the other hand causes exposure to other sources of risk, for example currency;
- the internalization of activity of business entities;
- the acceleration of technological progress, primarily by changes in the business entity environment;

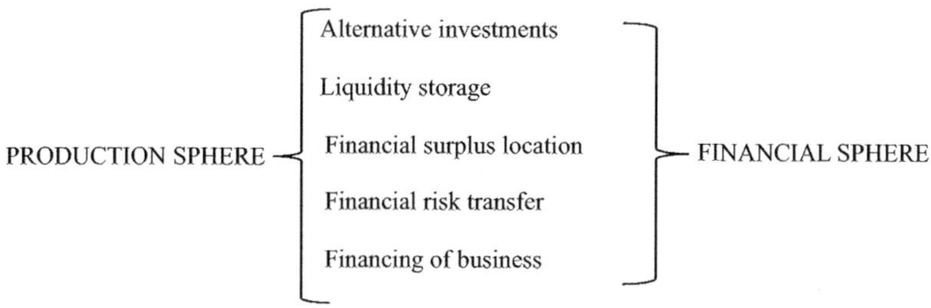

Figure 8.1 The form of financialization
Source: Author's description

- internalization means economic processes are becoming more complex, making it difficult to forecast events;
- growing importance of extreme events with a very low probability of occurrence and large resulting losses;
- increasing interdependence of various economic events and phenomena makes it difficult to isolate the sources of risk;
- underestimating the importance of reserves in risk management, shallow reserves may mean moving disparities within large areas of the economy. Reserves perform the function of specific shock absorbers, limiting the scope of economic turmoil.

The complexity of the phenomenon of financial risk, the wide range of factors determining its nature results in methodological difficulties in measuring financial risk:

- limited usefulness of econometric and mathematical models;
- limited usefulness of past events in predicting future;
- limited forecasting possibilities cause that attention should be focused on shaping the sensitivity of the subject to extreme events;
- the standard deviation cannot be regarded as a universal measure of risk;
- this causes excessive focus of attention on narrow measures;
- incomplete identification of risk sources causes an excessive amount of risk classifications;
- lack of understanding of the consequences of the risk leads to underestimation of risk management leading to, among others, the lack of real-time management.

Difficulties associated with the nature of financial risk cannot interfere with the search for methods, which nevertheless should allow the measurement of financial risk.

The dual character of financial risk management

The creator of the concept of ‘black swans’ drew attention to the fact that rare events, generating large losses, undermine the efficacy of traditional management methods, because very often one-off losses are much greater than the long-term benefits of classical methods.[6] Managing the risk should therefore direct attention to ensuring the viability of the business entity by eliminating all those elements in the functioning of the entity which are unstable, fragile.[7]

- All that is impermanent should be removed as soon as possible. Paradoxically, the more hidden risks there are in an action, the stronger the operator will become as a result. There is an analogy here to known processes of natural evolution. In life, only the strongest survive.

- Failing entities should not be supported (the socialization of losses), nor should profits be privatized. Subsidizing weak business entities prevents the removal of weak links from the economy and thus contributes to decrease of social management performance. On the other hand, taking over profitable private enterprises by the State undermines the fundamental principle of private economic initiative.
- In the economic processes, the elimination of erring executive assets should take place. People are a strategic factor in business, hence the appropriate selection of personnel – and not just for the executive positions – plays a key role in the running of any business.
- Incentive systems should avoid motivating people to undertake risky ventures. Projects involving numerous risks are burdened with the possibility of losses, thus preferring excessive risk may end disastrously for any business.
- Limiting financing through debt. The ability to repay debt depends on the ever fluent financial situation of the debtor. It introduces a form of moral hazard into the economic reality.
- One should use financial instruments that are understood by investors. Each activity in the financial market is associated with uncertainty as to the final results of these activities. This uncertainty increases with the erroneous use of financial instruments.
- The role of the trust should be limited within the realm of economy. Trust is a purely subjective category and therefore may become a source of all kinds of setbacks in objective reality.
- One should not use various forms of debt mitigation. The awareness that difficulties with the repayment of the debt may be alleviated by external factors may create an excessive tendency to debt.
- The living conditions of citizens should not depend on financial assets. A de-financialization of economic life should take place. Significant volatility in the capital markets may result in the need for accommodative financial resources of social policy.
- Gaining competitive advantage. Gaining a competitive edge by an operator facilitates the realization of economic goals undertaken by the operator.
- The deregulation of the economy. Deregulation is the primary trigger for the initiative of operators.
- Labour market flexibility. Labour market flexibility is one of the basic factors for the optimization of production costs, which are a major factor in labour costs.
- Renewal of the components of the economy should be performed using effective methods and means. The basic condition for investment decisions is the achievement of a positive net present value.

There are two forms of risk determined by the possibility of their quantification: the VaR calculation method which is affected by the properties of the normal distribution and the concept of 'black swans' rejecting any possibility of quantification. The problem lies in the fact that in each case the losses caused by the risk must be covered by equity. The source of equity is the economic efficiency and the ability to thereby generate appropriate economic surplus.

VaR quantification allows the separation of the part of the capital necessary to secure the losses resulting from this source. This part of the capital is called economic capital. Thus, the non-quantifiable remainder of the loss should be protected by a surplus of own funds over the level of economic capital.

Management effectiveness plays a key role in securing risk – that is, the ability to generate a surplus above the level of economic capital. Strategies for financial risk management may be recapitulated as follows: the aim is minimizing VaR, as this reduces the need for economic capital and thus allows a greater protection of unexpected losses by own funds.

In financial risk management, a lack of loss forecasting possibilities enforces the introduction of the so-called hybrid management system. On one hand, the economic capital is used for covering expected losses with a given probability, on the other the impossibility of determination of unexpected losses triggers a trend to maximize the surplus of own funds over the economic capital, as shown in Figure 8.2. The higher the excess, the greater the possibility of depreciation of extreme losses. This creates the following system of relations: the lower the risk exposure and lesser demand for economic capital, the greater the ability to generate a surplus over the economic capital.

The VaR concept is based on the adoption of the following breakdown (Neftci, 2004):

Risk is an objective phenomenon reflected in the ratio of the standard deviation. The coefficients k and $\sqrt{t}$ are subjectively adopted by the heads of the company and are subordinated on one side to corporate goals, and on the other to the nature of management in the chosen field.

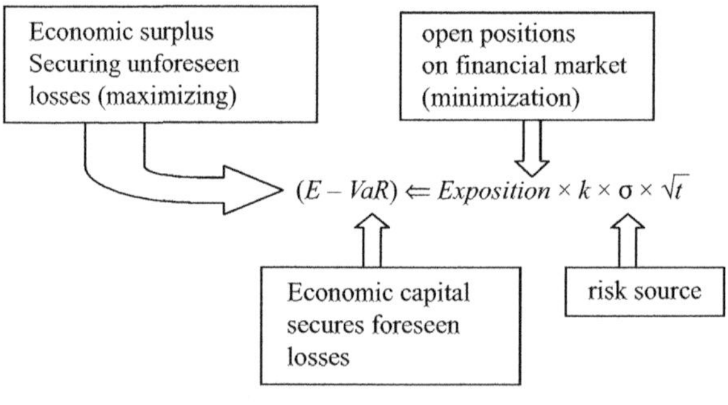

Figure 8.2 The risk formula
Source: Author's description

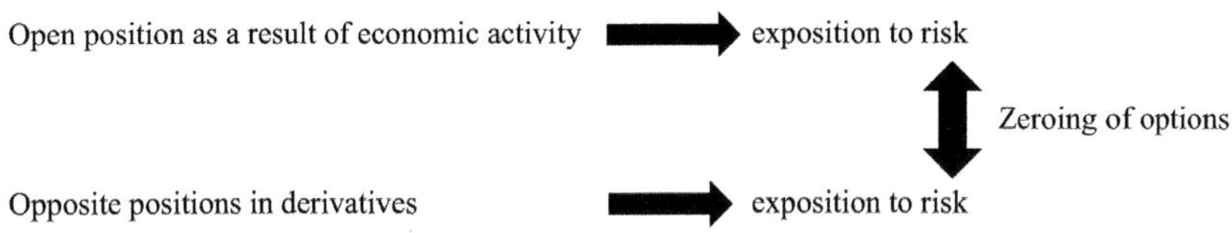

Figure 8.3 The essence of hedging
Source: Author's description

Exposure to risks, and thus the whole set of open positions, can be shaped by closing positions on the financial market. The possibility of closing open positions means minimizing exposure to financial risk. This depends mainly on the availability of financial instruments sensitive to the selected source of risk.

Closing of open positions is about combining opposite positions in instruments sensitive to the same source of risk. Hence, derivatives are used, generally in order to hedge against risk.

The essence of hedging – closing open positions – is shown in Figure 8.3.

The hybrid system of financial risk management

The dual nature of financial risk indicates that it is not possible to adopt a method of risk measurement, or it is necessary to seek methods of compromise towards this duality. The concept of black swans actually indicates an impossibility of financial risk measurement. Events extremely rare hinder, or even prevent, any prediction, and thus do not allow for quantification of future events related to financial risk.

The situation is different with the concept of VaR. This concept, starting from the properties of the normal distribution, tends to determine the size of the maximum values – for a given level of confidence – and expected, potential losses from the impact of a particular source of risk. This is the maximum expected value and therefore smaller than the potential maximum loss that can involve financial risk.

It can be illustrated by Figure 8.4.

Risks are secured with own funds. This dual nature of the risks allows the identification of two groups of own funds: part for securing the expected, potential loss, and part for securing the unknown and unexpected losses.

The main issue, therefore, in the management of financial risk is the desire on one hand to generate the maximum amount of funding and on the other to minimize the expected losses. These two trends guarantee the minimization of the consequences of the expected financial risk and thus secure the greatest possible degree of security of the business entity.

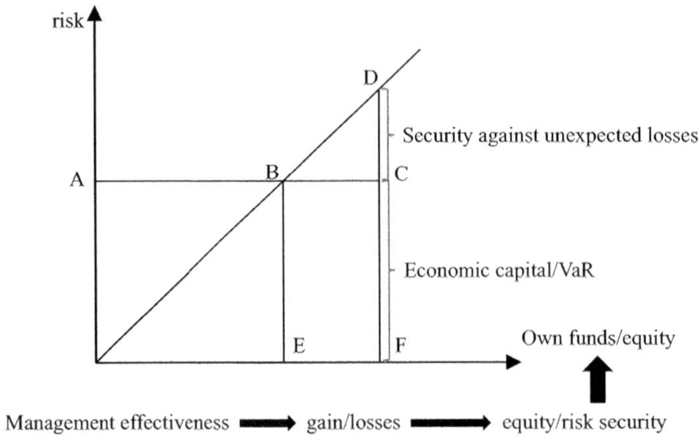

Figure 8.4 Structure and risk security
Source: Author's description

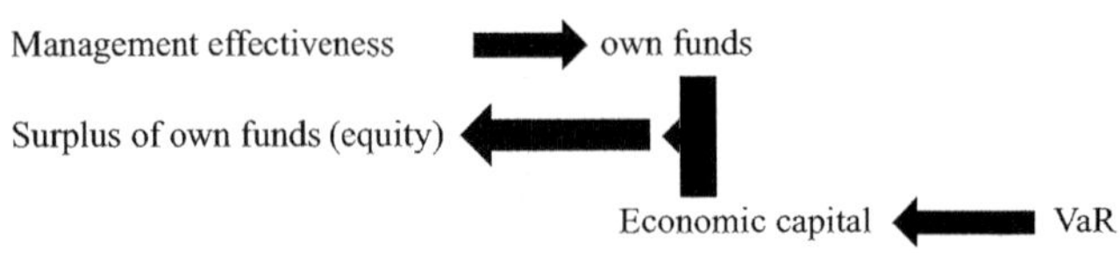

Figure 8.5 The interpretation of economic capital
Source: Author's description

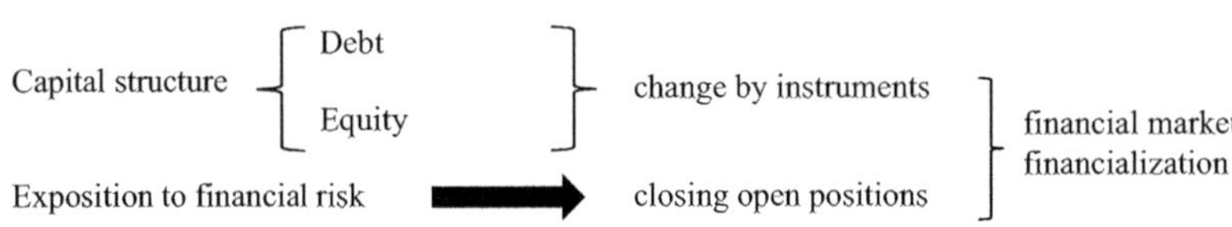

Figure 8.6 The source of financialization
Source: Author's description

The aim is therefore to manage as much as possible surplus of own funds above the amount of economic capital. The way to this is to not only through classic financial risk management by closing the open positions in the financial market, but above improving management efficiency.

Since own funds are a factor in neutralizing the consequences of the financial risk, an important role is played by the capital structure and possible change in this structure is served by a special group of financial instruments, such as convertible bonds and their reverse form. The value of own funds for hedging VaR depends on the ability to reduce exposure to risk by closing open positions on the financial market. This procedure reports, in turn, a demand for risk transfer instruments from the sphere of production to the sphere of finance.

Conclusion

The analysis of the relationship between financialization and financial risk presented above allows us to formulate the following theses:

- The increase in financial risk forces the subordination of the whole business enterprise managing to this phenomenon. This requires the use of both the relevant instruments available in the financial market, as well as the relevant procedures.
- Maximizing of the size of own funds may mean having to seek instruments to change the capital structure. The capital structure should be flexible enough to be able to adjust the size of the funds to secure the consequences.
- Classical financial risk management requires a search for financial instruments sensitive to sources of risk that are sensitive to the economic operator. Classical methods do not work in the case of rare events with significant consequences. This leads to the concept of 'black swans'.
- Protection against 'black swans' requires generating economic surplus, the size of which depends on the scope of protection against unexpected losses resulting from financial risk. This requires a completely different approach, both to the financial risk management process, as well as the functioning of the production company.

Notes

1 There is a certain analogy here to the 'fat tails' concept, and the extreme value theory (EVT) concept.
2 See: Szopa (2015), 'The "black swan" concept and the financial risk management'.
3 Of importance here is the fact of underestimation of reserves in risk management. Shallow reserves mean that, in case of any disturbances, they are distributed along a sizeable area of economy.
4 Assuming the easiest definition of Value at Risk:

$VaR = Exposal\ to\ risk \times k \times \sigma \times \sqrt{t}$ (see: J. P. Morgan/Reuters, 1996), where:
VaR – value at risk
Exposal to risk – economic activity area endangered by certain sources of risk

σ–risk source variable – (standard deviation)
$\sqrt{t}$ – period of occupying a market position
Hence economic capital (E) will equal:

E = VaR

5 The derivatives market is growing very rapidly throughout the world. At the moment, the highest turnovers are listed on the stock exchanges EUREX,

NYSE Liffe and OMX. The Warsaw Stock Exchange has a higher turnover than many European countries, e.g. Spain, Norway, Italy, Hungary and Greece. Such large interest in derivatives stems not only from their use for protecting against risks, but also for speculative purposes (large multiplier). See: NBP, 2014 and Wojciechowski, 2009.

6 For example, flood protection devices. Those devices are calculated for a certain level of flood water. In case of higher levels, this leads to large losses in state property.

7 There is a certain analogy here to natural evolution, which is based on the elimination of obsolete elements (Taleb, 2010).

References

Bailey, R. E., 2005. *The Economics of Financial Markets*. Cambridge: Cambridge University Press.

J. P. Morgan/Reuters, 1996. *Technical Document*. [Online] Available at: https://www.msci.com/documents/10199/5915b101-4206-4ba0-aee2-3449d5c7e95a [Accessed 5 December 2016].

NPB, 2014. *Turnover in the Domestic Foreign Exchange and OTC Derivatives Markets in April 2013*. Warszawa: Narodowy Bank Polski.

Neftci, S. N., 2004. *Principles of Financial Engineering*. London: Elsevier Academic Press.

Szopa, A., 2012. *Podstawy inżynierii finansowej*. Warszawa: Wolters Kluwer.

Szopa, A., 2015. Koncepcja 'czarnych łabędzi' a zarządzanie ryzykiem finansowym. In: *Zarządzanie w Przedsiębiorstwie i Regione, Nowe Wyzwania*. Sopot: Wydział Zarządzania Uniwersytet Gdański.

Taleb, N. N., 2010. *The Black Swan: The Impact of the Highly Improbable*. New York: Random House.

Wojciechowski, J., 2009. *Rynek giełdowych finansowych instrumentów pochodnych w Polsce. Rys historyczny, stan obecny i perspektywy*, Warszawa: s.n.

Part III

Financialization: impact on society, households and companies

9 Inequality in the twenty-first century – in need of a new theory?

Hanna K. Szymborska

Introduction

Over the past decades, income and wealth distribution in advanced countries has worsened dramatically, reaching the highest levels since the Great Depression. Economic studies have analysed the causes and consequences of growing inequality. However, most of these analyses are based on the standard conceptualization of income, obscuring the emergence of massive disparities in net wealth, understood as the difference between one's assets and liabilities. While empirical works have attempted to account for this aspect of inequality, economic theory seems to have lagged behind.

This is because the main theories of inequality are based on economic relations which have been fundamentally altered by changes in the nature of financial intermediation and the relationship between financial sector and real economy since the 1980s. An approach to inequality accounting for the distribution of net wealth in the light of this financial sector transformation necessitates a focus on the characteristics, dynamics and structures of balance sheets of different economic agents. Such analysis is largely absent from modern economic theory.

This chapter revisits the existing theories of inequality in order to answer the following questions. Are current theories capable of reproducing the trends in inequality experienced in the twenty-first century? How can the social phenomenon of inequality be adequately modelled in a formal manner? Is economics in need of a new theory of inequality? The first section describes how the transformation of financial sector operation has been associated with growing inequality in high-income countries since the 1980s by shaping different balance sheet compositions of households across the distribution. The next section discusses the existing theoretical explanations explicitly linking finance and inequality, focusing on the recent theory of Piketty as well as the Post Keynesian functional distribution models. It is argued that while both theories shed light on important structural factors related to inequality, neither of them explains what drives households to accumulate specific assets and liabilities. Next, the discussion is extended to theories of household portfolio decisions, finding that the Post Keynesian consumption theory, while relatively undeveloped, offers a better understanding of household behaviour in times of financialization than the neoclassical life-cycle hypothesis due to its emphasis on the social context of household consumption choices. The final section concludes, proposing an updated theory of inequality, postulating endogenous examination of household balance sheet decisions within the macroeconomic boundaries generated by financial sector transformation.

Finance and inequality since the 1980s

Financialization is a multidimensional processes occurring primarily in high-income economies since the late 1960s, accelerating in the 1980s under the neoliberal policies of Reagan in the USA and Thatcher in the UK (Sawyer, 2013, p. 13). It has been associated with deregulation of financial markets, securitization and financial innovation, privatization of public services and weakening of the labour power, all of which induced higher demand and supply of credit in the economy and greater involvement of households in financial markets. Financial intermediaries were eager to include more households in their services partly to compensate for diminishing deposits from non-financial firms (Dymski, 2009) and partly to generate more underlying assets for securitized instruments to keep pace with rapidly growing demand among financial investors (Goda and Lysandrou, 2011). In the process, many non-bank intermediaries took advantage of lax financial regulation and engaged in predatory lending practices by offering 'subprime' mortgages at extremely harsh conditions to social groups previously excluded from access to credit, such as women and ethnic minorities (Dymski *et al.*, 2013). Those subprime mortgages formed the lion's share of securitized assets, which resulted in unsustainable indebtedness for subprime borrowers and spread the burden of the crisis unequally between different race and gender groups (Young, 2010).

Consequently, processes of financialization directly affected the dynamics of income and wealth distribution in advanced countries. In the USA, where the trends are the most extreme, the Gini coefficient for income rose from 0.48 in 1982 to 0.57 in 2006 (Wolff, 2014, p. 27). Furthermore, as presented in Figure 9.1, the share of national income held by the richest 1 per cent in the USA increased by 131 per cent in a similar period, reaching 18.9 per cent in 2012. The growth in inequality at the top tail of the distribution was driven by the financial sector, with financial services sector employees accounting for 15–27 per cent of the top 0.1 per cent of the income distribution in the USA (and non-financial sector top executives representing only around 6 per cent (Kaplan and Rauh, 2010)). Simultaneously, due to wage growth lagging behind productivity growth, the share of worker compensation in GDP declined steadily from 62 per cent in 1980 to 56 per cent in 2013 in the USA (AMECO Database, 2016), suggesting redistribution of national income towards profits (specifically financial profits). Consequently, only the top 10 per cent of the US population experienced above average income growth between 1980 and 2010, with average annual growth rate of 3.2 per cent, while

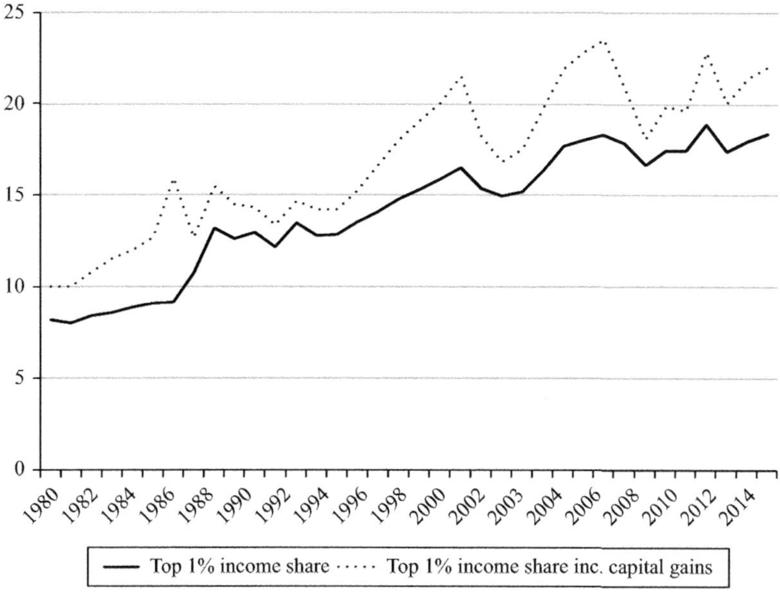

Figure 9.1 Evolution of the top 1 per cent income share in the USA, 1980–2015
Source: Author's calculations based on Alvaredo *et al.* (n.d.)

the bottom 90 per cent saw a mere 0.78 per cent average annual rate of growth of income in the same period (Bivens *et al.*, 2014).

In terms of wealth, the rise in wealth Gini in the USA has been less dynamic than that of income but its level has been persistently higher, reaching 0.87 in 2010 (Wolff, 2014). Deepening wealth inequality is further highlighted by the growing gap between the mean and median net worth (defined as marketable assets less current debt) – in the USA, the mean-median ratio increased from 3.9 in 1983 to 8.1 in 2010, presented in Figure 9.2. Asset composition and leverage levels had a key impact on US inequality, as shown in Figure 9.3. Middle- and low-income households rely more heavily on primary residence and high homeownership rates (67 per cent share of total assets compared to 31 per cent for all households) and greater relative indebtedness (debt-equity and debt-income ratio at 72 per cent and 135 per cent respectively compared to 21 per cent and 127 per cent for the whole sample) driven by mortgage debt, described in Table 9.1, making their balance sheets more vulnerable to financial shocks (ibid., p. 22). In particular, asset price movements and housing market collapse shortly before the Great Recession generated a massive drop in median wealth, while mean net worth suffered less and grew at a faster rate than the median in the whole period, indicating deepening inequality (ibid., p. 24). The fact that top quintiles directed most of their wealth

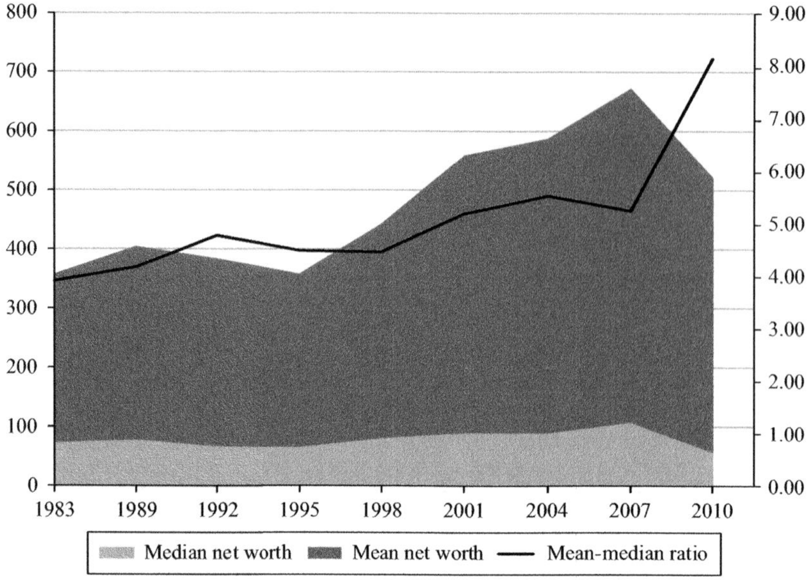

Figure 9.2 Mean and median net worth in the USA, 1983–2010
Source: Author's calculations based on Wolff (2014)

into financial assets meant that annual rates of return were comparatively higher for these wealth groups (ibid., pp. 30–31). Similarly to income, finance has been strongly associated with rising wealth inequality. Almost a third of the wealth of the rich listed on the Forbes 400 derives from finance, compared with around 10 per cent from manufacturing or technology (Foster and Holleman, 2010).

These dramatic trends in inequality were only briefly reversed during the 2007 recession. The top 1 per cent income share in the USA declined from 18.3 per cent in 2007 to 16.7 per cent in 2009, but it quickly recovered to 18.9 per cent in 2012. Importantly, fall in the top 1 per cent share of national income was redistributed within the top quintile, as the share of the top 10 per cent decreased by far less than the top 1 per cent share between 2007 and 2011 (Dufour and Orhangazi, 2016, p. 165). The overall Gini coefficient for income fell from 0.57 to 0.55 (Wolff, 2014, p. 27).

In contrast, while falling asset prices slightly diminished the stocks of wealth of the rich, the Gini coefficient for wealth increased by 0.035 Gini points in the post-crisis period (Wolff, 2014, p. 32). In fact, while median net wealth fell by 21.2 per cent from 2007 to 2010, mean net wealth saw only 6.5 per cent decline, suggesting an uneven burden of the crisis across the rich and the rest of the society (ibid., p. 24). Increase in wealth inequality during the crisis was due to different degrees of leverage across the population

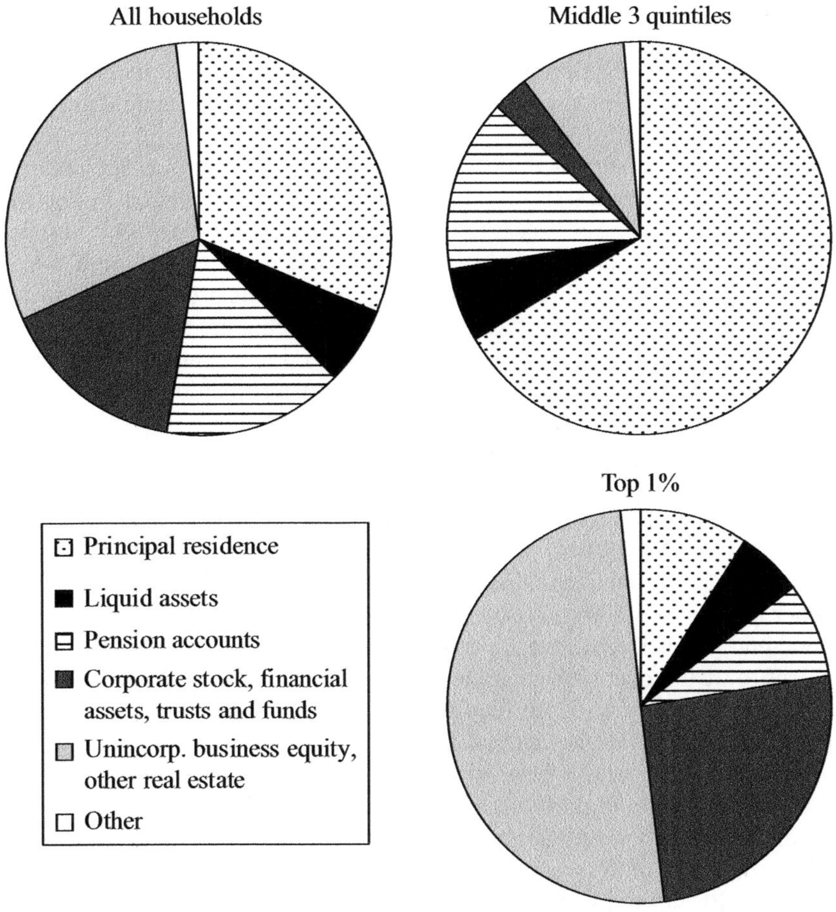

Figure 9.3 Portfolio composition by income decile in the USA, 2010
Source: Author's calculations based on Wolff (2014)

Table 9.1 Financial fragility indicators by percentile in the USA, 2010

	Debt to equity ratio	*Debt to income ratio*	*Principal residence loan to value ratio*
All households	21	127	41.2
Middle 3 quintiles	71.5	134.5	51.3
Top 1%	3.5	60.6	18.9

Source: Author's calculations based on Wolff (2014)

(ibid., p. 32). The ratios of debt to assets and income were unsustainable for the middle and bottom part of the distribution and amplified the asset price losses. Consequently, wealth gains experienced by this population group in the 1990s and early 2000s relied primarily on asset price inflation and increasing indebtedness, turning out to be illusory as the recession unfolded (Mian and Sufi, 2013).

Overall, data show that the rise in inequality since 1980s has been related to two underlying processes. First, wage growth has been seized by the top 10 per cent of earners as wages stagnated for the bottom 90 per cent. Second, the top 10 per cent have had access to high-yielding capital income, which further deepened inequality. Consequently, in the context of financial sector transformation, an important aspect of inequality emerges from the distribution of wealth. However, as shown in the next section, economic theory does not sufficiently account for wealth in inequality determination.

Finance and distribution – a theoretical perspective

The importance of wealth for analysing inequality is highlighted in the seminal work of Piketty (2014). The main premise of his *Capital in the Twenty-First Century* is that inequality is driven by accumulation of persistently higher returns to wealth (r) relative to the growth of income (g) (historically averaging at 5 per cent and 1 per cent respectively). Compounding of the returns to wealth over time generates higher income flows for the wealth holders and their inheritors (identified with the top 0.1–1 per cent) than for the rest of the society. Higher capital income in turn allows for greater saving, facilitating further wealth generation and perpetuating inequality.

Piketty's insight is particularly relevant in the age of financialization. Financial innovation and securitization influenced inequality by generating differential rates of return and degrees of volatility across the distribution. Large wealth holdings of the rich allowed them to invest in high-yielding financial instruments (often requiring large initial payments, which can only be afforded at high levels of net worth), generating sizeable capital income.

Despite the importance of its general conclusions, Piketty's work suffers from several drawbacks. First, his argument relies on comparing average growth rates of wealth and income. However, there is substantial variability in income and wealth trends across the distribution, which is particularly important when it comes to understanding the impact of financialization on inequality. As outlined in the previous section, differential degrees of leverage across the population turned out to be an important driver of inequality, particularly during the 2007 recession. Furthermore, theoretical explanation for inequality based on 'r greater than g' claim relies on the expectation that trends observed in the past would continue into the future (Pressman, 2016, p. 159). Hence, Piketty does not provide any explicit theoretical explanation why returns to wealth should always exceed the growth of income. Consequently, there is no formal link between inequality and financial sector transformation in Piketty's framework.

The alternative body of theoretical literature identified with the Post Keynesian functional distribution explicitly takes into account the link between financialization and distribution. It focuses on the macroeconomic impact of increasingly unequal distribution of national income between two factors of production – capital and labour – associated with higher propensity to save and consume respectively (Kalecki, 1971). Financialization is interpreted as rising shareholder value maximization leading to higher capital share of income (Van Treeck, 2009; Hein and Van Treeck, 2010; Palley, 2012; Hein, 2015). These models often draw from Bhaduri and Marglin (1990) argument that the macroeconomic effects of income transfers between wage and profit earners hinge on whether the economy is wage- or profit-led. Onaran *et al.* (2011) establish that the majority of advanced economies are wage-led, which implies that lower wage share in result of financial sector transformation has a negative impact on aggregate demand and growth by undercutting effective investment demand because resources are taken away from those who are more likely to spend them to those who are more likely to hoard them.

The issue with this theory, however, is that the transformation in the nature of financial intermediation has complexified the division of the society into two distinct categories. Both groups of 'workers' and 'capitalists' have become heterogeneous, which complicates their analytical usefulness. Workers became the recipients of capital income through homeownership and private pension schemes, while capitalists became the recipients of the highest wages in the economy. Hence, large disparities have emerged in the aggregate characteristics of each category, making the boundaries between them less clear.

Moreover, Post Keynesian models are traditionally focused on investment as the variable most important for macroeconomic growth, treating savings and consumption as residual and passive (Setterfield and Kim, 2013, p. 2). However, since the 1980s consumption has become much more volatile and thus more important as an independent source of aggregate demand. This is largely due to the development of financial sectors and massive expansion of credit to households, leading household spending to become increasingly disconnected from income.

Thus, there is a gap in the existing literature on inequality. On the one hand, Piketty's insight on the interplay between wealth and income is not fully developed on a theoretical level. On the other hand, the Post Keynesian theoretical literature does not sufficiently explore the role of wealth distribution for overall inequality dynamics. A new theory of inequality is needed, accounting for feedback mechanisms between macroeconomic processes and household balance sheet evolution in understanding distribution.

Finance and theories of household portfolio decisions

Household wealth has been traditionally understood in economic theory through consumption and saving decisions of households. Two strands of relevant economic theory seeking to understand the dynamics of wealth through examining household portfolio decisions can be identified. The first strand is associated with the life-cycle theory of consumption (LTC), originating in Modigliani and Brumberg (1954), and the permanent income hypothesis (PIH) developed by Friedman (1957). The second strand of the literature is associated with the contemporary Post Keynesian consumption theory.

In the LTC/PIH framework, wealth inequality is an expected phenomenon explained by households optimizing their consumption spending according to standard microeconomic behavioural assumptions, namely completeness, reflexivity, transitivity and non-satiation of preferences, yielding a continuous, quasi-concave and differentiable consumer utility function and a unique solution to utility maximization (Gravelle and Reese, 2012, pp. 12–19). Households engage in consumption smoothing to avoid large fluctuations in consumption over their life cycle, borrowing or running down assets in periods of lower-than-average income (when young), paying off loans, saving and accumulating assets in periods of higher-than-average income (associated with productive years) and dissaving (consuming out of accumulated savings) on retirement. Hence, saving rates should vary with income levels. Moreover, socio-demographic characteristics related to income expectations matter for consumer behaviour – e.g. college graduates should borrow more than blue-collar workers when young as their permanent income (defined as the expected long-run average income) is relatively higher (Bertola *et al.*, 2006, p. 6). These predictions have been generally rejected by empirical evidence (ibid.). Furthermore, at any point in time it is the wealthy households who take on more debt in terms of not only value but also participation. Fredriksen (2012) dismisses the prediction of hump-shaped evolution of net worth and financial asset holding along the life cycle, finding instead a steady increase with age. Deaton (1986) as well as Dynan *et al.* (2004) reject the dependency of savings on the position in the life cycle. Due to these empirical problems, the LTC/PIH framework has seen numerous extensions aiming to improve its explanatory power. The most relevant additions include the presence of liquidity constraints, precautionary savings and the bequest motive, where asymmetric information, uncertainty and altruistic motives help explain 'abnormal' household behaviour (Carroll, 1997; Gurrieri and Lorenzoni, 2011).

However, these extensions imply that financial deregulation and innovation are a relief to credit constrained households, decreasing information asymmetries and thus ensuring more optimal credit allocation, allowing households to achieve desired consumption smoothing patterns. Consequently, the LTC/PIH framework cannot encompass the concept of over-indebtedness and unsustainability of household consumption decisions. First, growth of indebtedness is interpreted as the prediction of future income rises (Bertola *et al.*, 2006, p. 33). Second, borrowing is seen as a rational response to changing income expectations and is assumed to generate a future flow of funds matching any amount of debt. Hence in theory no household should experience problems with loan repayment; no debt can be excessive. Default is only possible in case of external, unexpected shocks to income. Clearly, LTC/PIH is not suitable for the analysis of wealth distribution since the onset of financial sector transformation in the 1980s and within the context of the 2007 crisis.

Furthermore, LTC/PIH models do not explicitly take into account the heterogeneity of asset and liabilities in household portfolios along the distribution. The 'blame' of wealth inequalities is instead put on households, who exploit information advantages and are 'impatient' in their consumption by requesting credit in excess of their repayment capacities. This argument is devoid of understanding of the institutional changes in financial markets outlined at the beginning of this chapter and ignores the massive expansion in credit supply via predatory lending practices induced by high demand for securitized assets among financial investors.

The alternative Post Keynesian theories of consumer choice are based on radically different assumptions about consumer behaviour than LTC/PIH models, allowing for more realistic understanding of wealth distribution mechanisms in financialized economies. These have foundations in the work of Robinson, Pasinetti, Nell, Arestis and Eichner (Lavoie, 2014, pp. 95–96). Most importantly, the conventional assumptions of substitutability, transitivity and non-satiation are rejected in favour of social dependence, hierarchical ordering and satiability of consumption choices.

The first assumption referring to social dependence of consumption rejects the standard neoclassical notion that consumer preferences are transitive and respond in a predictable manner to price changes. Rather, preferences are socially shaped, which renders consumer choices inconsistent and unpredictable (Nell, 1992, p. 396). This idea draws from the relative income hypothesis (RIH), which emphasizes the importance of socio-institutional context in influencing household consumption behaviour (Veblen, 1899; Duesenberry, 1949).

The second assumption of Post Keynesian consumption theory concerns the separation and subordination of consumption choices. Since certain goods are observed to be more desirable than others, households order their consumption needs in a hierarchical way, which leads them not to consume a particular good after a certain threshold level of consumption has been reached (Robinson, 1956, pp. 251, 354; Pasinetti, 1981, p. 73). Thus, traditional substitution effects resulting from price changes are rendered invalid. Instead, it is argued that income effects are more powerful, inducing households to spend even more in times of perceived income increases (Eichner, 1986, p. 159; Arestis, 1992, p. 124). This further implies that consumption needs can be satiated so that once satisfied, they expand to incorporate new goods. Constant growth in consumption needs induced by rising social norms in consumption makes it impossible to capture household utility in a single measure, undermining utility maximization as the main motive of household portfolio decisions (Lavoie, 2014, pp. 98–99).

Thanks to these assumptions, Post Keynesian outlook on rising household debt is characterized by a drastically different interpretation of its nature and consequences. It provides a theoretical justification for growing wealth inequality since the 1980s in the institutional context of stagnant wages, privatization of social services and securitization, all of which forced households from middle and low wealth percentiles into excessive indebtedness.

In sum, the above review of theoretical literature highlights two points. First, it is crucial to explicitly model household portfolio structures in order to analyse the mechanisms of wealth distribution in high-income economies. Second, since LTC/PIH analyses encompass neither the institutional context of household portfolio decisions nor the unsustainability of excessive indebtedness, Post Keynesian consumption theory is more suitable to study wealth distribution in the age of financial sector transformation. However, its tenets have not been modelled in a coherent formal manner. Selected aspects, e.g. relative consumption, have been included in stock flow consistent models (SFCM) incorporating distributional concerns to study the impact of falling labour share of income on macroeconomic growth and stability (Setterfield and Kim, 2013; Caverzasi and Godin, 2015; Dafermos and Papatheodorou, 2015; Sawyer and Veronese Passarella, 2015). These constitute important attempts at including more complex behaviour into macroeconomic models; however, due to their level of aggregation SFCM cannot efficiently account for other determinants of household consumption behaviour identified in the Post Keynesian consumption literature. This is because the macroeconomic character of SFCM imposes a top-down structure of behaviour. While macroeconomic rigour is important, it may not be a suitable starting point for the analysis of inequality based on understanding what determines portfolio decisions of households and hence their balance sheet structures in the times of financialization. Agent-based dynamics (Gaffeo *et al.*, 2007; Delli Gatti *et al.*, 2011) offer an alternative approach informing the impact of household interactions with different social groups, employers and financial sector on distribution. These interactions result in emerging properties of the system influencing inequality determination, which are otherwise obscured in the aggregated macroeconomic approach. Hence, combination of SFCM and agent-based behaviour offers a richer analysis of the determinants of household balance sheet structures and hence inequality by endogenously modelling household portfolio decisions within the bounds of macroeconomic structures. It would allow for social and institutional context to influence how households decide on financing their expenditure. Importantly, combination of the macroeconomic SFCM framework alleviates problems of agent-based modelling (ABM) such as methodological individualism. A further issue with ABM is that due to the decentralized nature of the modelled systems, there is no analytical definition of the relationship between the micro- and macro-level of analysis (Carvalho and Di Guilmi, 2013, p. 3). Consequently, no precise causality between the two can be defined. Thus, the proposed integration of ABM into SFCM carries the advantage that macrostructures are clearly defined (Caiani *et al.*, 2016).

One may be tempted to ask whether such formal modelling of household behaviour is necessary, given its extreme complexity and dependency on socio-institutional factors. The author believes that a formal mathematical model of household behaviour and inequality in times of financial sector transformation is needed as an alternative to neoclassical models of household portfolio choices, which provide incorrect understanding of household financing decisions and are not capable of explaining inequality trends since the 1980s. It is important to provide a more accurate description of what determines household balance sheet structures along the distribution in order to understand the dramatic polarization of income and wealth in recent decades and formulate adequate policy solutions to achieve more equitable societies.

Conclusion

This chapter argues for a new theory of inequality in financialized economies. It shows how changes in the operation of the financial sector and its relation with the real economy since the 1980s influenced the distribution of income in favour of the rich. Wealth emerges as an important aspect driving overall inequality. The present theories of distribution were shown not to account sufficiently for differences in net wealth and balance sheet structures. However, the existing theories of household portfolio decisions are not helpful in understanding what drives households' financing choices because they ignore the socio-institutional conditions of household behaviour. Future research should focus on developing an alternative approach, based on Post Keynesian consumption theory, linking stock flow consistent modelling and agent-based dynamics, allowing for more complex modelling of household balance sheet decisions and their interactions with the macroeconomic environment. Although not without limits, such theory would contribute to a better understanding of the determinants of inequality in times of financialization.

References

Alvaredo, F., Atkinson, A. B., Piketty, T. and Saez, E., n.d. *The World Top Incomes Database.* [Online] Available at: http://topincomes.g-mond.parisschoolofeconomics.eu [Accessed 3 November 2016].

AMECO Database, 2016. *European Commission, Economic and Financial Affairs.* [Online] Available at: http://ec.europa.eu/economy_finance/ameco/user/serie/SelectSerie.cfm [Accessed 26 October 2016].

Arestis, P., 1992. *The Post-Keynesian Approach to Economics.* Aldershot: Edward Elgar Publishing.

Bertola, G., Disney, R. and Grant, C., 2006. The Economics of Consumer Credit Demand and Supply. In: G. Bertola, R. Disney and C. Grant, eds. *The Economics of Consumer Credit.* Cambridge, MA: The MIT Press.

Bhaduri, A. and Marglin, S., 1990. Unemployment and the Real Wage: The Economic Basis for Contesting Political Ideologies. *Cambridge Journal of Economics*, Issue 14, pp. 375–393.

Bivens, J., Gould, E., Mishel, L. and Shierholz, H., 2014. *Raising America's Pay: Why It's Our Central Economic Policy Challenge*. Washington: Economics Policy Institute Briefing Paper No. 378.

Caiani, A., Godin, A., Caverzasi, E. *et al.*, 2016. Agent Based-Stack Flow Consistent Macroeconomics: Towards a Benchmark Model. *Journal of Economic Dynamics and Control*, 69(August), pp. 375–408.

Carroll, C. D., 1997. Buffer-Stock Saving and the Life Cycle/Permanent Income Hypothesis. *Quarterly Journal of Economics*, 112(1), pp. 1–55.

Carvalho, L. and Di Guilmi, C., 2013. Macroeconomic Instability and Microeconomic Financial Fragility: A Stock-Flow Consistent Approach with Heterogeneous Agents. *Working Paper.*

Caverzasi, E. and Godin, A., 2015. Financialization and the Sub-Prime Crisis: A Stock-Flow Consistent Model. *European Journal of Economics and Economic Policies: Intervention*, 12(1), pp. 73–92.

Dafermos, Y. and Papatheodorou, C., 2015. Linking Functional with Personal Income Distribution: A Stock-Flow Consistent Approach. *International Review of Applied Economics*, 29(6), pp. 1–29.

Deaton, A., 1986. *Life-Cycle Models of Consumption: Is the Evidence Consistent with the Theory*. Cambridge, MA: NBER Working Paper No. 1910.

Delli Gatti, D., Desiderio, S., Gaffeo, E. *et al.*, 2011. *Macroeconomics from the Bottom-up*. Milan: Springer.

Duesenberry, J. S., 1949. *Income, Saving and the Theory of Consumption Behaviour*. Cambridge, MA: Harvard University Press.

Dufour, M. and Orhangazi, O., 2016. Growth and Distribution After the 2007–2008 US Financial Crisis: Who Shouldered the Burden of the Crisis? *Review of Keynesian Economics*, 4(2), pp. 151–174.

Dymski, G., 2009. Racial Exclusion and the Political Economy of the Subprime Crisis. *Historical Materialism*, Issue 17, pp. 149–179.

Dymski, G., Hernandez, J. and Mohanty, L., 2013. Race, Gender, Power and the US Subprime Mortgage and Foreclosure Crisis: A Meso Analysis. *Feminist Economics*, 112(2), pp. 124–151.

Dynan, K. E., Skinner, J. and Zeldes, S. P., 2004. Do the Rich Save More? *Journal of Political Economy*, 112(2), pp. 397–444.

Eichner, A. S., 1986. *Toward a New Economics: Essays in Post-Keynesian and Institutionalist Theory*. London: Macmillan.

Foster, J. B. and Holleman, H., 2010. The Financial Power Elite. *The Monthly Review*, 62(1).

Fredriksen, K. B., 2012. *Less Income Inequality and More Growth: Are They Compatible? Part 6. The Distribution of Wealth*, s.l.: OECD Economics Department Working Papers No. 929.

Friedman, M., 1957. *A Theory of the Consumption Function*. Princeton, NJ: Princeton University Press.

Gaffeo, E., Catalano, M., Clementi, F. *et al.*, 2007. Reflections on Modern Macroeconomics: Can We Travel Along a Safer Road? *Physica*, A(382), pp. 89–97.

Goda, T. and Lysandrou, P., 2011. *The Contribution of Wealth Concentration to the Subprime Crisis: A Quantitative Estimation*, s.l.: CIBS Working Paper No. 22.

Gravelle, H. and Reese, R., 2012. *Microeconomics*. 3rd Edition. Essex: Pearson Education Limited.

Gurrieri, V. and Lorenzoni, G., 2011. *Credit Crises, Precautionary Savings, and the Liquidity Trap*. Cambridge, MA: NBER Working Paper No. 17583.

Hein, E., 2015. Finance-Dominated Capitalism and Re-Distribution of Income: A Kaleckian Perspective. *Cambridge Journal of Economics*, 39(3), pp. 907–934.

Hein, E. and Van Treeck, T., 2010. Financialisation and Rising Shareholders Power in Kaleckian/Post-Kaleckian Models of Distribution and Growth. *Review of Political Economy*, 22(2), pp. 205–233.

Kalecki, M., 1971. *Selected Essays on the Dynamics of the Capitalist Economy*. Cambridge: Cambridge University Press.

Kaplan, S. N. and Rauh, J., 2010. Wall Street and Main Street: What Contributes to the Rise in the Highest Incomes? *The Review of Financial Studies*, 23(3), pp. 1004–1050.

Lavoie, M., 2014. *Post-Keynesian Economics: New Foundations*. Cheltenham: Edward Elgar Publishing.

Mian, A. and Sufi, A., 2013. *House of Debt*. Chicago: University of Chicago Press.

Modigliani, F. and Brumberg, R., 1954. Utility Analysis and the Consumption Function: An Interpretation of Cross-Section Data. In: K. Kurihara, ed. *Post Keynesian Economics*. New Brunswick: Rutgers University Press.

Nell, E. J., 1992. Demand, Pricing and Investment. In: E. J. Nell, ed. *Transformational Growth and Effective Demand: Economics After the Capital Critique*. London: Macmillan.

Onaran, O., Stackhammer, E. and Grafl, L., 2011. Financialisation, Income Distribution and Aggregate Demand in the USA. *Cambridge Journal of Economics*, Issue 35, pp. 637–661.

Palley, T., 2012. Wealth and Wealth Distribution in the Neo-Kaleckian Growth Model. *Journal of Post Keynesian Economics*, 34(3), pp. 453–474.

Pasinetti, L. L., 1981. *Structural Change and Economic Growth*. Cambridge: Cambridge University Press.

Piketty, T., 2014. *Capital in the Twenty-First Century*. Cambridge, MA: Harvard University Press.

Pressman, S., 2016. *Understanding Piketty's Capital in the Twenty-First Century*. Abingdon: Routledge.

Robinson, J., 1956. *The Accumulation of Capital*. London: Macmillan.

Sawyer, M., 2013. What is Financialisation? *International Journal of Political Economy*, 42(4), pp. 5–18.

Sawyer, M. and Veronese Passarella, M., 2015. The Monetary Circuit in the Age of Financialisation. Metroeconomica.

Setterfield, M. and Kim, Y. K., 2013. *Debt Servicing, Aggregate Consumption, and Growth*. Hartford, CT: Trinity College Department of Economics Working Paper 13–16.

Van Treeck, T., 2009. A Synthetic Stock-Flow Consistent Macroeconomic Model of Financialisation. *Cambridge Journal of Economics*, Issue 33, pp. 467–493.

Veblen, T., 1899. *The Theory of the Leisure Class*. New York: Macmillan.

Wolff, E. N., 2014. Household Wealth Trends in the United States, 1983–2010. *Oxford Review of Economic Policy*, 30(1), pp. 21–43.

Young, B., 2010. The Gendered Dimension of Money, Finance and the Subprime Crisis. In: C. Bauhardt and G. Caglar, eds. *Feministische Kritik der Politischen Oekonomie*. Wiesbaden: VS Verlag für Sozialwissenschaften.

10 Financialization and household debt in Poland

Agata Gemzik-Salwach

Introduction

Financialization means the growing role of financial markets and institutions in the economy (Epstein, 2005, p. 3). As a result of this process, the financial markets determine the behaviours of all subjects, including households, and affect numerous socio-economic categories and shape many areas of life, not always in a positive way (Dembiński and Beretta, 2014). Financialization causes a rapid increase in the number of financial institutions offering loans, while easily accessible money encourages households to borrow more, often beyond measure. As a result, households have problems with repayment of liabilities, which translates into a threat to the security of the entire financial system.

In order to increase the security of banks, as institutions of public trust, banking supervising regulators have introduced a whole new set of prudential regulations (Tonveronachi, 2016). On the one hand, the new prudential regulations support security of banks and stability of the entire financial system, and on the other hand, due to the fact that they impose restrictive prudential regulations, they hinder functioning of banks and inhibit the growth of banking. Strict prudential standards mean increased requirements towards customers and make it impossible for banks to give loans to some of their current customers, even though their financial situation has not changed. In the face of non-decreasing needs to use loan instruments by households there are grounds for believing that this activity moved to another sector of the market, namely to the sector of non-bank lending institutions.

The aim of this chapter is to show the relation between the new prudential regulations introduced in the banking sector and the level of household debt in the banking and non-bank lending institutions' sector in Poland. In this chapter a research hypothesis states: 'the emergence of new prudential regulations in the banking sector limited the access of some households to credits and loans taken in banks and therefore a transfer of these customers to the non-bank lending institutions sector followed'. With regard to such a hypothesis there were two adopted research problems:

Q1: What is the relation between the new prudential regulations introduced in the banking sector and the indebtedness of households in the banking sector in Poland?

Q2: What is the relation between the new prudential regulations introduced in the banking sector and the indebtedness of households in the non-bank lending institutions sector in Poland?

These issues are of fundamental importance in the context of answering the question about the true consequences of the introduction of new prudential regulations. Answers to these questions will help to show the impact of financialization on this very important aspect of functioning of the household market segment.

The adopted aim of the study, research problems and the hypothesis conditioned the structure of the elaboration. In the first part of the work a survey of empirical research already carried out on the undertaken subject was conducted, then the new prudential regulations, set by the banking supervisory authorities since 2010 in Poland, were selected. These regulations were analysed in the aspect of their importance to the debt structure of households. The succeeding part of the study was devoted to the description of changes that occurred over time in the level of indebtedness of households in banking and non-bank lending institutions sectors and their interconnections, with particular regard to the moments of introduction of new legal regulations.

Comparing the banking market with the market of loan institutions one should be aware of emerging information limitations and existing differences in business models. First of all, data concerning banks as entities regulated in detail are regularly publicized and monitored. In statistics of the banking sector one can find, among other things, detailed information on the state of indebtedness of households by virtue of consumer loans at the end of each month (PwC, 2013, p. 11). Quite different is the situation in the sector of non-bank lending institutions. Due to the fact that non-bank lending institutions are included in the shadow banking sector and identified with activities of the grey area in the financial market, many difficulties associated with access to the figures, lack of official statistics relating to shadow banks, etc. were encountered when writing this work.

The only part of institutions operating in the market of non-bank loans are members of professional organizations, and others operate only in the local market and do not participate in such initiatives. All this makes it impossible to create a full picture of activities of these institutions in the market. The obtained financial data concerning the non-banking sector are characterized by high incomparability with other data describing the banking sector or market conditions that occurred during a relevant period of time. Therefore, it was decided to analyse only some of the data obtained, and the time series subjected to tests were relatively short. Nevertheless, taking into account topicality of the subject, its importance and its economic, social and political dimensions a decision was taken to make an attempt to analyse this phenomenon.

Research on the impact of the new financial regulation on the banking and non-banking sector

Empirical research devoted to the analysis of the impact of the financial crisis and new financial regulations, that were introduced subsequently, on the level of indebtedness in banking and non-banking sectors is not particularly popular. Restrictions on access to credible data usually is an obstacle. Nevertheless, due to the importance of this subject, more and more attention is paid to these issues.

The undertaken research attempts can be divided into three groups – the studies on the impact of new regulations on the banking sector, the studies on the impact of new regulations on the non-bank lending institutions sector and the studies on the impact of new regulations on the sector of shadow banks, understood in various ways in different countries. In a narrow sense, this sector is identified with non-bank lending institutions and it means lending activity involving entities and activities carried out in full or in part outside the regulated banking system (Patterson, 2012; FSB, 2013). In a broader sense, it means a group of institutions operating in the financial markets and not subject to the state regulations and/or financial supervision (Srokosz, 2011; EC, 2012; Masiukiewicz 2012b). It, therefore, can be assumed with high probability that the studies on the impact of financial regulations on the shadow banking sector will refer both to non-bank lending institutions and to other financial institutions, such as, for example, money market funds and investment funds, special purpose vehicles (SPV), insurance and reinsurance institutions, and the like.

The impact of regulation on the stability of the banking sector was the subject of research conducted by Khan and Dewan (2013). Based on the analysis of data from 78 countries they concluded that it is the banking supervision that is a frequent cause of instability of the banking sector. The opposite conclusions were reached by Erdinç (2010) after analysing the situation in the Bulgarian banking system. He pointed to the stabilizing role of banking supervision thanks to which there was limited excessive credit expansion of banks in the period before the financial crisis. In Poland the impact of regulation of the banking sector on the changes occurring in it and on economic growth of the country was the subject of the work of Marcinkowska *et al.* (2014). The studies showed that stricter capital and liquidity requirements for banks have an impact on reduction of the scale of loan financing. Reduction of bank loan supply in Poland as a consequence of the financial crisis and its regulation is also indicated by the work of Łyziak *et al.* (2011).

The report concerning the changes taking place in the shadow banking sector in the world in 2009–2011 was prepared by the Financial Stability Board (FSB) (2012). The report implied that in this period the activity of the shadow banking sector constituted about 25 per cent of activities of all financial intermediation services, and the total size of the shadow banking sector was equal to half of the banking sector assets. Lysandrou and Nesvetailova (2013) showed the impact of the shadow banking sector on the financial crisis. They focused not so much on the activities of loan institutions but on the activities of such institutions of the shadow banking sector as hedge funds, investment funds and insurance institutions. The conclusion drawn from the conducted research is a statement that harder regulation of the shadow banking sector, per se, will not provide protection against further financial crises. The authors recommend here conducting a broader policy aimed at reducing the pressure on the banking system which led to the emergence of toxic assets in the previous crisis.

The non-bank lending sector, due to the lack of banking supervision, lacks transparency, and, as Farvaque *et al.* (2012) showed, it is the transparency that is the basis of efficiency in the banking sector. Financial exclusion as a derivative of globalization and the financial crisis was the subject of the analysis in the work of Dymski (2005). He showed that the strategic decisions of banks led to financial exclusion in various areas of financial markets. Similar correlation between financial exclusion and financial regulations introduced in Great Britain has been shown in research conducted by Chambers (2010).

In the Polish market the analyses of the impact of financial regulations on the market of non-bank lending institutions and the shadow banking sector were carried out by Masiukiewicz (2012a, 2012b). The aim of these studies was to determine the areas of competition and risk of non-bank lending institutions and their regulation in Poland. As a result, it was found that bankruptcies of non-bank lending institutions may be a factor of acceleration of the financial crisis and destabilization of financial security, hence the need for monitoring and supervision of their functioning.

There is also a number of publications associating the phenomenon of financial exclusion with the development of the sector of non-bank lending institutions. Buckland (2012) in his work shows that the fact of not using banking financial services is often a consequence of using the services of non-bank institutions.

Evolution of supervision over banks and non-bank lending institutions in Poland – selected aspects

The shape of the banking and non-bank lending institutions sectors in Poland is largely determined by prudential regulations introduced into this market (Marcinkowska *et al.*, 2014). The emerging new regulations directly influence the development of the banking sector which is required to comply with them.[1] Non-bank institutions are not subject to strict financial supervision and the new regulations are not mandatory for non-bank loan institutions, but they also affect their functioning. The created regulations seem to be beneficial for non-bank lending institutions which, through them, can capture a part of customers from banks.

The functioning of the sector of short-term loans and consumer loans is affected not only by the legal acts in force, but also recommendations of the Polish Financial Supervision Authority (PFSA) which are not binding. In the period from 1997 to 2014 in Poland a total of 18 recommendations were issued (from A to U), and in many of them significant modifications were made. They concern mainly the management of various types of risk in the bank. The juxtaposition of these regulations, which most strongly affected the market of consumer loans and shadow bank loans, is presented in Table 10.1.

Recommendation T was introduced on 23 February 2010 by the PFSA. A part of the guidelines had been in force since 23 August 2010 and a part since 23 December 2010. Recommendation T was passed in connection with the loosening of credit policy by banks in times of prosperity (increase of LtV, long periods of credit, easing the requirements in examination of creditworthiness). The loosening of credit policy was dictated by positive forecasts of the economic situation and Recommendation T was to lead to the re-tightening of credit granting criteria and to introduce the internal discipline (PwC, 2011, p. 25).

In its main assumptions Recommendation T was to create a mechanism that would make banks more closely look at the financial situation of their future borrower in order not to grant a loan whose instalment would be so high that it could prevent the borrower from repaying their obligations and simultaneous normal functioning in everyday life (PFSA, 2010). The aim of the recommendation was also ordering the principles of granting credits by banks, namely ensuring the correct measurement of credit risk and improving the methodology and organization of risk management.[2] The recommendation was also to eliminate situations where banks compete with one another in the level of security. At the same time Recommendation T complicated lending procedures by imposing the obligation to formally document the customer's income, for example, by a certificate of employment and earnings. Although Recommendation T did not constitute a binding law, it was so perceived by the PFSA, and banks' compliance with it was inspected during numerous periodical inspections (PwC, 2011, p. 25).

The changes initiated by the introduction of Recommendation T were strengthened by enactment of the Consumer Credit Act which was in force from 12 May 2011. This Act introduced various standards for banks and non-banking institutions in allowing credits and customer loans. On non-bank lending institutions, unlike banks, the obligation was not imposed to make the decision to grant a loan to the customer dependent on their level of credit risk.

All of these recommendations were somewhat mitigated by the introduction of the Resolution of PFSA of 2013 on issuing Recommendation T concerning good practices in management of risk of retail credit exposures which made the hitherto existing solutions more flexible and simplified the approach to risk management in some areas (PFSA, 2013b). The introduced changes

Table 10.1 Selected financial regulations and their impact on the development of the banking and non-bank lending institutions sectors, 2010–2013

Name of regulation	*Month and year of introduction*	*Descriptions of main changes*	*Impact on the level of indebtedness of households in the sectors:*	
			banking	*non-bank lending institutions*
Recommendation T	February 2010	Limit indicator for DTI (DTI – debt to income): established level of 50% retail customers whose income does not exceed the average level in economy and the 65% level for other debtors.	Negative stimulation	Positive stimulation
Consumer Credit Act	May 2011	Introduced various standards in granting consumer credits and loans for banks and non-bank lending institutions. In accordance with this act the non-bank institutions do not have the obligation to condition the decision on granting a loan to the customer on the level of the customer's credit risk.	Negative stimulation	Positive stimulation
Amendment of Recommendation T	February 2013	Previously introduced solutions made more flexible. Softened the approach to management of risk of retail credit exposures.	Positive stimulation	Negative stimulation

Source: Author's description

concerned standards of management of risk resulting from retail loans. At that time the regulatory limit of DTI was abolished, assuming that the maximum DTI for retail loans can be established individually by banks (NBP, 2014). Under the new recommendation a bank could assess the creditworthiness of the retail customer based on a scoring model and the customer's statement about the amount of their incomes and expenditures. Unlike the previous version of this recommendation, its amendment excluded from the object scope the credit exposures secured by mortgages and loans for purchase of securities, while the subject scope of the recommendation was extended to branches of credit institutions.

The most important changes arising from the discussed resolution include enabling the employment of simplified rules of creditworthiness rating, mainly for loans involving small amounts and short repayment terms. The possibility for the banks to apply simplified rules was introduced, for examining creditworthiness of customers in the case of loans for low amounts, i.e. loans whose values do not exceed singleness, and in the case of instalment loans quadruplicity of the average monthly salary in the business sector. With regard to customers maintaining a relationship with the bank for at least 6 and 12 months, the rules were simplified for examining creditworthiness when granting loans whose values do not exceed the amount 6 and 12 times higher than this salary respectively.

The relations between the new prudential regulations introduced in the banking sector and the indebtedness of households

There is a research hypothesis, that following the introduction of new prudential regulations, there has been an outflow from the banking sector to the non-banking sector of households in debt. In order to verify this hypothesis, a comparison about shaping the volume and rate of growth of loans in the two sectors (in the years 2008–2014) has been conducted. The market of non-bank short-term loans was compared with the market of bank consumer credits. In the category of consumer credit there were included various types of loans offered by banks to households, such as bank dues by virtue of credit cards, instalment loans for cars, other instalment loans and other consumer loans. In the research process, data concerning the sector of loan institutions was used, that was made available by the Confederation of Financial Enterprises in Poland – the Association of Employers (KPF) and data describing the banking sector published by the Polish Financial Supervision Authority (PFSA) and the National Bank of Poland (NBP).

Over the years one can observe diverse development of demand for funds coming from banks and non-bank lending institutions. In 2008–2009 there were already visible structural changes in the sources of financing consumption. The global financial crisis had taken place in 2008. It originated from the banking sector and had a particular effect on it. After this crisis in 2008–2009 the rate of growth of consumer loans granted by banks considerably reduced. This was a

Table 10.2 Characteristics of the market consumer credits in Poland, 2009–2014

	Consumer credits (banking sector with foreign branches)	*Consumer credits with stated loss of value*	*Consumer credits change m/m (in billions of PLN)*	*Consumer credits rate of growth y/y*	*Index of threatened credits for consumer credits*
31.12.2009	132 171 213 008	17 239 525 565	0.5	12.85%	13.04%
30.06.2010	134 151 126 516	21 260 767 442	−0.16	6.16%	15.85%
31.12.2010	134 057 206 724	23 164 761 187	−0.62	0.98%	17.28%
30.06.2011	129 766 655 435	23 193 318 115	−0.87	−2.52%	17.87%
31.12.2011	130 336 067 990	23 407 876 552	−1.26	−3.25%	17.96%
30.06.2012	126 215 165 409	22 484 232 698	−0.6	−3.1%	17.81%
31.12.2012	130 336 067 990	21 278 326 865	−1.2	−4.1%	17.24%
30.06.2013	122 089 708 367	19 615 772 682	−0.8	−2.9%	16.07%
31.12.2013	126 296 951 939	18 478 855 776	0.2	2.4%	14.63%
30.06.2014	128 496 182 933	18 127 844 795	0.6	5.5%	14.11%

Source: Author's calculations based on NBP and PFSA

result of self-regulatory activities of banks which reduced the supply of loans. At that time, in many banks, due to deterioration of the quality of consumer loans, it was necessary to create high write-downs. In 2008 the value of write-downs made in respect of consumer loans amounted to 3 billion zloty, and in 2009–2010 about 7 billion zloty (PFSA, 2013a). In 2011–2012 the decline in the value of consumer loans still resulted from the sale of a portion of the loan portfolio, the so-called 'clearing balance sheet' from the assets of poor quality and limitation of lending activities by a group of banks which in previous years suffered heavy losses in this segment.

The decreasing trend of issued consumer loans decreased further, strengthened by the introduction of Recommendation T and followed by the Consumer Credit Act, and it sustained until December 2012. The introduction of the Amendment to Recommendation T eased the previously introduced regulations and favoured the reversal of the downward trend. The data characterizing the volume of granted consumer loans are collected in Table 10.2 and presented in Figure 10.1.

At the time when the sector of bank consumer credits experienced the decline in the rate of growth, a strong increase occurred in competition from non-bank lending institutions. Since 2008 a dynamic growth in the value of loans provided by loan institutions could be observed on the market, strongly amplified since the introduction of Recommendation T. It should also be emphasized that the vast majority of loan institutions at that time already had advanced technologies for handling loan applications, therefore the time to launch such a loan was in most cases shorter than in banks. The selected data characterizing the development of the sector of loan institutions in Poland are gathered in Table 10.3, and the development of the value of granted loans and the portfolio of short-term loans is presented in Figure 10.2.

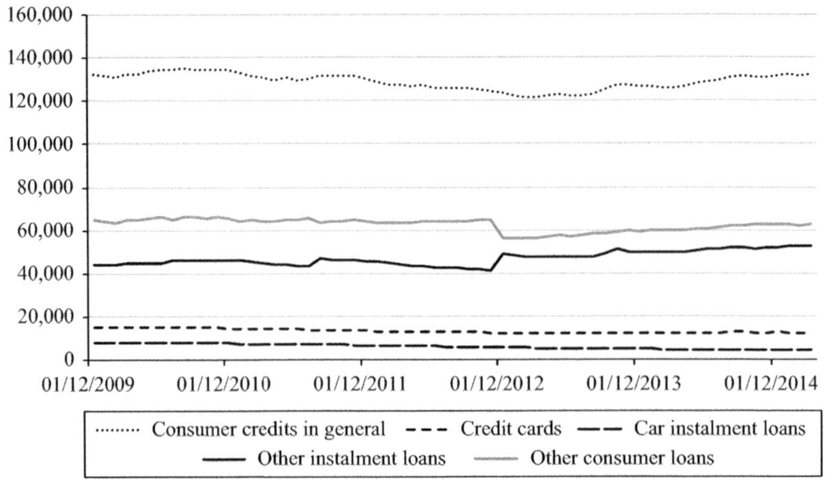

Figure 10.1 The value of granted consumer credits (including credit cards, car instalment loans, other instalment loans, other consumer loans), 2009–2015, in millions of PLN

Source: Author's calculations based on PFSA

It is worth noting that the dynamic development of the sector of non-bank lending institutions in the Polish economy is not necessarily perceived as a positive phenomenon. Non-bank lending institutions operating in Poland do not have a good reputation, they cause a lot of extreme emotions and due to numerous financial scandals with their participation they are identified with institutions preying on the poorest group of people and making use of the ignorance and difficult financial situation of their customers. Their customers are mostly people who would not get a credit in a banking institution because of their low level of income.

In this context, it can be stated that non-bank lending institutions perform an important function in the economy as financing providers in situations when banks do not provide and thereby reduce financial exclusion, understood as limited access to financial instruments of a particular social group (Leyshon and Thrift, 1995; EC, 2008; The World Bank, 2009). Financial exclusion is understood as difficulties experienced by people with low incomes and being in an adverse financial situation in the use of, among other things, a loan with an affordable interest rate (Anderloni and Carluccio, 2007). However, one should be aware of the fact that although access to capital is easier for the customer in shadow banks, it also involves more risk. Terms of granting loans or credits by financial institutions always depend on the level of credit risk related to the recipient (Stiglitz and Greenwald, 2003, p. 30), therefore in this case the cost of such a loan will be much higher. Thus, it increases the danger

Table 10.3 Characteristics of the market of non-bank short-term loans in Poland, 2008–2013

	Value of loans granted in half-year/year in total (in millions of PLN)	*Value of loans granted in half-year/year by members of KPF (in millions of PLN)*	*Value of portfolio of loans in total (in millions of PLN, status on the end of half-year/year)*	*Value of portfolio of loans of members of KPF (in millions of PLN, status on the end of half-year/year)*	*Number of served customers in total (in thousands, status on the end of half-year/year)*	*Number of customers served by members of KPF (in thousands, status on the end of half-year/year)*	*Number of loans granted in half-year/year by Members of KPF (in thousands of pc.)*
30.06.08	794	82	1366	337	951	73.7	46.4
31.12.08	1902	190	1501	404	958	101.5	109.7
30.06.09	739	91	1586	456	888	123	61.7
31.12.09	1792	196	1512	520	903	145.3	134.5
30.06.10	813	124	1707	577	927	165	88.7
31.12.10	2036	286	1657	642	998	216.2	218.6
30.06.11	876	180	1781	720	1081	275.4	176.2
31.12.11	2106	427	2105	858	1252	418.3	410.4
30.06.12	1105	299	2211	1008	1326	478.9	273.6
31.12.12	2284	647	2391	1210	1377	555.9	569.2
30.06.13	1270	369	2747	1369	1258	433.1	328.7
31.12.13	2729	833	3056	1648	1371	530.1	663.9

Source: Author's calculations based on KPF

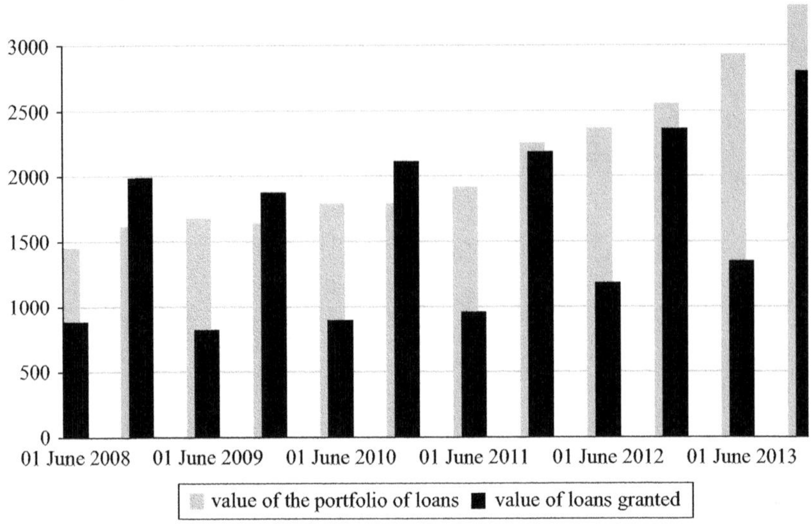

Figure 10.2 The value of loans granted and the value of the portfolio of loans in the sector of loan companies, 2008–2013, in millions of PLN

Source: Author's calculations based on KPF

of falling of a given household into a spiral of debt and raises a question about whether the customers who receive loans through non-bank lending institutions should actually receive them (Marcinkowska, 2013).

As can be seen from earlier analyses, the volumes of non-bank loans and consumer credits granted to households are closely connected with the introduced regulations in the financial market. Changes over time of the rate of growth of these categories and the moments of introduction of significant regulations in this area are shown in Figure 10.3.

Analysing the chart above, a fall can be seen in the rate of growth of consumer loans lasting from June 2009 to December 2012 and the dynamic development of the market of non-bank loans throughout the entire period analysed. The first distinct moment of acceleration of the rate of growth of this market came after the introduction of Recommendation T. On this basis it can be assumed that the recommendation contributed to a slowdown in the development of the market of consumer credits and to the increase in competitiveness of the non-bank lending institutions sector to which these regulations did not apply. Taking into account the narrow subject scope of Recommendation T and the minuteness of detail of its provisions one can state that it contributed to unfair competition between the banking and non-banking sectors, obviously in favour of the latter. Moreover, the introduction of this recommendation, through the fact that it forced banks to change procedures, credit agreements and internal policies, also contributed to the

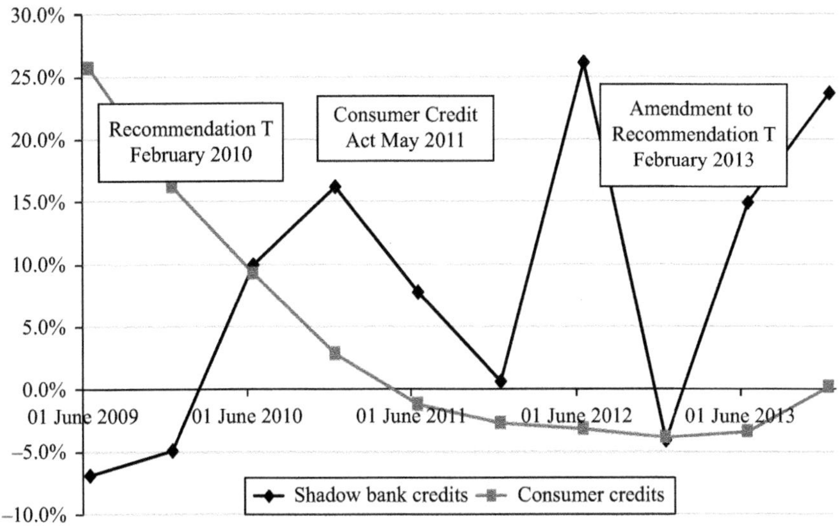

Figure 10.3 The rate of growth of consumer credits and loans issued by non-bank lending institutions, 2009–2013

Source: Author's calculations based on KPF and NBP

increase in costs in the banking sector. At that time an outflow of customers from the banking sector to the sector of non-bank lending institutions occurred.

Another important regulation stimulating the development of the market of banks and non-bank lending institutions is the Consumer Credit Act. After its introduction, part of banks or their parent entities, observing the phenomena occurring in the market, decided to run non-bank lending activity within the same capital group. The aim was to avoid the need to comply with regulatory requirements. The analyses of the PFSA show that as a result of this process the state of credits decreased by 4.7 billion zloty in 2011 and by 5.3 billion zloty in 2012. Such activities were negatively assessed by banking supervision authorities in Poland which pointed to the increase in the risk of compliance and reputation of banks or their capital groups due to transfer of credit risk to other places, reduction of transparency of activities, as well as the negative competitive pressure (PFSA, 2013a, p. 7). However, looking at this phenomenon from the households' point of view, it can be recognized as neutral, as only the sales channel was changed, through which the funds were supplied.

The revival of consumer credit took place with the advent of the Recommendation T amendment in 2013. In the first half of 2014 the data available through the Credit Information Bureau (BIK) pointed to the record level of sales of consumer loans. Another increase in the banking credit action

Table 10.4 Correlation coefficients between the growth rate of consumer loans and the rate of increase in the value of loans, the loans granted by members of the KFP and the total value of the portfolio of loans

	Rate of growth of value of consumer credits	*Statistical significance*
Rate of growth of loans granted	−0.53	0.112
Rate of value of loans granted by members of KPF	−0.74	0.014
Value of portfolio of loans in total (in millions of PLN)	−0.43	0.219

Source: Author's calculations based on KPF and NBP

had taken place, as well as the 'return of banks to the market' which, due to previous regulatory solutions, had transferred lending to other entities. In addition, some banks made modifications in the strategy of activities towards a greater share of short-term loans for retail customers.

The rate of growth of the lending sector did not end with the loosening of the regulations imposed in the form of Recommendation T, which proves the demand for this product. The increase in credit and lending action carried out by the two groups of subjects was also enhanced by the recovery of the economy and reduction of interest rates on loans and bank credits.

The analysis above shows that changes in the demand for capital from these banks and non-bank lending institutions were closely interconnected. The correlation coefficients between different categories depicting the situation in these markets are presented in Table 10.4.

All the presented correlation coefficients take negative value. On this basis it can be stated that the development of the non-bank short-term loans market in Poland was accompanied by a slowdown in the rate of growth of bank consumer credits.

Conclusion

The occurrence of the phenomenon of financialization had a definite influence on the development of the non-bank lending institutions sector in Poland. The conducted analysis confirmed the validity of the adopted hypothesis that the emergence of new prudential regulations in the banking sector limited the access of some households to credits and loans taken in banks and therefore a transfer of those customers to the non-bank lending institutions sector. The obvious purpose of introduction of new regulations was to improve the standards of lending to people by banks. However, excessive tightening of legal regulations and prudential mechanisms in the field of the classical banking sector caused a mass exodus of customers of banks to non-bank lending institutions and the dynamic development of the latter entities which – because of their flexibility and attractiveness – were an alternative and competition to the banking entities.

If the intention of supervisors was to protect low-income consumers against getting indebted to the point where 'the normal functioning' is impossible and against the risk of falling into a spiral of debt, then this attempt should be regarded as completely unsuccessful. As the quoted numbers show, households which failed to get a bank credit turned to non-bank lending institutions, where they received financing in the form of loans. As the loans in non-bank institutions have a much higher interest rate than bank credits and additionally they involve more risk, the risk of such a customer falling into a spiral of debt additionally increased.

The education of the society is of key importance for solving this problem. Selected aspects of personal finance management, including talking about the need to maintain an appropriate balance between the amount of incomes and indebtedness, should be a part of school education from an early age. In the face of overwhelming financialization the understanding of mechanisms of financial instruments offered in markets and the ability to correctly assess and choose them are not to be overestimated.

Notes

1 See: Marszałek and Janc (2016).

2 In a way Recommendation T constituted a supplement of earlier Recommendation S which assumed stricter methods of assessment of creditworthiness of persons applying for granting a foreign currency loan in comparison with credits in zloty. However, Recommendation S did not define maximum level of indebtedness in zloty.

References

Anderloni, L. and Carluccio, E. M., 2007. Access to Bank Account and Payment Services. In: L. Anderloni, M. D. Braga and E. M. Carluccio, eds. *New Frontiers in Banking Services: Emerging Needs and Tailored Products for Untapped Markets*. Berlin: Springer.

Buckland, J., 2012. *Hard Choices: Financial Exclusion, Fringe Banks and Poverty in Urban Canada*. Toronto: University of Toronto Press.

Chambers, C., 2010. *Financial Exclusion and Banking Regulations in the UK: Template Analysis*. Saarbrücken: Lambert Academic Publishing.

Dembiński, P. H. and Beretta, S., 2014. *Kryzys ekonomiczny i kryzys wartości*. Kraków: Wydawnictwo M.

Dymski, G. A., 2005. Financial Globalization, Social Exclusion and Financial Crisis. *International Review of Applied Economics*, 19(4), pp. 439–457.

EC, 2008. *Financial Services Provision and Prevention of Financial Exclusion*. [Online] Available at: http://ec.europa.eu/social/BlobServlet?docId=760&langId=en [Accessed 28 December 2015].

EC, 2012. *Green Paper. Shadow Banking*. [Online] Available at: http://ec.europa.eu/internal_market/bank/docs/shadow/green-paper_en.pdf [Accessed 20 December 2015].

Epstein, G., 2005. *Financialization and the World Economy*. Cheltenham and Northampton: Edward Elgar Publishing.

Erdinç, D., 2010. Does a Credit Boom Increase Bank Fragility? Transitional Challenges in Bulgarian Banking, 1999–2008. *Eastern European Economics*, 48(3), pp. 68–87.

Farvaque, E., Refait-Alexandre, C. and Weill, L., 2012. Are Transparent Banks More Efficient? Evidence from Russia. *Eastern European Economics*, 50(4), pp. 60–77.

FSB, 2012. *Global Shadow Banking Monitoring Report 2012*. [Online] Available at: www.financialstabilityboard.org/publications/r_121118c.pdf [Accessed 20 December 2015].

FSB, 2013. *Strengthening Oversight and Regulation of Shadow Banking – Policy Framework for Strengthening Oversight and Regulation of Shadow Banking Entities.* [Online] Available at: www.fsb.org/wp-content/uploads/r_130829c.pdf?page_moved=1 [Accessed 20 December 2015].

Khan, A. H. and Dewan, H., 2013. Who Should Supervise Banks for the Banking Sector Stability? *Applied Economics Letters*, 20(17), pp. 1531–1537.

Leyshon, A. and Thrift, N., 1995. Geographies of Financial Exclusion: Financial Abandonment in Britain and United States, Transactions of the Institute of British Geographers. *New Series*, Issue 20, pp. 312–341.

Lysandrou, P. and Nesvetailova, A., 2013. *The Shadow Banking System and the Financial Crisis: A Securities Production Function View*. Leeds: FESSUD Working Paper Series No. 5.

Łyziak, T., Przystupa, J., Stanisławska, E. and Wróbel, E., 2011. Monetary Policy Transmission Disturbances During the Financial Crisis. A Case of an Emerging Market Economy. *Eastern European Economics*, 49(5), pp. 75–96.

Marcinkowska, M., 2013. *Kapitał relacyjny banku.* Tom II: Relacje Banku z Kluczowymi Interesariuszami, ed. Łódź: Wydawnictwo Uniwersytetu Łódzkiego.

Marcinkowska, M., Wdowiński, P., Flejterski, S. *et al.*, 2014. *Wpływ regulacji sektora bankowego na wzrost gospodarczy – wnioski dla Polski.* Warszawa: Materiały i Studia 305, NBP.

Marszałek, P. and Janc, A., 2016. Financial Regulation in Poland. In: J. Kregel, R. Tonveronachi and R. Kattel, eds. *Financial Regulation in the European Union.* London and New York: Routledge.

Masiukiewicz, P., 2012a. Instytucjonalny system bezpieczeństwa finansowego w Polsce. In: I. Lichniak, ed. *Kryzys, i co dalej?* Warszawa: OW SGH.

Masiukiewicz, P., 2012b. Regulacje a ryzyko shadow banking w Polsce. *Zarządzanie i Finanse*, 4(2), pp. 5–22.

NBP, 2014. *Rozwój systemu finansowego w Polsce w 2013 r*. Warszawa: Narodowy Bank Polski.

Patterson, R., 2012. *Kompendium terminów z zakresu bankowości po Polsku i Angielsku.* Kraków: Zielona Sowa.

PFSA, 2010. *Rekomendacja T dotycząca dobrych praktyk w zakresie zarządzania ryzykiem detalicznych ekspozycji kredytowych*. Warszawa: KNF.

PFSA, 2013a. *Raport o sytuacji banków w 2012 r*. Warszawa: KNF.

PFSA, 2013b. *Rekomendacja T dotycząca dobrych praktyk w zakresie zarządzania ryzykiem detalicznych ekspozycji kredytowych*. Warszawa: KNF.

PwC, 2011. *Szukając nowych kierunków. Raport o rynku consumer finance w Polsce.* [Online] Available at: www.pwc.pl/pl/publikacje/2011/consumer-finance-2011.html [Accessed 20 December 2015].

PwC, 2013. *Rynek firm pożyczkowych w Polsce.* [Online] Available at: www.pwc.pl/pl/publikacje/assets/pwc_raport_rynek_firm_pozyczkowych.pdf [Accessed 20 December 2015].

Srokosz, W., 2011. *Instytucje parabankowe w Polsce*. Warszawa: WoltersKluwer Polska.

Stiglitz, J. and Greenwald, B., 2003. *Towards a New Paradigm in Monetary Economics*. Cambridge: Cambridge University Press.

The World Bank, 2009. *Banking the Poor*. Washington: The World Bank.

Tonveronachi, M., 2016. Post-Crisis International Regulatory Standards and their Inclusion in the European Framework. In: J. Kregel, M. Tonveronachi and R. Kattel, eds. *Financial Regulation in the European Union*. London and New York: Routledge.

11 Financial exclusion and rationality of financial behaviour in view of financialization

Marta Maciejasz-Świątkiewicz

Introduction

Financialization is the term that describes the increasing role of financial motives, financial markets, financial actors and financial institutions in the operation of the domestic and international economies and is concerned with the increasing domination of capital-oriented financial systems over banked-based financial systems, growing political and economic share of specific social groups such as rentiers, explosion of financial exchange using a multitude of new financial instruments, and patterns of accumulation in which profit making occurs increasingly through financial channels rather than through trade and commodity production (Epstein, 2005). What does this term mean for regular citizens? First of all it means that without finance it is impossible to operate properly. What is more, we have contact with financial activities every day, which occur all around the world, so it is impossible currently to live without contact with finances. People who cannot benefit from financial services market offer might be vulnerable to financial exclusion, the situation in which citizens encounter difficulties accessing and/or using financial products and services in the context of the mainstream market that are appropriate to their needs and allow them to lead a normal financial life in the financial citizenship they belong to (European Commission, 2008). This definition suggests that financial exclusion is a result of external limits which are largely beyond the influence of the person. What is more, considering the financial exclusion as negative (use of the word 'difficulties') suggests that people who are subject to it do not act in a streamlined way in the market and they cannot maximize their benefits. In practice it is easy to notice that some people consciously do not use the financial services offer. They choose a self-exclusion rather than buying financial products or services. The question appears as to whether financial exclusion could be rational? Could someone's behaviour, who consciously decides not to use specific products or financial services, be rational? The answer to this is not explicit because it is the justification of choice which is vital.

The aim of this chapter is description of different financial behaviours in the context of their rationality. According to mainstream economy and finance theories people are rational and behave in a rational way. So it is interesting to see if rationality or its lack can affect the financialization process. The main hypothesis stated at the beginning of this chapter is that lack of perfect rationality is one of the reasons of financial exclusion and has a negative impact on the financialization process.

What is rationality and rational behaviour?

Rationality is a key concept related to individual behaviour in the economic meaning. It means that a person always tends towards maximum fulfilment of their needs. The aim of this action is to maximize the satisfaction, pleasure or other individually sensed experiences possible to achieve under specific circumstances thanks to acting in a particular way. The pleasure experienced subjectively related to specific behaviour, for instance consumption of goods or services, is called utility (Klimczak, 2011). An individual who behaves rationally calculates advantages and disadvantages (loss and gain) coming from specific behaviour and tends to maximize benefits while reducing losses. The rational behaviour is when an individual has their own preferences and is able to indicate their own intentions within particular limits, is able to make comprehensible arrangement of their own intentions in an internally coherent manner and makes internally coherent choices to maximize their own satisfaction. Therefore irrational behaviour displays a lack of comprehensible arrangement and is contradictory to individual business (Kamerschen *et al.*, 1993).

In the theory of economy different types of rationality are described. The description mentioned above applies to a narrow concept of rationality, which was implemented by M. Weber and is specific for conscious targeted action. It reflects relations between means, which were used, and goals and it occurs when the choice of constituents is accurate. There is also the concept of subject rationality which takes place when constituents' choice suits the goal and is adjusted to the present situation. Methodological rationality takes place when the choice of constituents to achieve the goal is a result of the decision maker's knowledge (Kieżel, 2004).

Within the context of achieving rationality there is the theory of bounded usability (rationality) by Herbert Simon. He stated that individuals and organizations do not possess unlimited possibilities to process information which is necessary to achieve full rationality. They are limited by multiple goals within the time limits, lack of complete information about all alternatives and their features or shortage of opportunities to perform all essential calculations and comparisons. It is caused by the fact that a man is a cognitive miser, who tries to think and solve problems in simpler and less effortful ways. In the place of 'homo oeconomicus' H. Simon implements the concept of 'homo satisfaciendus', and instead of the optimization rule he introduces the satisfaction rule, which stems from the fact that possibilities of human thinking are limited. Complexity of surroundings in which human lives causes that people must be satisfied with finding 'good enough' solutions of their problems and 'good enough' manners of working. That means the exploration of the good enough option for the decision maker. He does not examine all options, but stops when he finds one which sufficiently satisfies his requirements (Simon, 1955).

Other theory which negates perfect rationality is the theory of selective rationality of Harvey Leibenstein according to which calculation made by subjects could be of a strict nature (rigorous) or casual (sketchy). In conditions of perfect rationality, calculation is rigorous, whereas in conditions of selective rationality calculation is only approximate and, in fact, it is used in the majority of cases. In other words people graduate a range of rationality in their action and they behave as they want, as they think they should behave or they choose another indirect solution. It does not mean that they behave irrationally, because there is no necessity to take maximal effort while making a decision (Leibenstein, 1988).

A rational decision is being made according to a decision algorithm which consists of the following stages (Robbins, 2005):

- problem diagnosing and defining;
- determining of decision-making criteria;
- determining of criteria importance;
- formulating possible solutions;
- evaluating each possible solution;
- choosing the highest evaluated solution.

A different way of presenting those stages is as follows (Maison, 2004):

- problem diagnosing and – as an effect – formation of needs;
- searching information about available possibilities and their evaluation in terms of essential factors for the decision maker;
- eliminating those options which do not suit the assumptions;
- making the right choice;
- post-decision-making evaluation.

Both schemes indicate the same mentioned above elements and importance of keeping them in the right order, which is included in the algorithm shown in Figure 11.1.

Only obedience to the presented algorithm ensures deciding on optimal choice in the conditions of full rationality. However, in the conditions of limited rationality, the choice is made based on heuristics, in other words simplified schemes of decision making.

Additionally it should be underlined that perfect rationality means that the individual makes a decision in the terms of certainty. In fact the aforementioned terms are impossible to arrange in reality and uncertainty accompanies people's choices. In real life it is much more probable that one of the situations specified below may occur (Forlicz, 2001):

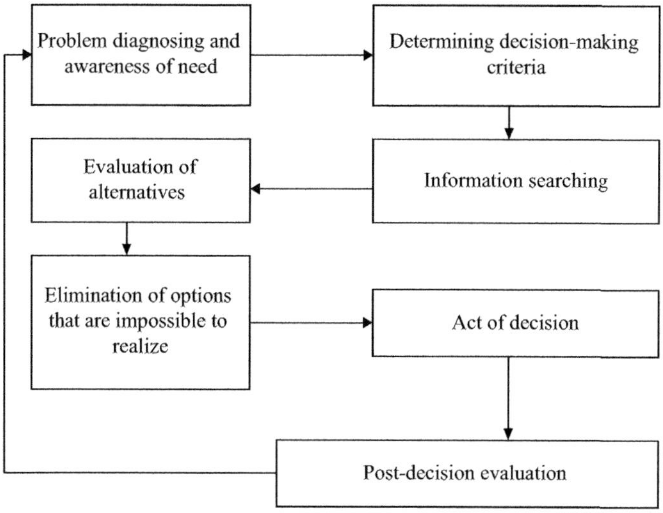

Figure 11.1 Process of decision making
Source: Author's description

- making a decision in the conditions of risk, when the decision maker is acquainted with all possible options and probability of their occurrence;
- making a decision in the conditions of uncertainty, when the decision maker is acquainted with all possible options, however they do not know the probability of their occurrence;
- making a decision in the condition of ignorance, when the decision maker is not acquainted with all possible options, opportunities and results of their own behaviour;
- making a decision in the condition of conflict, when the situation is a result of a decision made by another individual who fulfils his own goals.

To sum up the foregoing, achieving full rationality is very difficult, if possible. These difficulties are general and concern all life problems and decisions, including financial ones.

Financial behaviours and their rationality

Financial behaviours are types of individual behaviour and their particularity consists in applying to a specific object – money and incidents related to it. Similarly, like in other behaviours, their basis is appearance of the specific need, financial need in this case. It could be need connected with an access to money (earning, saving, cash management), need related to arranging insurance for personal property (own insurance), need related to money transfer

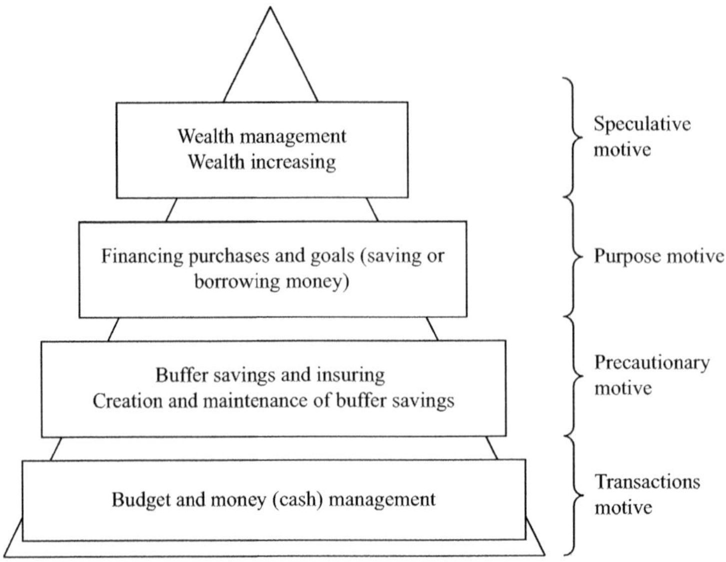

Figure 11.2 Hierarchy of financial behaviours
Source: Author's description

between subjects, need related to delaying payment (undertaken commitments) or need related to financial consulting concerning increased demand for information and advice to maximize optimization of purchasing decision.

Those behaviours might occur in a few levels creating so-called behaviour hierarchy which articulates the general tendency to consumer engagement in higher levels of behaviour only after performing on lower levels (Antonides and Fred van Raaij, 2003). It means that among the financial behaviours we can distinguish those which are perceived as fundamental and concern a vast group of individuals, e.g. saving, and those of an advanced nature and related to a narrower group, e.g. wealth management. Particular behaviours might occur at the same time or in altered, to the mentioned before, order. This is a very individual matter, therefore the behaviour hierarchy could not be treated as absolutely obtained by all individuals in the same way. Levels of financial behaviours are presented in Figure 11.2.

Budget and cash management (budget and money management) involves current coordination of own money. 'Rest' savings or transitory indebtedness, e.g. current account overdraft, might be an effect of the above mentioned management. Cash flow management takes into account foreseeable situations which may cause both generating incomes (e.g. job) and spending (e.g. eatables, electricity, heating or phone bills).

Buffer savings and coverages (creating and maintaining buffer stock) are in the group of behaviours including gathering resources to protect against happenings that are unforeseeable (liquidity buffer, security pillow). This level of behaviour requires self-control and ability of postponing satisfaction originating from current consumption. Therefore not every individual is able to achieve this level. The most popular instrument of gathering this kind of saving is bank deposit thanks to which saving of general purpose appears.

Financing purchases and goals requires self-control and setting own task hierarchy no matter if it involves gathering saving or taking loans. In both instances it is necessary to collect funds, however in the case of saving it takes place before spending, while in the case of loans it happens after. Wealth management (wealth increasing) is the highest and the most advanced level of financial behaviours. It concerns only those individuals who managed to gather any surpluses before. Basing on this, individuals want to sustain or increase the value of assets they possess and protect them from decrease of value caused by inflation.

Financial behaviours, presented above, could be related to the money demand motives which were distinguished by J. Keynes: transactions motive (budget and cash management), precautionary motive (buffer stock and coverage) and speculative motive (wealth management). Financing purchases and goals which involves planned gathering of sources or gaining them from outside, could be related to the purpose motive in money demand.

In approach of mainstream economy the human is rational, so his financial behaviours should be rational too. With references to behaviours, it means that everyone should have determined preferences and could indicate their own intentions, should know how to arrange them in an internally consistent manner and, what is more, make internally consistent choices to maximize their own satisfaction. Additionally, those choices should be made according to the algorithm presented above.

In terms of financial behaviours it appears that economic criteria are not always decisive. For example in the situation of saving, some believe that it is psychologically interesting that it does not have anything to do either with foresight or postponed consumption – even though it may arise so out of rationalizing saving attributions – but it becomes a goal in and of itself … behaviour is awarded internally, saving is then done because of itself and is self-awarding (Górniak, 2000). It could mean that no external factors decide about saving (including economic ones), only the internal predispositions of the individual, e.g. personality. One of its factors is self-control – a feature that manifests itself through self-discipline which is responsible for the ability to begin tasks and finish them. People with high results on the scale of self-discipline have the ability to motivate themselves towards different tasks, on the other hand people with low results will delay beginning the task and easily drop out (Siuta, 2009). Could we recognize that behaviour, which is motivated by personality attributes, is rational in an economic sense? In terms of mainstream economy perhaps not, however in the meaning of simplified rationality – yes. If the necessity of overcoming one's own limits and boundaries is presumed as a loss of this behaviour, which additionally could generate higher loss than benefits coming from the behaviour – then withholding from saving is rational.

Applying to making commitments, the factor outlining rationality of behaviour is the state of indebtedness, which is the result of providing more and more consumption and investment goods. Not entering the state of indebtedness depends on correct recognition of one's own needs. For this purpose adequate perspective is needed to evaluate the real usability of goods which are planned to be bought by the individual on credit. Thus evaluation of rationality concerns mainly the fact whether increase in household debt will not make household liability much higher than income. In such case this behaviour cannot be recognized without any hesitations as rational.

In relation to insuring, it is believed that everyone should be interested in taking care of himself, his family and amassed wealth. What is more also insuring all those elements against negative actions of different factors. Unfortunately in practice it occurs that tendency to acquire insurance is very individual. It may result from the differences in risk perception and estimation of expected utility, which is subjective as well. Other way of explaining this behaviour is perceiving value in time which is determined by discounted utility. According to it, monies received earlier have bigger usability than those gained later (Wilkinson and Klaes, 2008). What is more, the person who insures oneself will, without any hesitation, sooner or later claim a loss, when the profit is surely uncertain. The profit here is receiving compensation and lack of any expenses for removal effects of past happening. It means that the balance of profits and losses is negative.

Acquiring insurance could be explained as a lottery, where the winner is the person who will contribute to the system the least but will acquire the most. The loser then will be the person who paid high fees and will never receive any compensation. Nobody likes to lose and thus there are people who do not obtain any insurance at all because they believe that it is better not to lose anything, since compensation is uncertain. Others misappropriate compensations to gain the win. It means that acquiring insurance is a result of risk calculation concerning possibility of happenings occurring. When the result of those calculations is negative, then the person resigns from insuring and it should be seen as rational behaviour (Maciejasz-Świątkiewicz, 2012).

Referring to taxes, and particularly to the tendency to avoid them, tax fraud could be perceived as a choice between loss of money paid to the IRS (Internal Revenue System) and a lottery in which it is possible not to lose or the loss could be higher than, the previously mentioned, loss of money. In this meaning tendency to tax fraud depends on: amount of expected fine and probability of review, whereas agreement on paying taxes depends on: strictness of fiscal policy (stated through relations between the tax-payer and IRS which consists of: amount of paid taxes, types of punitive sanctions and inquisitiveness of tax service) and will to cooperate (so called: tax mentality emerging from individual evaluation of the tax system and individual attitude towards taxes) (Niesiobędzka, 2004). Tax fraud could be regarded as well as a decision which is encumbered by alternative cost. When the person pays taxes, the alternative cost of not making a decision about not paying the tax is part of the income loss. In the event of not paying the taxes the alternative cost will be found in the necessity of discharging the higher taxes compared to the regular tax obligation.[1] Therefore tax fraud could bring some benefits like non-taxable income. The transaction costs, paid due to the attempt of concealing income, still cannot be omitted. They could turn out to be high enough to outrun the expected benefit. What is more, financial measurability could be trifling. Summing up, not paying taxes could be an expression of rational financial behaviour.

The explanations presented above have cognitive specifics and are based on the assumption that people are trying to be rational and each time they estimate the economic consequences of their behaviours. In practice, more often people are basing on their subjective feelings and their emotions. Some people rationalize their behaviours which could be explained as finding rational arguments to motivate their own acts and conducts rooting from feelings and motives that are hard to admit to. Outwardly it could seem like a rational explanation but it takes place after the behaviour happened so it does not fulfil the rational assumption.

Considering rationality of financial behaviours there are four types that can be distinguished:

- rational behaviour when the individual, to make the best decision, searches, analyses and processes information;
- habitual behaviour when the individual stops searching for information in order to behave as he used to do in the past;
- impulsive behaviour when the individual acts spontaneously ignoring the phase of gathering information;
- behaviour determined by social reasons when the individual acts under the influence of particular norms and social values specific to his environment. (Swoboda, 2004).

While the first type of behaviour has features of rationality, the remaining ones could be the subject of rationalization but they are not rational. Examples of those behaviours are presented in Table 11.1.

Planning process relates to how predictable specific financial behaviour is and if it is possible to take preliminary activities to prepare for certain behaviour.

Need for information refers to the level of information demand concerning the decision subject, intensity of processing this information and the level of usage logic rules in the decisive process. Need for information directly

Table 11.1 Financial behaviours considering rationality of making decision

	Rational behaviours	*Habitual behaviours*	*Impulsive behaviours*	*Behaviours determined by social reasons*
Planning process	planned	planned/ unplanned	unplanned	planned
Need for information	Large need for information	Low, acting automatically	Low, acting spontaneously, fast	Low, acting under the influence of view, opinion and value system of other people or institution
Emotional involvement	Low	Low	High	Medium
Involvement of cognitive process	High	Low	Low	Low
Examples	Choice of loan based on thorough search for the best offer	Choice of loan in the bank with long history of cooperation (e.g. current account)	Choice of loan while shopping or under the influence of advertisement	Choice of loan in the bank, basing on the social environment's opinion that this is the only honest bank

Source: Author's description

influences the behaviour pace. The lower the need for information is, the faster the behaviour may occur without any previous preparation.

Emotional involvement relates to the strength of feeling accompanying behaviour. According to knowable works, low emotional involvement favours rationality of decision, because it permits substantive consideration of all arguments.

Presented in the chart, involvement of cognitive process indicates conscious receiving and consideration of given information, researching and evaluating preceding decision making. The person concerned cognitively receives, rates, processes information and transforms them into attitude, particularly:

- receives information from environment, e.g. in the form of an advert;
- interprets information according to foregoing experience, opinions, personal characteristics;
- searches for additional information;
- evaluates available options which could satisfy the demand;

- creates own beliefs, attitude and purpose;
- acts under influence of inner forcefulness while exploiting chosen option;
- re-evaluates own attitudes and purposes depending on level of satisfying own needs;
- preserves own attitudes and purposes to use them in the future.

On the other hand the person with a low level of cognitive involvement behaves differently:

- exploits existing information to a lesser extent;
- presents very little indication that they make a decision based on rational processing;
- uses the product to obtain information about and to evaluate it;
- purchases products which have many common qualities, which permits them to narrow researching of information and enables making a decision based on experience;
- when making a choice takes into the consideration situation factors and information sources available at the purchase place (Foxall and Goldsmith, 1998).

Financial self-exclusion as an expression of conscious decision process

In the modern world it is expected that people express financial behaviours. But in real life there are some who do not do this. This group of people is called financially excluded. Some of them don't use financial products because they can't and some because they don't want to. This last group is called financially self-excluded.

In the definition of financial self-exclusion two areas could be pointed out: exclusion from access to financial services and exclusion from using them. The first case refers to those individuals who, for various reasons, cannot, even if they would want to, use the offer. On the other hand the second case refers to individuals who do not use the above mentioned services, because they do not want to. It occurs because, for example, they perceive this financial offer as unsuitable for their needs, inadequately attractive or unprofitable. Presented aspects of exclusion allow some types of it to be distinguished, as T. Beck, A. Demirgüç-Kunt and P. Honohan (Beck *et al.*, 2009) point out, financial exclusion according to its origin criterion could be voluntary (self-exclusion) or obligatory. Voluntarily excluded are individuals who stop using financial institutions' offers, while forcibly excluded are those who cannot use the offers, even if they would like to. Factors which could be qualified to obligatory exclusion are of an economic nature (lack of sufficient financial means, unemployment), legal factors (such as: limited ability to act in law, being sentenced, business failure, homelessness), psychological factors (addictions, chronic diseases, lack of financial knowledge), technological factors (lack of access to services because of adequate infrastructure, lack of internet access) or social-demographic factors (such as: age, place of living).

Factors deciding on voluntary choice of exclusion are: economic factors (high prices of products, unsuitable offer, lack of marketing information), social-cultural factors (upbringing, current stereotypes, prejudice and habits, beliefs originated from religion or from being a part of specific social group), legal factors (desire to hide the fact of possessing financial means which, for instance, come from illegal sources, or on purpose to obtain social benefits by fraud) or psychological factors (lack of trust towards the financial system).

Self-exclusion can be treated as an example of financial behaviour and may have a conscious or unconscious character. A conscious character means that an individual knows that he cannot take advantage of a financial offer, while in the other case doesn't know that the offer for him even exists. Some people think that they could cope perfectly without using the financial institution offer.

Voluntary exclusion (self-exclusion) could be regarded as an expression of freedom of choice rule. It is known as so called 'alternative every-day reality' and is connected with 'alternative rationality', in the range of which the decision maker reasons this situation as advantageous in the given circumstances (Maciejasz-Świątkiewicz, 2013). The question arising is if this situation could be regarded as exclusion? Out of exclusion definition could be derived as the fact that it is about participation impossibility and lack of reluctance. However it could be acknowledged that reluctance to participate in any area of social functioning results from this area unfamiliarity, and thus it cannot be treated as fully conscious choice. Classification of financial exclusion in the term of voluntariness is presented in Figure 11.3.

In this structure self-exclusion was divided into two categories: rational and irrational. Rational self-exclusion is a consequence of a fully conscious process of decision making performed before taking an action, based on loss and profit calculation connected with specific financial behaviours which were mentioned in the previous section and presented in the second section decision-making algorithm. Irrational self-exclusion is a consequence of cultural, religious, social or psychological factors. Psychological factors are responsible for the existence of a group, so-called 'financialphobes' who are distinguished by specific dysfunction – feeling anxiety (phobia) in using financial products. It could be a result of the overall difficulties in learning during the standard education process, based on popular methods of teaching, among people with average intelligence and living in favourable socio-cultural conditions. What is more it could result in disorders of fundamental cognitive functions in relation to individual financial behaviours. Those disorders could apply to perception of seeing which results in seeing but not recognizing proper information and/or phonological perception which is hearing but not listening to this information. This disorder could be emotionally based (Chambers, 2010). Lack of financial need could be an expression of rationality as well as irrationality which depends on consciousness level in this area

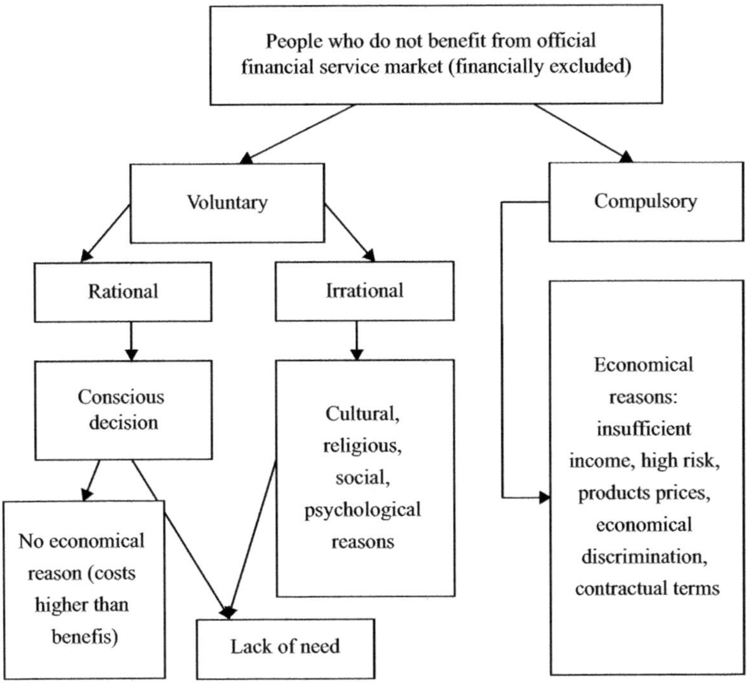

Figure 11.3 Framework of people financially excluded in regard of voluntariness of behaviours

Source: Author's description

and conducted in this context analysis. Sometimes declaration about the lack of need of financial products and services is an easy excuse for aversion to time-consuming and demanding evaluation of their profitability.

Conclusion

As it arises from being presented in these chapter considerations, rational behaviour is rather a particular case than a rule and thus it should be recognized that rational self-exclusion is rather a particular case of self-exclusion but at no time a rule. Consequently financial exclusion should be recognized as an expression of lack of rationality rather than a fully justified and motivated action realized on the basis of the decision-making algorithm. Indeed, there are probably situations when a person does a fully correct decision-making process, including all circumstances and all economic calculations, and on this basis decides that using particular financial products or services does not maximize their personal usability. This person decides then on financial self-exclusion which is fully justified financially and it should not be eliminated.

Occurrence of this type of exclusion could be advantageous for marketing of financial services and could be a stimulus for its development thanks to pointing out to financial institutions those areas which are rated negatively from the potential client.

The aim of this chapter was connected with presenting financial behaviours in the context of rationality. As it was described financial behaviours can be rational, but it is very difficult to obtain perfect rationality. Especially it is very difficult to obtain rational self-exclusion.

Finally, referring to the hypothesis stated in the introduction and coming back to the process of financialization – rational self-exclusion is not, paradoxically, an expression of inability to use the financial services market, but the expression of good knowledge of one's own financial needs and ability of evaluating expenses and benefits coming from an offer of the financial services market. This means that self-exclusion can have both positive and negative impact at the financialization process. It is quite a useful conclusion as it shows that knowledge about financial behaviours and financial literacy should be promoted as they can, under some circumstances, positively correspond with the financialization process. Rational self-exclusion is mainly a consequence of good knowledge about the financial market.

Because this chapter is conceptual it would be very interesting and welcome to carry out a survey which can explain in what way people become self-excluded and who does it in a rational way. This problem has never been described before in literature.

Note

1 In Poland according to personal income tax revenue stake of revenue derived from unnamed source amounts to 75 per cent of income.

References

Antonides, G. and Fred van Raaij, W., 2003. *Zachowanie konsumenta. Podręcznik akademicki.* Warszawa: Wydawnictwo Naukowe PWN.

Beck, T., Demirgüç-Kunt, A. and Honohan, P., 2009. Access to Financial Services: Measurement, Impact and Policies. *The World Bank Research Observer*, 24(1).

Chambers, C., 2010. *Financial Exclusion and Banking Regulations in the UK: Template Analysis.* Saarbrucken: Lambert Academic Publishing.

Epstein, E., 2005. *Financialization and the World Economy.* Cheltenham, Northampton: Edward Elgar Publishing.

European Commission, 2008. *Financial Services Provision and Prevention of Financial Exclusion*, s.l.: European Commission.

Forlicz, S., 2001. *Niedoskonała wiedza podmiotów rynkowych.* Warszawa: Wydawnicwo Naukowe PWN.

Foxall, G. and Goldsmith, R., 1998. *Psychologia konsumenta dla menedżera marketingu.* Warszawa: Wydawnictwo Naukowe PWN.

Górniak, J., 2000. *My i nasze pieniądze.* Kraków: Aureus.

Kamerschen, D., McKenzie, R. and Nardinelli, C., 1993. *Ekonomia*. Gdańsk: Fundacja Gospodarcza NSZZ 'Solidarność'.

Kieżel, E., 2004. *Racjonalność konsumpcji i zachowań konsumentów*. Warszawa: PWE.

Klimczak, B., 2011. *Mikroekonomia*. Wrocław: Uniwersytet Ekonomiczny we Wrocławiu.

Korenik, D., 2003. *Oszczędzanie indywidualne w Polsce- produkty różnych pośredników i ich atrakcyjność*. Wrocław: Akademia Ekonomiczna we Wrocławiu.

Leibenstein, H., 1988. *Poza schematem homo oeconomicus*. Warszawa: Wydawnictwo Naukowe PWN.

Maciejasz-Świątkiewicz, M., 2012. Psychologiczne aspekty ubezpieczania się przed ryzykiem. In: E. Bogacka- Kisiel, ed. *Finanse osobiste. Zachowania- produkty- strategie*. Warszawa: Wydawnictwo Naukowe PWN.

Maciejasz-Świątkiewicz, M., 2013. *Wykluczenie finansowe i narzędzia jego ograniczania*. Opole: Uniwersytet Opolski.

Maison, D., 2004. *Utajone postawy konsumenckie*. Gdańsk: GWP.

Niesiobędzka, M., 2004. Podatki. In: T. Tyszka, ed. *Psychologia ekonomiczna*. Opole: Uniwersytet Opolski.

Robbins, S., 2005. *Skuteczne podejmowanie decyzji*. Warszawa: PWE.

Simon, H., 1955. A Behavioural Model of Rational Choice. *Quarterly Journal of Economics*, 69(1), pp. 99–118.

Siuta, J., 2009. *Inwentarz osobowości NEO-PI-R Paula T. Costy Jr i Roberta R. McCrae*. Warszawa: PTP.

Swoboda, U., 2004. *Bankowość detaliczna*. Warszawa: CeDeWu.

Wilkinson, N. and Klaes, M., 2008. *An Introduction to Behavioural Economics*. Hampshire: Palgrave Macmillan.

12 The sources of corporate savings in the era of financialization

Anna Białek-Jaworska

Introduction

This chapter aims to explain the reasons behind the increase in corporate savings in the era of financialization. The International Monetary Fund indicates that there has been a significant increase in financial assets held by enterprises from the world's most influential countries. In Poland, corporate savings rose from 9.1 per cent of GDP in 2007, up to 15.8 per cent of GDP in 2013 (GUS, 2015). During the last decade we can observe a change in enterprises approach, from rational management through investment which generates profit or increases the equity value to an approach where the entity just accumulates the financial surplus. This chapter tries to disclose what caused such tendencies analysing the relevance of the measurement of corporate savings used for calculating National Accounts and carrying out panel and logit analyses of determinants of non-financial companies' savings. This study explores if the opportunity to improve the financial situation due to valuation at fair value encourages companies to increase their scale of financial investment and create or develop business groups. Valuation at fair value, by virtue of the Polish Accounting Act, concerns financial investment and investment property. The research covers 784 non-financial companies listed on the Warsaw Stock Exchange (WSE) on the main or alternative – the NewConnect – trading floor, based on the Notoria database. In this study, data from financial statements concerning balance sheet, profit and loss statement and cash flow statement, as well as additional information and closing market prices of companies at the end of each of the analysed years from the 2008–2014 period are used. The research excludes the insurance, banking and financial institutions sectors, the activity of which involves collecting and keeping or investing cash, trade in receivables or providing loans.

Definition and motives of corporate savings

Savings are defined as cash holdings that are a sum of at hand or in bank and marketable securities (Opler *et al.*, 1999; Drobetz and Grüninger, 2007; Bates *et al.*, 2009). Whereas willingness for saving is defined as a difference between cash holdings in the *t* and (*t-1*) periods (Riddick and Whited, 2009), which at the same time, based on a relation between balance sheet and cash flow statement, is the value of cash flows from three types of activities: operating, investment and financial. This approach enables a focus on the dynamic nature of savings' accumulation phenomenon by non-financial companies, and it seems that this approach enables us to answer the question of what determines the accumulation of corporate savings more accurately. This methodology is used for a logit analysis of determinants of non-financial companies' willingness for saving in this chapter. The dependent variable is a dummy variable that takes the value of 1 if a company is willing to save, i.e. when the change in cash holdings between *t* and (*t-1*) is positive.

The literature in the field of economy and corporate finance provides the following motives for corporate savings' accumulation (Bates *et al.*, 2009):

- The transaction motive related to transaction costs due to conversion of non-monetary financial assets into cash used for payments for purchases of goods and services. Due to economies of scale related to the transaction motive, large companies hold less cash (Mulligan, 1997).
- The precautionary motive – enterprises hold cash in order to manage negative shock effects, when access to capital markets is too costly. Companies with higher operating risk (higher volatility of cash flows) and limited access to external capital, hold more cash (Riddick and Whited, 2009). Companies with better investment opportunities (measured by market_to_book ratio, or expenses for R&D) also save more because limited access to funding is more costly for them.
- The tax motive – multinational corporations hold higher cash resources (savings), which were generated abroad, in order to avoid taxes upon repatriation (Foley *et al.*, 2007).
- The agency motive – managers with more experience and longer seniority prefer to keep their cash holdings rather than to increase the dividends' payouts for shareholders especially when the company has poor investment opportunity (Jensen, 1986; Pinkowitz *et al.*, 2006). Experienced managers are more willing to accumulate savings, but at the same time tend to spend excess cash very quickly (Dittmar and Mahrt-Smith, 2007; Harford *et al.*, 2008).

Financial assets are not only a capital conservation buffer in case of shock liquidity changes, but also a speculative component of investors' portfolio because assets' rate of return is as high as non-financial investments', for which financial assets became a substitute. For non-financial companies, a positive direction of the precautionary motive's impact and the negative impact of speculative motive counterbalance each other (Kaplan *et al.*, 2006).

More indebted companies and those with better access to financing from the capital market, hold less cash (Kim *et al.*, 1998; Deloof, 2001; Ozkan and Ozkan, 2004; Bansal and Bansal, 2012). While companies that have limited access to capital market's financing accumulate higher amount of savings. Companies keep a cash holding in order to be independent on external funding (Opler *et al.*, 1999). But the limitation in access to financing does not impact the level of savings that much because it depends not only on the creditworthiness, but also on the size of the cash flows compared to investment capability. Entities with limited access to financing hold more cash if future growth opportunities are more profitable (Almeida *et al.*, 2004). Companies aim for an individually set level of long-term balance in cash holdings with average annual speed of approx. 24–28 per cent (Bruinshoofd and Kool, 2004). The higher speed of adjusting current level of cash holdings to the targeted level occurs due to the bigger problems with asymmetric information, agency costs and higher external financing costs (Garcia-Teruel and Martinez-Solano, 2008). Good relationships with banks and other financial institutions reduce the agency costs and limit the savings kept by the companies (Drobetz and Grüninger, 2007; Garcia-Teruel and Martinez-Solano, 2008; Fresard, 2012). However, the alternative cost of keeping cash holdings increases along with the value of debt (Drobetz and Grüninger, 2007) and the maturity of liabilities (Garcia-Teruel and Martinez-Solano, 2008). Rationing loans and information asymmetry creates companies' demand for liquid assets in order to hedge against an imperfect capital market (Kaplan *et al.*, 2006), and keeping adequate working capital enables avoiding high cost of loans and insolvency risk (Abbadi and Abbadi, 2013).

Literature review on determinants of corporate savings

Investment opportunities have a considerably positive impact on cash resources (Kim *et al.*, 1998; Opler *et al.*, 1999; Ferreira and Vilela, 2004; Ozkan and Ozkan, 2004). Companies which are small, exposed to an increased risk of bankruptcy and not paying dividends are accumulating more cash (Baum *et al.*, 2012). The increase in savings also resulted from conducting R&D activities (Dittmar *et al.*, 2003; Baum *et al.*, 2012), for which it is extremely difficult to get financing from a bank. Thus, companies with high growth opportunity under conditions of asymmetric information and rising borrowing costs hold higher savings (Drobetz and Grüninger, 2007; Garcia-Teruel and Martinez-Solano, 2008).

According to the pecking order theory a company prefers to finance future investments from internal sources of financing, including own cash resources (Deloof, 2001; Garcia-Teruel and Martinez-Solano, 2008). Companies that intend to expand their operations in the future or companies that have underestimated market value hold lower savings (Lins *et al.*, 2010). Savings are determined by managers' expectations on the prospects for future growth opportunity and future financing costs (Fresard, 2012). Surplus in funds from operations (cash flow) is negatively correlated with savings of enterprises (Kim *et al.*, 1998; Ozkan and Ozkan, 2004), while Dittmar *et al.* (2003), Ferreira and Vilela (2004) and Garcia-Teruel and Martinez-Solano (2008) showed a positive correlation. Enterprises hold higher cash reserves for a decrease in cash flow (Opler *et al.*, 1999); low or negative financial surplus in cash from operating activities (Lins *et al.*, 2010). Companies should increase savings in response to positive changes in cash flows from operations, if they face funding constraints, while estimated savings sensitivity to changes in cash flows of companies with unlimited access to financing is close to zero. However, the savings behaviour patterns vary in different phases of the life cycle. At higher limits of access to financing from the capital market corporate, cash resources are more sensitive to changes in the cash flows (Baum *et al.*, 2012), while companies are more likely to save, especially in conditions of unstable economic situation (Almeida *et al.*, 2004). Expectations for future financial situation have a positive impact on cash resources (Kim *et al.*, 1998; Ferreira and Vilela, 2004; Ozkan and Ozkan, 2004). The main reason for the increase in cash holdings is the decrease of inventories and capital spending and increase of the risk (variability of cash flow from operations). Companies hold more cash resources in case of the expected expenditure on R&D (Bates *et al.*, 2009) than when they expect capital expenditures in fixed assets. The mechanism interacts particularly strongly in enterprises more exposed to the risk of bankruptcy, i.e. the smaller firms, that almost do not pay dividends (Baum *et al.*, 2012).

The increase in cash is also concentrated in companies that do not pay dividends or have recently carried out the first issue of shares (IPO) (Bates *et al.*, 2009). A small positive correlation between dividend payments and savings may be due to the reluctance of entrepreneurs to limit dividend payments with an increase in cash resources (Drobetz and Grüninger, 2007). Corporate governance also has a significant impact on the cash holdings level (Yarram, 2012).

The sources of non-financial corporate savings in Poland

In order to identify the sources of non-financial corporate savings in Poland we conduct a decomposition of changes in cash holdings between the beginning and the end of the financial year, for 784 listed companies in total, in Figure 12.1. Using a cash flow statement structure prepared on the basis of the indirect method, we determine directions of cash flows on balance, i.e. the difference between inflows and expenses from investment and financial activities. Figure 12.1 shows the share of sources of corporate savings (inflows) in cash flow statement from the entire activity: operating, investment and financial activities and opposing share of cash outflows, in total change of balance sheet cash holdings.

Due to the conducted analysis, operating cash flow was reduced with expenses connected with repurchase of own shares and payment of dividends, using National Accounts methodology (GUS, 2013) to calculate savings of non-financial enterprises, while net profit is replaced with cash flow from operations. Results in Figure 12.1 indicate that in the periods of 2008–2010

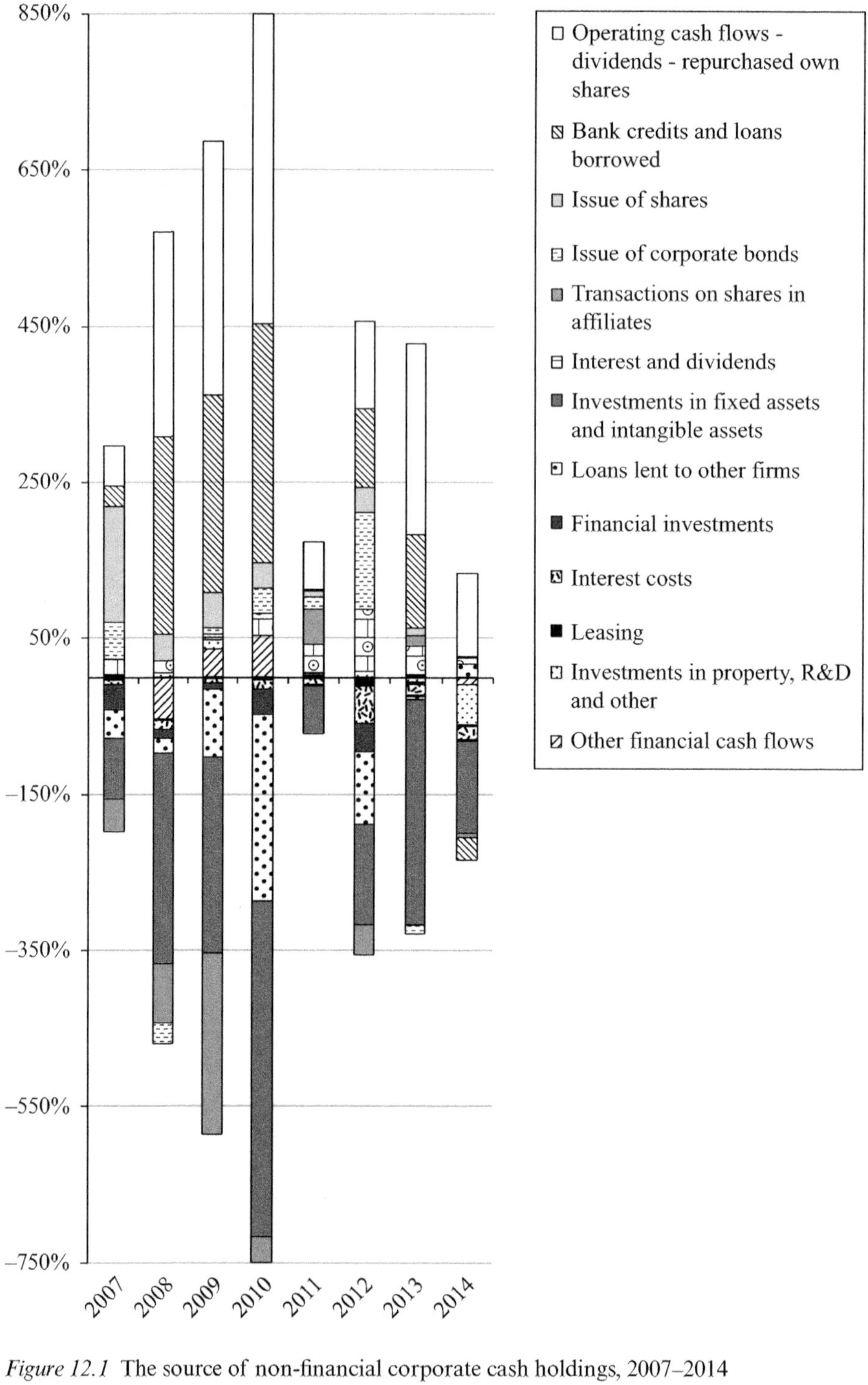

Figure 12.1 The source of non-financial corporate cash holdings, 2007–2014
Source: Author's calculation based on Notoria database

and 2012–2013, the main sources of savings of non-financial corporations were: financial surplus from operations and inflows from loans and borrowings (above outflows), in 2007 inflows from issuing shares, in 2007 and 2012 issuing bonds, and in 2011 inflows from disposal of shares in related companies. Inflows from interest and dividends had more influence in the period of 2011–2013. In the analysed time frame only in 2014 did expenses on repayment of loans and borrowings exceed inflows from debt financing, besides low interest rates. In 2014 non-financial companies listed on the WSE, when analysed together, showed negative cash flow from entire activity: operating, investment and financial.

National Accounts methodology for corporate savings measurement

As in the National Accounts methodology (GUS, 2013), non-financial corporate savings are calculated based on net profit, less the payment of dividends and repurchase of own shares. Figure 12.2 shows the comparison between the corporate savings calculated as in the National Accounts and an author's proposal of corporate savings' estimation, based on financial (cash) surplus (i.e. financial result calculated on the basis of cash accounting principle, that is without valuation effects and accrual principle), less the payment of dividends and repurchase of own shares as well. I propose the measurement of financial surplus (similar to cash flow = inflows – outflows) as an alternative method for calculating corporate savings on the basis of the net financial result. My proposal considers differences between the net financial result and

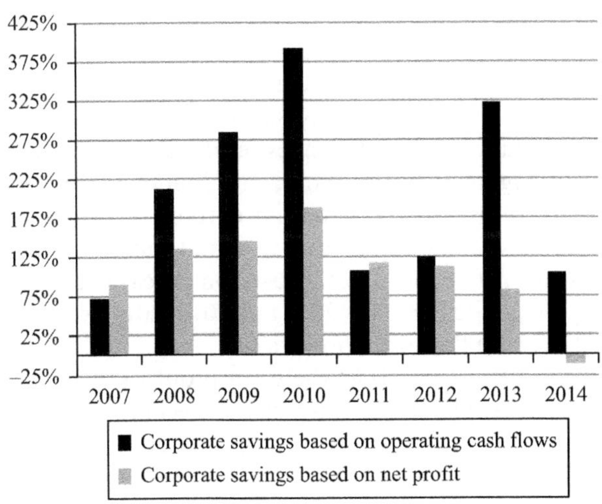

Figure 12.2 Non-financial corporate savings relative to the total cash flow, 2007–2014
Source: Author's calculation based on Notoria database

cash flow. This approach to the savings measurement suggests the following steps in the calculation: 1) adjust the net financial result for valuation effects; 2) adjust for accrual principle; 3) do not exclude the following from the financial result: foreign exchange differences, interest costs and income, dividends and investment activities results. Figure 12.2 compares corporate savings' measurements described above on the basis of net profit (GUS, 2013) with the author's approach based on cash flow (in relation to total cash flow from operating, investment and financial activities all together). Underestimation of savings in the National Accounts methodology results from reduction of financial result due to depreciation which is not generating expenses, using the accrual principle (consideration of costs instead of expenses and income instead of inflows). This approach omits cash inflow from last year's receivables repayment, lowers expenses paid, rather than costs, due to the deferral of current liability or the impairment of assets, reserves, foreign exchange differences on balance sheet valuation, and the effects of valuation at fair value which does not produce cash inflows or outflows.

Due to revaluation as at the balance statement day and accrual principle, significant differences between both measurements occur mainly in 2008–2009 and in 2014, as shown in Figures 12.2 and 12.3. Differences in 2010 and 2013–2014 are mainly caused by effects of depreciation (cost without cash outflow). Small differences in 2007 and 2011 result from negative impact of the accrual principle (e.g. inventories increase, reserves decline) over depreciation, while in 2012 it is mainly due to depreciation shown in Figure 12.3. Financing at suppliers' expense (higher trade credit taken than trade credit provided) at least partly explains a considerable difference between methods used for calculating corporate savings in 2008 (higher trade payables than receivables) (Białek-Jaworska and Nehrebecka, 2016).

However, in the period of 2009–2010 these differences are due to a higher value of net trade credit provided (higher trade receivables than payables). It may also result from valuation at fair value or inclusion of impairment loss, caused by the economic situation (subprime mortgage loans' crisis, euro-zone crisis, Russian embargo), in financial result (changes resulting from application of accrual principle in Figure 12.3). Summarizing, Figure 12.2 shows weaknesses of measurement of Polish non-financial corporate savings on the basis of National Accounts methodology due to significant differences between net profit and adjusted net financial result based on the cash accounting principle. Especially in the periods of 2008–2010 and 2013–2014 net profit is considerably lower than net cash flow from operations.

This can be particularly observed in 2014, where net profit less payment of dividends and expenses on repurchase of own shares became an actual loss (below the axis in Figure 12.2, and 'negative adjusted net income' in Figure 12.3) mainly due to high depreciation and effects of the accrual principle, as presented in Figure 12.3. Figure 12.4 shows that the 2008 transactions connected with the repurchase of shares already owned decreased the savings of non-financial companies resulting from the uncertainty and

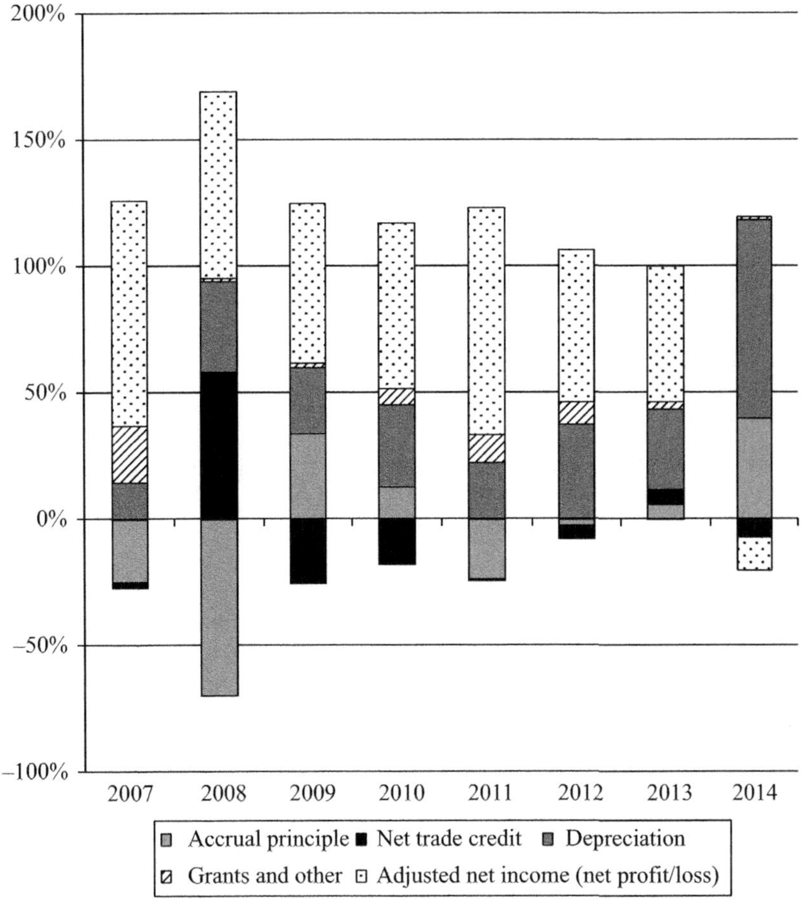

Figure 12.3 The measurement of non-financial corporate savings based on operating cash flows, 2007–2014

Source: Author's calculation based on Notoria database

increased investment risk due to the related subprime mortgage loans crisis. However, expenses connected with payment of dividends reduced corporate savings in 2007–2010 and in 2013, while in 2011 and 2014 at lower cash flows from operations there were almost no dividends paid.

Empirical study on determinants of corporate savings

We analyse determinants of non-financial corporate savings and their propensity to save with use of data for 784 non-financial companies listed on the main or alternative floor of the WSE, collected from the Notoria database. We

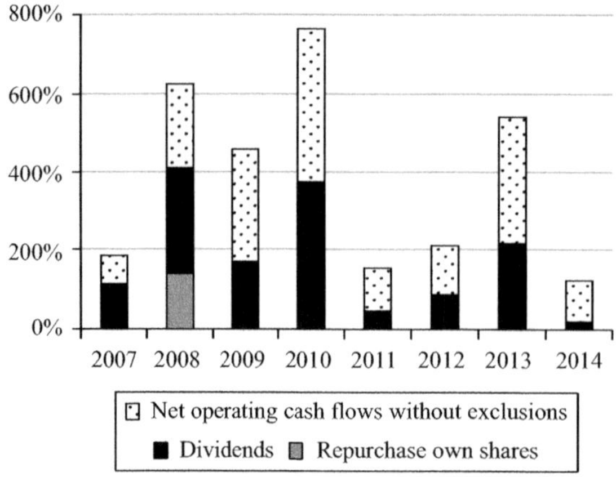

Figure 12.4 Repurchase of own shares and payment of dividends in non-financial companies, 2007–2014

Source: Author's calculation based on Notoria database

use the Drisc/Kraay estimator to solve problems with heteroscedasticity and autocorrelation. The following sectors were excluded from the study: banking, insurance and financial institutions, because their activities involve the collection and storage of, or investing cash, debt trading and lending. We use also data on shares trading that were collected manually from the StockWatch portal. Definitions of variables used in the panel and logit models are shown in Table 12.1. Before conducting the panel and logistic regression, descriptive statistics and the correlation between the explanatory variables were analysed. Table 12.2 shows the results of panel models estimation and the estimation of logit models with marginal effects. These findings indicate that companies creating and expanding corporate groups through the acquisition of shares in related parties (the acquisition_activity variable) and companies with a higher propensity to save (dcash) accumulate higher savings. Corporate cash holding is determined by a company's higher ability to generate cash financial surplus from operations (cash_ flow_oper) and the higher operational risk (higher variability of cash flows from operating activities). Use of derivatives increases the accumulated savings of companies, as one can assume, due to their activities associated with a higher risk encouraging companies to hedge risk exposures. Issue of shares increases the savings of listed companies, as well as pursuit of a policy of paying dividends does. Higher investment opportunities (measured by market_to_book ratio) and higher investment in fixed assets and intangible assets (CAPEX) reduce corporate savings. The opposite results were obtained by Dittmar *et al.* (2003) and Baum *et al.* (2012), where carrying out R&D activities, for which it is difficult to get external financing, explains the increase in savings. This may indicate that Polish companies are less likely

Table 12.1 Definitions of variables used in the panel and logistic analysis

Variable	*Definition*
cash_ratio	(cash in hand and bank account + short-term financial assets) / total assets
cash_holding	binary variable equals to 1 if the cash flow (change in cash and equivalents between years *t* and (*t-1*)) > 0; and 0 otherwise
acquisition_activity	expenditure on the acquisition of shares in related parties / total assets
capex	expenditure on purchase of tangible and intangible assets / total assets
cash_flow_operating	cash flow from operations
dcash	*cash_ratio* in year *t* – *cash ratio* in year *(t-1)*
derivatives	derivatives (as part of financial assets) / total assets
dividend_dummy	dummy variable equals to 1 if the shares in profit paid to shareholders of the parent company > 0; and 0 otherwise
share_issue_dummy	dummy variable that takes the value of 1 if the inflows from share issue > 0; and 0 otherwise
leverage	(long-term debt + short-term debt) / total assets
operational_risk	the standard deviation of cash flows from operations over the past five years or less if not available
loss	dummy variable that takes the value of 1 if the net financial result < 0; and 0 otherwise
market_to_book	(book value of total assets – book value of equity + market value of equity (share price x number of shares)) / book value of total assets
net_debt_issue	(annual inflows of loans and corporate bonds issue – annual expenditure on repayment of loans and redemption of corporate bonds) / total assets
net_equity_issue	(annual inflows from share issue – annual expenditure on the purchase of own shares) / total assets
net_leverage	*leverage – cash_ratio*
firm_size	ln(total assets)
r&d_intensity	expenditure on R&D activities / sales
bonds_issue	dummy variable equals to 1 if the inflows from the corporate bonds issue > 0; and 0 otherwise
fair_value	dummy variable that takes the value of 0 if the (unrealized profit on investments + net change the values of assets) = 0; and 1 otherwise
fin_inv_real_estate	dummy variable that takes the value of 1 if the (long-term financial assets + investment properties) > 0; and 0 otherwise
donations_cf	dummy variable equals to 1 if the other financial cash flows > 0; and 0 otherwise
donations_uzg	dummy variable equals to 1 while other financial flows > 0 and other operating revenues > 0; and 0 otherwise

Source: Author's description

Table 12.2 Results of panel models on determinants of non-financial corporate savings and logistic regressions of their propensity to save

	cash_ratio Fixed effects	*cash_ratio Drisc/Kraay*	*cash_ratio Fixed effects*	*cash_ratio Drisc/Kraay*	*cash_holding logit*	*marginal effects dy/dx*	*cash_holding logit*	*marginal effects dy/dx*
acquisition_activity	0.0454892**	0.1015815	0.1261054***	0.1844313**				
	(0.023043)	(0.0786029)	(0.0258563)	(0.0493546)				
capex	−0.1198919***	−0.1044058***			0.1139487***	0.4001191***	0.099893***	0.4560088***
	(0.0044309)	(0.0107628)			(0.1260618)	(0.0315)	(0.1162933)	(0.02903)
cash_flow_operating	3.85e-09	3.46e-09***						
	(5.65e-09)	(6.12e-10)						
dcash	0.4713***	0.52736***	0.4844731***	0.5325491***				
	(0.0111364)	(0.018196)	(0.011613)	(0.0191918)				
cash_ratio (logit)					1.78157***	0.4451835***	1.59588***	0.3984248***
					(0.2197181)	(0.05492)	(0.2382245)	(0.0595)
operational_risk			−4.61e-10	2.16e-08***			−6.76e-08	−1.69e-08
			(1.66e-08)	(1.77e-09)			(9.39e-08)	(0.00000)
derivatives			1.710283***	1.561933***				
			(0.0627075)	(0.0512274)				
dividend_dummy	0.005689	0.0302435***	0.0153282**	0.0344888***				
	(0.0058748)	(0.0034179)	(0.0061611)	(0.0015509)				
share_issue_dummy	0.0039981	0.0071891**	−0.0044472	0.0093267***	0.6115019***	0.1512971***	0.4741516***	0.1179118***
	(0.0047008)	(0.0021039)	(0.0049203)	(0.0015543)	(0.0823632)	(0.01991)	(0.0936702)	(0.02301)
loss	−0.0106021**	0.0004034	−0.0101805**	0.0036685	−0.387971***	−0.096372***	−0.414817***	−0.102791***
	(0.0047365)	(0.0033632)	(0.0049603)	(0.0058871)	(0.0772209)	(0.01898)	(0.0851034)	(0.02083)
market_to_book	7.42e-10	−2.13e-09**	−1.11e-10	−2.58e-09***				
	(2.11e-09)	(5.50e-10)	(1.95e-09)	(1.45e-10)				
net_debt_issue bonds_issue*	−0.0271167*	−0.03458**	−0.0430078***	−0.0659846***	0.2919002***	0.0727648***	0.2079065*	0.0519298*
	(0.0152068)	(0.0088577)	(0.0152785)	(0.0112662)	(0.1088456)	(0.02694)	(0.1165774)	(0.02906)
net_equity_issue	−0.0253415***	−0.0246854##	−0.033047***	−0.035198***				
	(0.0083332)	(0.0136768)	(0.0084184)	(0.0061355)				
net_leverage	−0.0025986*	−0.014912						
	(0.0013904)	(0.0114767)						

leverage			0.0012313	−0.0024614##				
			(0.0012987)	(0.0012954)				
firm_size	0.0076467**	−0.0193955***	−0.0063609*	−0.0246631***				
	(0.0030826)	(0.0034609)	(0.0037177)	(0.0013266)				
fair_value	−0.0119762#	−0.0044161	−0.0125599##	−0.005748	−0.1294133	−0.0322611	−0.1767945	−0.0439218
	(0.0095999)	(0.0093505)	(0.0094355)	(0.0069019)	(0.1501461)	(0.0373)	(0.1585543)	(0.03911)
donations_uzg	0.0118085**	0.0082355*	0.0132558**	0.0070528#	0.1369134##	0.0342149##	0.1169239	0.0292109
donations_cf*	(0.0051845)	(0.0040086)	(0.0052445)	(0.0048627)	(0.0887943)	(0.02217)	0.0969786	(0.02423)
fin_inv_real estate			−0.0040188	0.0221801***				
			(0.0060189)	(0.0026241)				
r&d_intensity			3.15e-07	−1.54e-07				
			(7.80e-07)	(1.48e-07)				
cons	0.0413128#	0.3178011***	0.1883626***	0.3576506***	−0.371337***			−0.299161***
	(0.0329936)	(0.0421404)	(0.03978)	(0.0166814)	(0.0585949)			(0.0655899)
observations	3350	3350	2685	2685	3350		2685	
Groups	693	693	690	690				
R2	0.3388	0.4448	0.4311	0.4649	0.180		0.150	
Root MSE		0.1485		0.1510				
F Test	340.40***	374.77***		5363.93***				
F test that all u_i = 0	9.64***		11.33***					
Sargan-Hansen	159.024***		53.433***					
Wooldridge test for autocorrelation	556.488***		258.434***					
Modified Wald test	1.1e+14***		1.3e+33***					
Pr(y) (predict)					0.48916836		0.48151479	
Correct classif					59.97%		59.11%	
LR					176.02***		110.04***	
Pearson chi2					3343.30		2687.30	

(*continued*)

Table 12.2 (cont.)

	cash_ratio Fixed effects	*cash_ratio Drisc/Kraay*	*cash_ratio Fixed effects*	*cash_ratio Drisc/Kraay*	*cash_holding logit*	*marginal effects dy/dx*	*cash_holding logit*	*marginal effects dy/dx*
LR chi2(2)					181.59***		112.58***	
Log likelihood					−2230.2937		−1802.9082	
_hat					1.07275***		1.036305***	
					(0.0847047)		(0.1012292)	
hatsq					−0.2588301**		−0.2336308	
					(0.1062759)		(0.1427644)	
cons					0.0578104#		0.0416598	
					(0.0431458)		(0.0477666)	

Significant at 1% ***, 5% **, 10% *, 15% #, 20% ##. * in logistic regression

Source: Author's calculation in STATA ver. 13

to invest in R&D activity. In addition, in this study it has been shown that better credit conditions and access to finance (reflected in a greater ability to raise funding by issuing shares on the capital market (net_equity_issue), the issuance of corporate bonds, and/or the taking out of bank loans (net_debt_issue)) reduces non-financial corporate savings. Similar results were achieved by Kim *et al.* (1998), Deloof (2001), Ozkan and Ozkan (2004) and Bansal and Bansal (2012). Larger enterprises (firm_size) hold lower savings due to economies of scale and transaction motive (Mulligan, 1997), and greater opportunities to obtain external funding when favourable investment opportunities appear. The results revealed a significant effect of donations on corporate cash holdings, probably because of limited possibility of using them often due to grant project budget restrictions and project objectives. Similarly Bilgrami and Nishat (1990) indicate that obtaining subsidies explains the increase in corporate savings.

The second model of corporate savings identifies a positive impact of corporate long-term financial and real estate investments on the explained variable. However, the research did not reveal any significant impact of the fair value estimation effects on the cash holding. This may indicate that the Polish listed companies which accumulate savings, hedge against macroeconomic uncertainty by investing in long-term financial assets or investment property. Hence, their investment decisions are not motivated by the fair value use, but by the potential to achieve income from interest, rent and dividends or share in the profits of other companies.

The results of the logit regression of non-financial corporations' propensity to save, presented in Table 12.2, show that companies incurring financial losses (loss) have a lower propensity to save and it is less likely that they are able to increase cash resources. For American companies significant relationship between savings and financial losses was not confirmed (Bates *et al.*, 2009). In addition, logistic regression results indicate that companies incurring capital expenditure (CAPEX) have a higher propensity to save. The increase in expenditure on tangible and intangible assets by the unit increases the propensity to save by 11.39 pp. The issue of shares and corporate bonds by non-financial companies increased their propensity to save, but the share of cash and short-term financial assets in total assets (cash ratio) has the greatest impact on the corporate propensity to save. The increase in the cash ratio by 1 per cent increases the propensity to save by 39.8–44.5 pp. At the 15 per cent significance level, the use of donations increases the propensity to save, which may be related to the legal restrictions to immediately engage them in profitable investments.

Conclusion

This author's research contributes to the knowledge of financialization in the scope of measurement of the corporate savings and the identification of sources and determinants of non-financial corporate cash holdings. The main savings sources of non-financial companies listed on the WSE are: cash financial surplus from operations, inflows from taking out bank loans (overspending on their repayment), inflows from issuance of shares or corporate bonds, and in 2011 inflows from the sale of shares in affiliates. The importance of inflows from interest and dividends has been increasing in 2011–2013. It seems that the source of savings, such as bank loans or grants, set up legal restrictions on their immediate spending for the investment that could generate profit. Despite the weakness of non-financial companies' savings measure, used in the National Accounts (GUS, 2013), the increase of listed companies' savings until 2013 is not something illusory, but rather it reflects companies' protection against risk (Riddick and Whited, 2009), also reflected by the use of derivatives for hedging. Significant and relatively stable expenses associated with lending money to other companies or financial investments indicate a shift of a non-financial business paradigm from the unit that manages rationally and invests in fixed assets to gain profits or to increase the value for the shareholders, to the unit that accumulates surplus funds.

The results of the panel analysis showed a positive effect of long-term financial investment or investment property on the accumulation of savings, but the impact of the effects of fair value estimation became irrelevant. This suggests that for listed companies in Poland, possibility of valuation at fair value plays a relatively less important role than the potential income from interest, rent and dividends. It seems that the Polish listed companies accumulating savings, by investing in long-term financial assets or investment property, are more likely to hedge against macroeconomic uncertainty than apply the valuation at fair value. Based on positive correlations between expenditure for acquisition of shares in affiliates and corporate savings, we can say that the chance to improve the financial situation due to the valuation at fair value encourages companies to expand the scale of financial investment and the business groups.

Future research could be aimed at identifying the sources of non-financial private companies' savings. Extending research on the determinants of cash holding for private enterprises will diagnose the impact of asymmetric information and limited access to finance sources on corporate behaviour. It is important to investigate if the non-financial private companies accumulate higher or lower savings than non-financial public companies with better access to finance from the capital market.

References

Abbadi, R. T. and Abbadi, S. M., 2013. The Determinants of Working Capital Requirements in Palestinian Industrial Corporations. *International Journal of Economics and Finance*, 5(1), pp. 65–75.

Almeida, H., Campello, M. and Weisbach, M., 2004. The Cash Flow Sensitivity of Cash. *Journal of Finance*, 59(4), pp. 1777–1804.

Bansal, R. and Bansal, V., 2012. A Research Paper on Determinants of Corporate Liquidity in India. *International Journal of Marketing and Technology*, 2(4), pp. 103–117.

Bates, T., Kahle, K. and Stulz, R., 2009. Why do U.S. Firms Hold So Much More Cash Than They Used To? *Journal of Finance*, 64(5), pp. 1985–2021.

Baum, C. F., Caglayan, F. and Talavera, O., 2012. *The Effects of Future Capital Investment and R&D Expenditures on Firms' Liquidity*. Boston: Boston College Working Papers in Economics No. 712.

Białek-Jaworska, A. and Nehrebecka, N., 2016. The Role of Trade Credit in Business Operations. *Argumenta Oeconomica*, 2(37), pp. 189–231.

Bilgrami, N. and Nishat, M., 1990. The Determinants of Corporate Savings in Pakistan: A Case Study of Companies Registered with Karachi Stock Exchange. *Pakistan Economic and Social Review*, 28(1), pp. 9–39.

Bruinshoofd, W. A. and Kool, C. J., 2004. Dutch Corporate Liquidity Management: New Evidence on Aggregation. *Journal of Applied Economics*, 7(2), pp. 195–230.

Deloof, M., 2001. Belgian Intragroup Relations and the Determinants of Corporate Liquid Reserves. *European Financial Management*, 7(3), pp. 375–392.

Dittmar, A. and Mahrt-Smith, J., 2007. Corporate Governance and the Value of Cash Holdings. *Journal of Financial Economics*, 83(3), pp. 599–634.

Dittmar, A., Mahrt-Smith, J. and Servaes, H., 2003. International Corporate Governance and Corporate Cash Holdings. *Journal of Quantitative and Financial Analysis*, 13(1), pp. 111–133.

Drobetz, W. and Grüninger, M. C., 2007. Corporate Cash Holdings: Evidence from Switzerland. *Financial Market Portfolio Management*, 21(3), pp. 293–324.

Ferreira, M. A. and Vilela, A. S., 2004. Why Do Firms Hold Cash? Evidence from EMU Countries. *European Financial Management*, 10(2), pp. 295–319.

Foley, C., Hartzell, J. H., Titman, S. and Twite, G. J., 2007. Why Do Firms Hold So Much Cash? A Tax-based Explanation. *Journal of Financial Economics*, 86(3), pp. 579–607.

Fresard, L., 2012. Cash Savings and Stock Price Informativeness. *Review of Finance*, 16(4), pp. 985–1012.

Garcia-Teruel, P. and Martinez-Solano, P., 2008. On the Determinants of SME Cash Holdings: Evidence from Spain. *Journal of Business Finance and Accounting*, 35(1), pp. 127–149.

GUS, 2013. *Rachunki narodowe według sektorów i podsektorów instytucjonalnych w latach 2008–2011, Studia i analizy statystyczne*. Warszawa: GUS.

GUS, 2015. *Rachunki narodowe według sektorów i podsektorów instytucjonalnych w latach 2010–2013, Studia i analizy statystyczne*. Warszawa: GUS.

Harford, J., Mansi, S. and Maxwell, W., 2008. Corporate Governance and a Firm's Cash Holdings. *Journal of Financial Economics*, 87(3), pp. 535–555.

Jensen, M., 1986. Agency Costs of Free Cash Flow, Corporate Finance and Takeovers. *American Economic Review*, 76(2), pp. 323–329.

Kaplan, C., Özmen, E. and Yalcin, C., 2006. *The Determinants and Implications of Financial Asset Holdings of Non-Financial Firms in Turkey: An Empirical Investigation*. Ankara: Central Bank of the Republic of Turkey.

Kim, C. S., Mauer, D. C. and Sherman, A. E., 1998. The Determinants of Corporate Liquidity: Theory and Evidence. *Journal of Financial and Quantitative Analysis*, 33(3), pp. 335–359.

Lins, K. V., Servaes, H. and Tufano, P., 2010. What Drives Corporate Liquidity? An International Survey of Cash Holdings and Lines of Credit. *Journal of Financial Economics*, 98(1), pp. 160–176.

Mulligan, C. B., 1997. Scale Economies, the Value of Time, and the Demand for Money: Longitudinal Evidence from Firms. *Journal of Political Economy*, 105(5), pp. 1061–1079.

Opler, T., Pinkowitz, L., Stulz, R. and Williamson, R., 1999. The Determinants and Implications of Corporate Cash Holdings. *Journal of Financial Economics*, 52(1), pp. 3–46.

Ozkan, A. and Ozkan, N., 2004. Corporate Cash Holdings: An Empirical Investigation of UK Companies. *Journal of Banking & Finance*, 28(9), pp. 2103–2134.

Pinkowitz, L., Stulz, R. and Williamson, R., 2006. Do Firms in Countries with Poor Protection of Investor Rights Hold More Cash? *Journal of Finance*, 61(6), pp. 2725–2751.

Riddick, L. and Whited, T., 2009. The Corporate Propensity to Save. *Journal of the American Finance Association*, 64(4), pp. 1729–1766.

Yarram, S. R., 2012. Corporate Governance, Cash Holdings and Value of a Firm: Evidence from Australian Firms. *Information Management and Business Review*, 4(12), pp. 606–614.

Index

Page numbers in *italics* refer to figures; those in **bold** refer to tables.

For Product Safety Concerns and Information please contact our EU representative GPSR@taylorandfrancis.com Taylor & Francis Verlag GmbH, Kaufingerstraße 24, 80331 München, Germany

Batch number: 09184780

Printed by Printforce, the Netherlands